EMPIRE
OF
MUD

The new iron dome of the US Capitol rising in 1859.

EMPIRE OF MUD

THE SECRET HISTORY OF WASHINGTON, DC

J. D. DICKEY

LYONS PRESS
Guilford, Connecticut
An imprint of Globe Pequot Press

To my parents

Lyons Press is an imprint of Globe Pequot Press.

Frontispiece photo courtesy of the Library of Congress Prints and Photographs Division. Photos
on pp. 2, 6, 36, 43, 46, 59, 71, 72 (top and bottom), 76, 83, 93, 114, 122, 125, 142, 153, 174, 187, 189,
216, 235, and 238 courtesy of the Library of Congress Prints and Photographs Division. Photos
on pp. 16 and 201 (all) courtesy of the National Archives and Records Administration. Photos on
pp. 113, 183, 231, and 244 courtesy of the Historical Society of Washington, DC. Photos on pp.
9, 38, 62, 106, 111, 137, 149, 164, 170, 176, 197, 203, 206, and 211 courtesy of DC Public Library,
Washingtoniana Division. Photo on p. 98 from a private collection. Photos on pp. 120 and 156 by
the author.

Maps by Daniel Rosen and Melissa Baker © Morris Book Publishing, LLC
Project editor: Meredith Dias
Layout: Melissa Evarts

Library of Congress Cataloging-in-Publication Data

Dickey, Jeff.
  Empire of mud : the secret history of Washington, DC / J. D. Dickey.
    pages cm
  Includes bibliographical references and index.
  ISBN 978-0-7627-8701-2
  1. Washington (D.C.)—History. I. Title. II. Title: Secret history of Washington, DC.
  F197.D53 2014
  975.3—dc23

                                                                                    2014015136

Printed in the United States of America

CONTENTS

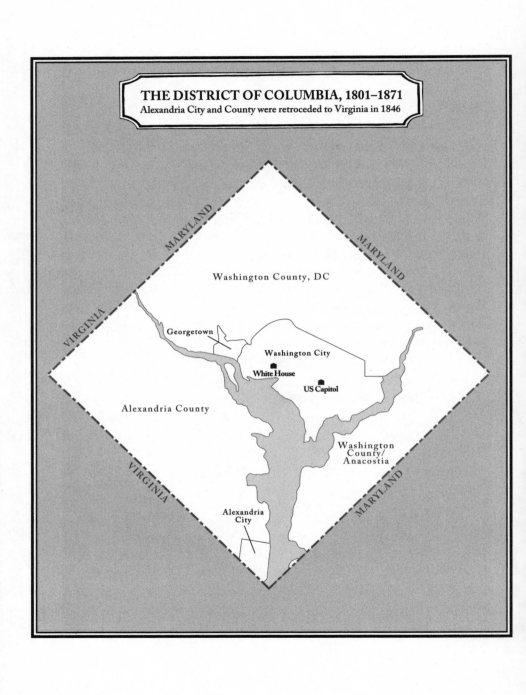

THE DISTRICT OF COLUMBIA, 1801–1871
Alexandria City and County were retroceded to Virginia in 1846

A NOTE ON MAPS OF WASHINGTON CITY

Few reliable sources indicate how the District of Columbia appeared when it became the site of the nation's capital. Most of the depictions created by Pierre L'Enfant, Andrew Ellicott, and their imitators present plans for the city rather than descriptive diagrams. Not until Albert Boschke's highly detailed 1857 map of the District did any comprehensive view—as it was, rather than as it should have been—achieve widespread dissemination. After later editions of Boschke's work and that of other cartographers, the District's urban landscape was depicted more accurately.

Yet how the District actually looked in the beginning remained a mystery until recently. Tee Loftin, Joseph Passonneau, Don Hawkins, and the Imaging Research Center have filled in some of the gaps. Daniel Rosen's 1801 map of Washington City (pages 26–27) draws from these sources and period accounts such as reminiscences by Christian Hines and other firsthand witnesses. This book's 1860s map (pages 160–61) draws from the 1861 edition of the Boschke map, providing a clearer view of the downtown area where most of the capital activity occurred. For the years between, especially circa 1830, no accurate, detailed representation of the District exists. Jacksonian-era Washington still awaits its modern cartographer.

A NOTE ON GEOGRAPHICAL TERMS

Alexandria: Tobacco port and slave-trading city founded in the eighteenth century; included in the District of Columbia from 1801 until its retrocession to the state of Virginia in 1846.

Alexandria County: Largely unincorporated land surrounding Alexandria, west of the Potomac River; included in the District of Columbia from 1801 until its retrocession to the state of Virginia in 1846; since renamed Arlington County.

District of Columbia: The ten-mile square encompassing former parts of Maryland and, until 1846, Virginia; selected by George Washington and designated by Congress as the federal capital of America.

Georgetown: Maryland port city founded in the mid-eighteenth century; included in the District of Columbia from 1801 to the present. In 1871 Congress revoked its charter and designated it as a neighborhood in the District.

Territory of the District of Columbia: Short-lived experiment, from 1871 to 1874, to reorganize the District as a US territory under the control of a federal governor.

Washington City: Independent city founded in 1802; synonymous with the federal capital for much of the nineteenth century and home to most of its key sites. Congress revoked its charter in 1871 and consolidated it into the District.

Washington County: Largely unincorporated land surrounding Washington City east of the Potomac River and a constituent part of the District starting in 1801. Congress consolidated it into the District in 1871.

Washington, DC: Name for the capital in use since the early days of the republic. Since 1871 there has been no official city of Washington—only the District of Columbia—so the term has been both misleading and redundant for nearly 150 years.

INTRODUCTION

CAPITAL MOVERS

Washington is not the official capital of America. Maps include a place called Washington, everyone refers to the seat of federal power as Washington, and the city's homegrown politicians, celebrities, and athletes all claim to hail from Washington. But according to the law—and law is very important in the capital—such a place doesn't exist. There is only the District of Columbia, and it's been that way for nearly a century and a half.

A Washington City did exist once, though, and this older version of the capital, its life span from 1802 to 1871, is the primary subject of this book. But "Washington City" was always a misnomer. When that was its legal name in the nineteenth century, it was hardly a town, let alone a city. By the time it emerged as a city in the Gilded Age, Congress had abolished it and consolidated it into the District of Columbia. Thus, as with so much about the place in its early years, its planners even got the name wrong.

Familiar Origins

The usual story of the origin of the federal capital goes back to two key events: the Residence Act of 1790, by which Congress designated the general site for the future American capital, and Pierre L'Enfant's 1791 presentation of his survey map, which outlined the street plan of that capital. The maneuvers and machinations that led to those events form part of a convoluted tale of nation building that historians have recounted well and often in recent years: political wrangling to choose a suitable site, contentious debates between surveyor and city commissioners, bureaucratic conflicts and inevitable lawsuits.*

---

* In a nutshell: The founders placed the national capital close to the geographical center of the country but still in the South as a concession to Southern states in exchange for the federal assumption of state debt, most of which the Northern states held.

However, the genesis of the idea of a federal capital began nearly a decade before L'Enfant presented his map. It is a tale that, if not quite the stuff of legend, at least makes for a good yarn with a decent measure of adventure and intrigue. More importantly, it helps explain why Washington City, instead of Philadelphia or New York, became the US capital and why this new capital—far from a citadel of democracy—emerged as a fiefdom ruled by national politicians, and why its citizens were denied the right to vote for those politicians.

The Intrigues of June

In the summer of 1783, all seemed to be going well for the fledgling American states in their fight for independence. The British army still occupied New York City, but a peace treaty looked to be signed in a matter of months, and the nascent republic already had a functional legislature, burgeoning industries from timber harvesting to shipbuilding, and a fateful taste for westward expansion. So it was more than a little surprising that at this moment—when the states finally emerged triumphant from their eight-year struggle against their British overlords—the army of citizens who had done so much to defeat the Royal Army turned against its own leaders and held them captive at the point of bayonets.

Discontent in the soldiers' ranks was nothing new. From 1779 to 1781 Pennsylvania militia members and soldiers engaged in periodic riots and mutinies over inadequate pay and unfair terms of service. In March 1783, Officer John Armstrong Jr., an ally of General Horatio Gates, encouraged veteran soldiers not to disband until their demands for fair treatment were addressed. George Washington himself suppressed this challenge, which became known as the Newburgh Conspiracy—one of the most serious threats to civilian control of the army during the war—by personally stepping in to address the officers' demands.[1]

Three months later a much greater conflict erupted. Congress (aka the Congress of the Confederation) had passed a resolution furloughing the soldiers of the Pennsylvania Line, drawn largely from that state. A group of sergeants wrote to Congress: "We will not accept your furloughs and demand a settlement."[2] When the legislature didn't respond adequately to their demands, on June 17 a group of eighty to a hundred soldiers made for Philadelphia, then the locus of federal as well as state power.

Word of the soldiers' approach stirred the fears of politicians and gave rise to rumors of what the troops would do once they got there—*perhaps even joining with other bands of renegades and robbing the mighty Bank of North America to get their money!*[3] Key power brokers, such as finance chief Robert Morris and Representative Alexander Hamilton, demanded that John Dickinson, president of the Pennsylvania Supreme Executive Council, call out the militia to stop them. But Dickinson balked, doubting the threat of violence from the soldiers as well as the loyalty of the dodgy, homegrown militia. As historian Kenneth Bowling writes, "Pennsylvania, which had exclusive jurisdiction over affairs within its boundaries, had made its decision; Congress, which had no jurisdiction over the capital of the United States at Philadelphia, had to obey Pennsylvania's decision."[4]

Not surprisingly, Hamilton seethed, decrying the state's "weak and disgusting position," and charged Assistant Secretary of War William Jackson with stopping the soldiers' march without resorting to force—a task that predictably failed. The troops arrived at their barracks in Philadelphia on Friday, June 20, ready to bring their case before the Pennsylvania State House. But their audience would consist of state legislators, not federal ones, since the national Congress didn't meet on Saturday, and in any case "Pennsylvania was simply wealthier and more important than the federal government."[5]

The night before they planned to march on the State House, however, the soldiers received a curious group of guests: Jackson, Hamilton, and Gouverneur Morris, the assistant superintendent of finance. History doesn't record the details of who said what at the meeting, but after the national leaders left, the soldiers had grown even angrier than before, no doubt insulted by the trio's patronizing attitude and cheap offer of buying off the men with a month's pay in cash.[6] Thus, enraged by the furloughs and inadequate pay for their lengthy service, mocked by the smug attitudes of national politicians, and nearly given a pass by their state's leaders, the men of the Pennsylvania Line marched on the Pennsylvania legislature—straight into Hamilton's trap.

In 1783 Hamilton hadn't yet achieved most of his fame in the annals of the republic: champion of the Federalist Party, first secretary of the US Treasury, victim of Aaron Burr's bullet. Instead, after his wartime service as a battalion commander, he was serving as a freshman representative from New York . . . albeit one with an unusual amount of pull and a Machiavellian sense of cunning. He could see the strategic opportunity that came with crisis, and he had a great opportunity with the crisis at hand.

The soldiers arrived at the State House on June 21, and their mutiny played out in melodramatic, almost ridiculous fashion. They marched defiantly and flashed their guns. Taverns sold liquor, drunken crowds cheered, politicians cowered. Further entreaties for Dickinson to call out the militia failed, and the Pennsylvania Line surrounded the state legislature. Some feared they might hold the politicians hostage.[7]

However, the troops were after the state politicians, not the federal ones, and the national body, the Congress of the Confederation, didn't even convene on the weekend. But Hamilton knew how insulting it would be if this historic mutiny *didn't* attack Congress: The underfunded national legislature would look pathetic, not even worthy of a soldiers' march! More importantly, his idea of a strong, central American government would look laughable. So he had Elias Boudinot, president of Congress, call the legislature into session, making it appear the mutineers were assaulting the federal government and by implication the nation itself.

What exactly the members of Congress were supposed to do in a building surrounded by armed troops wasn't clear, and in any case only thirteen members showed up, not even enough for a quorum. The scene that greeted them was more *commedia dell'arte* than coup d'état. Fired up by cheap booze, the soldiers swore loudly and brandished their bayonets, joined by townsfolk who added to the drinking and shouting. James Madison judged the danger as less "premeditated violence" and more "hasty excess."[8]

By the time congressional leaders rounded up enough members for an official session that evening, the chaos had ebbed. The mutinous troops had returned to their barracks, leaving no violence in their wake. Despite the debauchery, no state or federal legislators sustained attack or were even kept from entering or leaving the building.[9] The Pennsylvania Line had made a show of force more suitable for a village tavern than a national legislature.

For the members of Congress meeting that Saturday night, however, the identity of the villains in the story had shifted from the "grumbling band" of soldiers to the Pennsylvania leaders too scared to do anything about them. Boudinot announced that "this wound to the dignity of the Federal Government will not go unpunished." Congress followed by ordering Washington's own troops to quash the mutiny . . . and by fleeing the state altogether.[10] Its resolutions were kept secret, however, and revealed only when the politicians had safely reached their new home: Princeton, New Jersey.

In the ensuing national debate, Hamilton performed at his best—or worst, depending on your persuasion. He claimed that the soldiers' fury targeted Congress itself, and in the face of danger the national body wrote its steely resolutions with the mutineers laying siege to the building. Dickinson indicated that Congress never faced any real danger, but Hamilton took exception. The impassioned statesman blamed Pennsylvania as much as the soldiers for the debacle, seeing it as an attack not just on the national legislature but on the very notion of legitimate authority. In his view, this "deliberate mutiny of an incensed soldiery carried to the utmost point of outrage" involved an "armed banditti of four to five hundred men" who had the potential to "make the city a scene of plunder and massacre."[11]

As historian William di Giacomantonio writes, "Hamilton converted the appearance of the episode from a demonstration against a state to one against the federal government. Observers came away with an enduring lesson that Congress required immunity from the policing powers of a state government in order to preserve its own dignity and independence."[12] But by that time the mutiny had long ended.

When Dickinson finally called out the militia, a few days after Congress skipped town, the uprising collapsed. The mutineers submitted to government authority without a shot being fired, a person injured, or property damaged.[13] Indeed, for all their supposed threats of plunder and massacre, most of the mutineers received pardons. Congress addressed the soldiers' pay and furlough concerns in July and disbanded the army in October after the Treaty of Paris ended the Revolution.

For all their bluster, the soldiers turned out to be dupes, pawns in the hands of clever political operators who used them to advance their own strategy. Hamilton and his allies, especially, used the spectacle of the splendid little mutiny to advance the cause of increasing the power and privilege of the central government. Although no proof exists that Hamilton himself engineered the revolt, his opponents suspected greater machinations behind his strategy and accused him and his followers of deceit in raising fears that mutineers and armed mobs would subject a weak Congress to attack. Madison saw "profound darkness" behind the affair, and Judge James Mercer placed the blame on unnamed but strongly implied "Capital movers in this nefarious business."[14]

In the end, as with most issues in his political career, Hamilton won. But it wasn't easy relocating the capital or convincing a wary public to support a powerful central government—indeed, it took another four years of struggle.[15] By the time of the 1787 adoption of the Constitution, Hamilton got his way: Congress planned a ten-mile-square federal district, in which the federal government would have exclusive jurisdiction, to prevent "the folly of dependence upon any state for the protection of the national capital."[16] Three years later, the Residence Act of 1790 established the new American capital along the Potomac River between Maryland and Virginia—the exact site chosen by George Washington—and it opened for business within ten years. In 1801, under the District of Columbia Organic Act, Congress gained full control over the capital and organized its constituent cities and counties—and its residents lost their federal voting rights with no recourse to Congress or any other elected body.

At the time of these historic changes, the memory of the Philadelphia mutiny of 1783 had faded only partly, and was still used as an object lesson of how any threat to public order could overwhelm a weak legislature. The story, if anything, grew even more exaggerated: The rogue troops had become "enraged assassins"; John Dickinson, a spineless ninny, dithered while the soldiers and their allied street mobs attacked with ferocity; and Congress did the only sensible thing it could by escaping town before anarchy prevailed. Even today, this view of the mutiny prevails for most historians who mention it.[17]

Many factors ultimately led to the conception of Washington—constitutional, political, sectional—but the mutiny provided the earliest reason for relocating the capital from Philadelphia and the only one that involved fear. The threat was clear: The nation's leaders always stood in jeopardy, and the only way to ensure their safety was to keep the locals on a tight leash.

Despite this foundation, for most of the history of Washington City, residents of the capital could still vote for their local officials because Congress adopted a rather relaxed, even indifferent policy toward the District. After all, it could overrule any municipal policies it didn't like. The appointed commissioners, who had ruled so maladroitly in the 1790s, were replaced in 1802 by popularly elected Washington City councilors and a presidentially appointed mayor, and in 1820 the locals got to vote for mayor too. This partial enfranchisement held until the tumultuous days of Reconstruction, when a new version of the city arose with a Republican-majority Congress and large black voting popula-tion. As we'll see, this dramatic shift in the political calculus had an unexpected effect, which eventually resulted in the total abrogation of local voting rights and the disenfranchisement of District residents for a century.

The City of Angles

In the meantime, however, the creation of Washington presented a strange capstone to the struggle for American independence. The logic of the Revolution primarily involved securing individual rights by checking the powers of the state—the right to prevent unfair taxation in the years leading up to the War of Independence; the rights to "life, liberty, and the pursuit of happiness" embodied in the Declaration of Independence; the separation of powers laid out in the Constitution; the enumeration of individual liberties in the Bill of Rights. Yet, at the very time these con-cepts were codified into law, their antithesis was on the drawing boards just upriver from George Washington's plantation.

Contrary to the blueprints of a nation designed around the popu-lar control of government, the federal Leviathan wielded absolute power over its own turf. Against the idea that all people have self-evident liber-ties that cannot be taken from them by the state, the residents of Wash-ington couldn't vote for their national leaders. Unlike Jefferson's idea of a rustic capital to guide a nation of sovereign states and "yeoman farmers," Washington would embody a vast, centralized bureaucracy, imagined as a massive neoclassical metropolis with giant radial avenues and boulevards. Some even sketched plans for giant statues like those toppled by the revo-lutionaries a dozen years before.

Backed by all this federal power, Washington should have emerged as a hub of national power and pride—or at least an object of jealousy for those whose cities had been denied the same prestige and largesse. Instead, Hamilton's Federalists squandered their chance to realize their grand design for the capital, overwhelmed by greedy landowners and incompetent city planners. By the time the city was ready for business at the turn of the nineteenth century, their archrivals in the Democratic-Republican party controlled its levers of power. True to form, Jefferson and his successors had such contempt for Federalist notions of what the District should be like, that whether through neglect or disregard they adopted many policies to ensure the city would fail in embryo.

Even some Federalists later had second thoughts about the whole enterprise. Timothy Pickering, still mulling the lessons of the 1783 mutiny, noted in his journal that if John Dickinson had managed to call up his militia, "Philadelphia would have remained the capital of the United States; America would have saved not only the millions it had wasted by building Washington, DC, but would also have avoided the disastrous measures adopted during the presidencies of Thomas Jefferson and James Madison."[18]

So, instead of a functional municipal government and coherent social planning, what sprang up was a place of near-complete dysfunction. In its early years, real estate bubbles inflated and burst, development was random and scattered, and everything from roads to streetlights either didn't exist or didn't work. By the middle of the nineteenth century, the town only faintly resembled L'Enfant's conception of it, with a great deal of ugliness on view—open sewers doubling as canals, slums doubling as workers' housing, unfinished monuments doubling as city attractions—not to mention an abundance of con men, prostitutes, slave traders, cockfighters, and, of course, politicians. The men and women who lived within the city's sharp angles struggled for decades against its disorder and built it into something worthy of its namesake only near the end of the nineteenth century, by which time the city had experienced many crippling decades of corruption and mismanagement. The capital's emergence as a world icon proved painfully awkward, embarrassing, and slow.

Unearthing Washington City

This book doesn't present the familiar story of Washington so well known to readers of popular history: the horse trading between North and South to create the capital, the Old World stylings of L'Enfant's blueprint, the high-minded rhetoric of politicians, the various doings of presidents and potentates, the grand architectural projects. Such a narrative is warm and comforting, like an old friend spinning a tale by firelight—the heroes of the Revolution engaged in a grand project for the ages, forging a city founded on their ideals. This book takes no interest in roasting these tasty chestnuts of American history.

Instead, this book presents an alternative history of Washington City that shows the actual character of the capital: what it looked like, how it functioned, who controlled its power—and why. In the story, we'll see how the national capital, founded on noble ideals and with a few sparkling public buildings, devolved into an urban dystopia by the time of the Civil War, when British novelist Anthony Trollope memorably described it as "the empire of King Mud," both literally and figuratively, "the Augean stables through which some American Hercules must turn a purifying river before the American people can justly boast either of their capital or of their government."[19]

This book aims to reimagine this forgotten city, a place of dramatic contrasts—landed wealth and desperate poverty, civic liberty and racial oppression, genteel society and shocking squalor. The narrative begins in the 1790s and ends in 1878, describing in between how a visitor might have experienced the town, traversing its miles of unfinished roads that led through swamps and farmland, gambling on cards or cocks in the dusty streets, watching nightly battles between volunteer firefighters, and plunging into the chaotic markets, taverns, and slave depots that held as much importance to the city's social world as its drawing rooms, parlors, and assembly halls.

These days, Washington, DC, scarcely resembles the squalid little town that limped along through the early decades of American history. Bordellos and gambling halls have given way to superblocks. Towering neoclassical monuments dot the landscape. L'Enfant's urban design has taken full shape with magnificent boulevards and avenues. The city has emerged as the urban showpiece, focus of national politics, and center of world power that Hamilton and his cohorts once imagined it could be.

To many Americans, though, the city remains a fearsome metropolis, a place forever to be criticized, satirized, and campaigned against. Such antipathy is nothing new. From the beginning, Americans cast a wary eye on their capital, whether for its concentration of federal power, its suspicious cosmopolitanism, or its pretensions to glory. Indeed, without the original sin of Hamilton's "deliberate distortions" of an obscure mutiny, the place might never have come into existence—no concentration of federal power, no supreme federal district, no citizens stripped of their votes. If we still suspect our capital of dark designs, our fears are embedded in the city's DNA.

ONE

THE CAPITAL ARCHIPELAGO

The new American capital came with quite a pedigree when it opened for business in the summer of 1800: plotted by and named for a conquering hero and president, designed and surveyed to grand effect by a talented Frenchman, and redesigned by a man who mapped a good part of the early nation. What George Washington, Pierre L'Enfant, and Andrew Ellicott couldn't have imagined, though, was just how dismal the place would turn out to be in its first decades or how much work would have to go into making it a place worth living in, or even visiting.

William Thornton, designer of the US Capitol, had predicted that this proud new citadel of the republic would quickly become home to some 160,000 people and would flourish in accord with the fledgling country's inevitable growth. He was right about the country—but Washington City was another matter. At the turn of the nineteenth century, it barely held three thousand people and could scarcely bear comparison to any other national capital of the era.[1]

Certainly, no other such place had "avenues" consisting of little more than alleys of cleared forest,[2] roads with mud furrows "cavernous enough to hide robbers"[3] and strewn with garbage and the refuse of cows and hogs,[4] swamps that incubated mosquitoes carrying malaria and other diseases, or a landscape littered mostly with "brick kilns and temporary huts for labourers,"[5] or a near-complete lack of civic amenities, from a water supply and police force to street lighting and even sidewalks. Disgusted by the whole enterprise, Pierre L'Enfant ultimately called the place a "mere contemptible hamlet,"[6] and his contemporaries weren't much kinder. Treasury Secretary Oliver Wolcott observed, "The people are poor, and as far as I can judge they live like fishes by eating each other."[7]

But how could a place with so much promise spend its inaugural decades as a shadow of what it was meant to be, a phantom city fallen to ruin without ever having risen? The roots of this trouble lay within the land itself and the people who came to dominate it.

A Trojan Capital

The Residence Act of 1790 gave President Washington the authority to select the site for the American capital, which he did about sixteen miles upstream from his Mount Vernon estate, offering a variety of reasons for locating it here (as we'll see in the next chapter). Amid this landscape

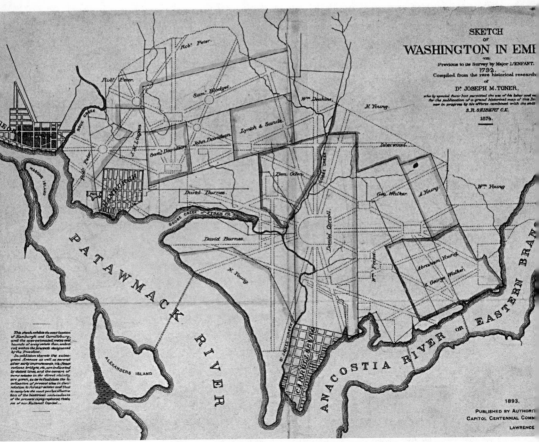

The names and property holdings of the original capital proprietors.

landowners had carved out a few agricultural tracts and plantations with idiosyncratic, often romantic names: The Adventure, Chance, Flint's Discovery, The Hogpen Enlarged, Jamaica, The Nock, Orme's Luck, Port Royal, The Vineyard, and Widow's Mite, among others.[8] Unfortunately, these whimsical labels applied to terrain so overworked by more than a century of tobacco exploitation that much of it lay in ruin, little more than abandoned fields, collapsing barns, and pastures without fences amid plentiful forestland.[9] Hardly a logical place on which to build a national capital from scratch.

The creators of this new city, however, didn't let that stop them. Envisioning a site on which a great capital could rise, L'Enfant admired the tract of Daniel Carroll, pronouncing Jenkins Hill at its center "a pedestal awaiting a monument"[10]—his way of describing an eighty-eight-foot-high mound covered with trees. More warily, Ellicott remarked that the site had "no more proportion to the country about Philadelphia and Germantown, for either wealth or fertility, than a crane does to a stall-fed ox."[11]

The capital mostly rose on ground ceded from Maryland, one of the few bastions of Catholicism in early America. Daniel Carroll's domain had roots in an eighteen-hundred-acre property grant from Lord Baltimore in 1663,[12] and his family was just this side of legendary, producing a US senator, the country's first Roman Catholic bishop, and signers of the Declaration of Independence and Constitution. However, keeping track of all their doings posed a bit of a problem, even for later historians, since, like all good aristocratic families, they desperately lacked originality: No fewer than four of them were named Daniel, and about as many shared the name Charles.[13]

One of these Daniel Carrolls ("of Duddington") was more than happy to relinquish his five hundred acres of what some called New Troy* to the American government in 1791. He'd been trying for more than two decades to attract developer interest to his land, and now the US capital itself would sit on his front porch and the city center would rise around it. Carroll celebrated his victory by becoming a property speculator.

---

* How this inauspicious moniker ever came to identify the land around what is now Capitol Hill is a bit of a mystery, although its prescience impresses. The British played the role of the Greeks in 1814 by burning it to the ground. It was just one of the classical pretensions in the area. A smaller, neighboring estate was named Rome and a large creek the Tiber.

The Bubble Economy

While today's history books present the early history of Washington City as a careful exercise in political negotiation, high-minded ideals, and daring architectural planning, something much more prosaic—and, to modern eyes, depressing—drove the development of the capital: housing bubbles.

Carroll wasn't alone in thinking his plantation held almost infinite value; his fellow landowners felt the same about theirs. In March 1791, they cut a deal with the commissioners overseeing the development of the capital, letting the government pay them for half their lots and retaining the rest for their own profit. When an auction took place in October of the same year, they appeared to have hit the jackpot. The going rate became $265 per full lot, more than five times its previous value.[14] A speculative frenzy began as the humble planters imagined themselves as lords holding sway over what surely would become the choicest turf in America.

However, despite the auction's promise of raising huge sums for the government and the landowners, only thirty-one lots sold.[15] But Carroll didn't let this stop him, as the appeal of charging exorbitant prices for exhausted agricultural land and forests proved irresistible. Whether he had any buyers at the beginning didn't much matter because it would be only a matter of time before the real boom began. He proudly kept his holdings on Jenkins Hill—i.e., Capitol Hill—among the most expensive in town. His fellow profiteers followed his example by keeping their prices high as well, perhaps fantasizing about all the starry-eyed patriots who would pay top dollar for old tobacco barns and mudflats.

But there weren't enough rubes in America to make the proprietors rich. Real estate sales remained sluggish, and the growth of the future capital site sagged. Instead of recognizing the situation and lowering their prices like proper businessmen, the planters held out and capital development slackened even more. By 1793 the nascent city desperately needed financing, and what little development there was ended up being haphazard and piecemeal.[16] The means of finding new investment capital fell to the city commissioners. One of them was Daniel Carroll of Rock Creek, uncle of Daniel Carroll of Duddington.

Magic Mushrooms

George Washington had selected this Daniel Carroll and his two equally respected fellow commissioners, Thomas Johnson and David Stuart, to manage the surveying of the capital site and to oversee its development and growth.[17] As commission leader, Johnson in particular had a reputation for probity and acumen as a US Supreme Court justice and former Maryland governor. But the capital was desperate for financing, and he knew he had to entertain almost any new idea or source of cash to get the city built.

When twenty-eight-year-old Boston merchant James Greenleaf presented an offer to purchase three thousand lots of real estate from the government—later doubling the offer—Johnson had his opportunity. In exchange for Greenleaf's beneficence, he would give the venture capitalist the bargain rate of $66 per lot with a payback period of seven years, instead of the usual rate of $300 per lot over three years—a 78 percent discount. As a bonus, Greenleaf and his partners, John Nicholson and Robert Morris, would agree to build ten homes a year in the capital and deposit $2,660 a month into the commissioners' coffers. Greenleaf also would purchase $13,300 worth of Maryland land holdings that Johnson was trying to unload.[18] All in all, the commissioner judged it a fair deal for the city and a lucrative deal for himself. It was hard to imagine its failure; Morris himself had helped finance the Revolution!

But Johnson had a surprise waiting for him. Greenleaf hadn't secured the bank loan from Holland to buy the property, nor had he imagined the scale of the chicanery that Greenleaf and his partners had engineered. Instead of improving the capital property, they looked to mortgage their unpaid-for Washington City lots to obtain a further loan to purchase six million acres of Appalachian wilderness, a colossal tract of land that held just as much promise to the Greenleaf syndicate, and yielded roughly the same results, as Florida swampland did to later generations of investors.[19] To achieve this end, the men established a web of financial trickery, sweetheart deals, and bluff and intrigue that historians still have a hard time unraveling two centuries later.

Some knew better. Greenleaf's brother-in-law, famed lexicographer Noah Webster, described his relative's employees as little more than "rogues and whores," and in 1795 George Washington questioned the

intelligence of his commissioners in accepting the credit of such speculators in lieu of real bank deposits, especially when they brazenly had
resold some of their unpurchased lots at a handsome profit.[20] Increasingly
frustrated, the president wrote to Carroll that "the continual disappoint-
ments" of the speculators "are really painful."[21]

What Greenleaf lacked in ethics, he made up for in rhetoric. To anyone questioning his motives, he hyperventilated about the rise of the "New
Jerusalem," a veritable City of God to tower over the republic. All this hot

Financial trickster and Ponzi schemer James Greenleaf.

air didn't convince everyone, but it was enough to fire up Thomas Law, a former officer of the East India Company, to offer as much as $133,000 to purchase property around Capitol Hill, which of course Greenleaf had never legally acquired.[22] The deal went sour, and Law soon found himself deep in litigation with the syndicate, which even held claim to the first mansion where he lived (at 6th and N Streets SW) as it made off with much of his fortune.[23] But Law was a different kind of speculator. Unlike his counterparts' houses, Law had paid for his in pounds sterling instead of credit. He followed all the building requirements and built them solidly (most notably the "10 Buildings" row houses in Southeast DC). By contrast, after Nicholson and Morris held a barbecue for two hundred people to celebrate their own development taking shape on New Jersey Avenue (the "20 Buildings"), they never bothered completing the structures, which remained unfinished and eventually collapsed.[24]

By this point the syndicate was running out of options. The money it received from buyers like Law didn't go to reimburse the federal government but rather to private creditors on whose loans it had defaulted. As Greenleaf's rhetoric became loftier, the pyramid scheme grew larger and more byzantine, until it collapsed in 1797 when his organization finally went bankrupt.[25] The syndicate controlled up to a third of all the available lots in town, though, so countless legal battles remained, and turmoil resulted: Illegitimate owners sold unimproved lots. Rival claimants struggled for control of overlapping or identical properties. Federal officials seized ownership of some lots and re-auctioned them, sometimes to the same people who had defaulted on paying for them in the first place. A litigious nightmare resulted for anyone attempting to venture into Washington City real estate. Court battles continued for decades. Even if land was available with clean title, prices were still outlandish, and, thanks to European wars and financial crises throughout the 1790s, little investment capital was available to pay for it anyway. As a result of the legal quagmire, even into the 1840s, buyers could take hold of the disputed tracts for less than a penny per square foot or forty-seven dollars per lot—for anyone foolhardy enough to take the risk.[26]

Not surprisingly, very little was built. Some isolated tracts did emerge, with bland names like the Six Buildings and the Seven Buildings, but the original plantation owners continued to sit on roughly half

the lots available in town, unhappily for most of them, it turned out.[27]
Daniel Carroll of Duddington saw his income dwindle and his estate
wither, and in 1820 he declared bankruptcy. He spent most of his later
years as a recluse in his Duddington estate, dying in 1849. (One of his
few successful developments, Carroll Row, lasted much longer, first as a
row of fashionable boardinghouses, then as a Union prison in the Civil
War.)[28]

The real victim of the speculative frenzy, though, was the capital itself.
After all the financial tumult, the city, enormous on paper, contained very
few actual buildings, and those that did exist were often half-built, following the "magic appearance of uninhabited structures like mushrooms
after a shower."[29] As Secretary Wolcott observed, immense sums "have
been squandered in buildings which are but partly finished" and in the
end never were.[30] The English writer Charles Janson added that speculation was "the life of the American," and, apart from the buildings set aside
for government use:

> the remainder of this boasted city is a mere wilderness of wood and
> stunted shrubs, the occupants of barren land. Strangers, after viewing
> the offices of state, are apt to enquire for the city, while they are in its
> very centre . . . some of the few houses which were then building [ten
> years ago], are now falling to ruin, the unfortunate owner having
> been ruined before he could get them roofed.[31]

Janson wrote these words in 1806, nearly a decade after the Greenleaf
syndicate had collapsed, eight years after its principals had been locked up
in a Philadelphia debtors prison, and five years after the federal government officially had moved to the District.[32]

The Wrath of Mr. Burnes

Thanks in part to Daniel Carroll's attempted profiteering on Capitol Hill,
the site that the founders intended for the center of town sat mired in
lawsuits and speculative chaos. The most reasonable alternative for the
builders lay westward, around what L'Enfant had imagined as the "Grand
Avenue" between the Capitol and the Executive Mansion.[33] But an angry
old farmer stood in their way.

David Burnes and his contingent of slaves grew rye, tobacco, wheat, oats, and corn on 527 hardscrabble acres bundled into tracts with evocative names like The Gleaning, Elinor, Burnes's Discovery, and the less exciting Resurvey on Part of Beall's Levels.[34] Some of it contained arable land, part of it sat on a floodplain, and the rest was swamps or mudflats—not an obvious place to build a city.

The crotchety Burnes had a long list of grievances going back to the birth of the capital. George Washington had tried to induce him to surrender his land on the cheap, often through land agents and subterfuge. Burnes constantly battled with the commissioners over the valuation of his property, and he resisted the creation of a new city in the middle of his homestead. A second lieutenant during the Revolution, Burnes also didn't particularly like Washington, dismissing him as the "Geographer General."[35]

More than anything, though, he fumed about the deal that the land proprietors had cut with the government back in 1791 and which he had signed. While the planters did receive $66.67 for each lot used for public buildings—and half the future proceeds of lots auctioned to the public—they got nothing for any streets, avenues, and alleys that cut through their

Humble residence of planter David Burnes, who sowed trouble for city founders.

land.[36] Few expected, then, that the transit corridors would end up as huge as they emerged on the L'Enfant plan, up to 160 feet wide, devouring even more of the proprietors' land but giving them nothing in return. The placement of 17th Street near his ramshackle cottage especially rankled him since it led to Commissioners Wharf, one of the first on the Tiber, a fitting symbol of the type of development and politicians he scorned. The most important one soon would be living just a few blocks north, in what Burnes called the "President's Palace."[37]

Signs of Burnes's wrath arose practically everywhere in the 1790s: open grievances against the commissioners, threats to sue the government, public indignation at the taking down of his fences to clear more land for avenues, and newspaper postings that served as the early American equivalent of *"Get off my lawn!"*:

> *I hereby forewarn all persons from hunting with Dog or Gun, within my inclosures or along my shores; likewise, cutting down Timbers, Saplings, Bushes, or Wood of any Kind, carrying off and burning Fence logs, any old wood on the shores, or in the woods. If I should find any person trespassing as above, I will write to my attorney, and suits will be commenced against the trespassers in the general Courts.[38]*

Burnes proved so stubborn that Jefferson thought city planners needed an alternative to the L'Enfant plan to deal with the bullheaded planter. In fact, Burnes continued to plant crops on Pennsylvania Avenue long after it was sited as the key road linking the White House and the Capitol, making it difficult to build a town center while corn was growing there.[39] Only after his death in 1799 did the full development of his holdings become possible, when they emerged as a viable site for the urban growth that should have been occurring on Capitol Hill. In an ironic twist, the daughter of this bitter old farmer, Marcia Burnes Van Ness, later became one of the capital's great society hostesses and one of the richest women in the country.[40]

Jerry-Buildings

As if dealing with angry farmers and rampant real estate speculation wasn't enough, builders found themselves confronted by a set of construction rules that assumed acres of wilderness would magically transform into stylish row houses and Georgian manors overnight. The regulations were supposed to make the capital look grand and upstanding, like Georgetown and Alexandria, the other prominent parts of the District of Columbia. But no one could graft the tasteful look of those old port towns onto forest groves and fallow farmland easily, no matter how rigorous the building codes—and in 1791 these rules weren't just rigorous, they were rigid: Only sturdy structures of brick and stone were to be erected, and no vulgar wood-framed houses. Buildings had to stand at least thirty-five feet tall but not taller than forty if on a major road. They had to lie "parallel thereto and . . . advanced to the line of the street." Tasteful row housing was the favored style.[41]

The first test of the regulations came in August 1791, when Daniel Carroll of Rock Creek set about creating a handsome new estate for his nephew, Daniel Carroll of Duddington, helpfully called Duddington.[42] The mansion mistakenly wound up seven feet in the path of New Jersey Avenue, a clear violation of a rule outlawing building walls projecting onto public throughways. To correct this transgression, L'Enfant quickly had those walls razed—and Duddington Daniel Carroll seethed. The error had been his own fault, but the French architect took the blame. L'Enfant first received a reprimand, and then, thanks to the efforts of Uncle Daniel and other city commissioners, who had unsuccessfully tried to make L'Enfant submit to their authority in this and other matters, Washington fired him.[43] The government paid Carroll an indemnity of four thousand dollars, and Duddington soon rose in proud Federal style.[44] It was only the first example of how the rigidity of the rules in Washington varied inversely to the power of those they affected.

Yet imposing such conditions mostly proved a failure because, without incentives or assistance with building codes or costs—such as those provided to real estate speculators—private builders hardly erected any structures. On noticing the capital's glacial growth, and realizing its pace was due in part to their own rules, government administrators decided to act. According to James Sterling Young, they changed the regulations to allow for wooden and single-story dwellings, which had an unexpectedly dreadful effect:

*a mushrooming of workers' shantytowns, one such appearing on the
very grounds of the executive mansion . . . jerry-built houses which,
being too expensive for resident laborers, remained unoccupied and fell
victim to vandals and the elements. When the government arrived in
1800 . . . The commissioners then reported 372 dwellings as "habit-
able," but, as a cabinet officer noted, "most of them are small miserable
huts."[45]*

By that point nothing the government did helped, and the capital
grew uglier. Countless visitors found its ramshackle appearance and its
emptiness shocking, one of them reporting in 1796 that "a spectator can
scarcely perceive any thing like a town."[46] But financial and regulatory
problems weren't the only factors holding the city back. Other difficul-
ties related to the curious beliefs of the Founding Fathers in general, and
Thomas Jefferson in particular.

A City of Yeoman Farmers

Planters and their society dominated the Potomac region, like much of
the Upper South, emphasizing social caste and proper etiquette while
employing draconian methods to turn a profit—foremost among them
slavery. Jefferson served as a leading exponent of these beliefs and saw the
country as a nation of "yeoman farmers," in which the virtue of American
government derived from the strength of its agricultural society as long as
there were vacant lands left to exploit.[47] He predictably held a wary view
of urban growth.

Ever since serving as secretary of state in the Washington administration, Jefferson thought the capital should be a humble little "federal
town" in dramatic contrast to Washington's view of a highly urbanized
and muscular "grand capital city" and "Metropolis of America."[48] Moreover, the letters that he wrote to Washington regarding the shape of the
capital contained no endorsement of the L'Enfant plan; he preferred a
more traditional grid system.[49] While in Europe, Jefferson could do little
to prevent the capital plan from taking shape other than arguing against
its imperial outlines from the comfort of a Paris salon. But that soon
changed.

Pyramid Schemes

The Jeffersonians (i.e., the Democratic-Republican Party) employed more than just pastoral ideology to guide their strategy. Good old-fashioned partisan politics also played a role. Since America was predominantly rural, Jefferson and his followers exploited the straw-man image of the corrupted, European metropolis against their Federalist rivals . . . who just happened to represent the most urbanized parts of the country. It also helped that the adversaries of the Democratic-Republicans kept giving them ripe opportunities to make political mischief.

A prime opportunity came in the late 1790s, when the federal government, seeing construction funds depleted on the hugely expensive Capitol and Executive Mansion, had to chip in and fund its less-than-humble abodes. In the kind of political firestorm that often repeated itself in American history, federal loan guarantees of $300,000 to complete the buildings provoked one of the country's first antigovernment reactions. Jefferson's faction raised hell and organized protest rallies, and indignant newspaper editors wrote scathing editorials laced with doggerel that decried

> *the ship of state on rocky ground*
> *and fools to pay for Federal Towns.*[50]

The situation worsened after George Washington died in 1799 and his Federalist followers proposed a 150-foot-high mausoleum to honor the fallen president.

The Federalist Congress rubber-stamped a weird, giant pyramid with a planned cost of $200,000, and Jefferson's anti-Federalists used the ensuing public controversy to their advantage.[51] The man from Monticello thus swept to power in one of the great electoral victories in American history and swiftly ended the mausoleum project.

The effect of this public reaction was a paradox. The outcry targeted leaders who wanted to enlarge the scope of federal power and spend freely on great public monuments. But despite rhetoric to the contrary, the Jeffersonians arrogated federal power anyway and, other than the mausoleum, built those monuments in full. What suffered was the rest of the city where it all took place. While American voters certainly weren't demanding that Washington City's streets remain unpaved, its garbage go uncollected, or its streets lay enveloped in darkness, that's ultimately what happened. Jefferson's party took power in 1801 and closed the tap for urban improvements for several long, bleak decades.

While he did secure the funding for the Navy Yard on the Eastern Branch, in most other areas the third president cut spending and kept the capital's areas of settlement disconnected from one another, preventing them from forming a coherent urban grid. Behind the scenes, he pushed against congressional bills meant to improve the District's infrastructure and follow the centralized contours of the L'Enfant plan. From the viewpoint of British diplomat Augustus John Foster, Jefferson's attitude toward the city had the effect of forcing members of Congress to rely on visiting the president's house for their "amusement and relief" from public affairs, or else be forced "to live like bears."[52]

Capital Sorrows

Jefferson's successors James Madison and James Monroe continued his policies in the first decades of the nineteenth century. It was a miserable time for the District, rife with incompetent city planning and blatant federal indifference, as the capital engendered little sense of community or civic purpose beyond the creation of government bureaucracy. Outside of the political class, the small, itinerant population struggled with living conditions that were as socially alienated as they were economically strained—and prone to occasional bouts of horrific violence. As a fitting symbol of the era, one of the town's biggest spectacles wasn't a noble ceremony or parade but a public execution gone wrong.

In 1802, James McGirk, an Irish immigrant and bricklayer, came home one evening after a round of heavy drinking and beat his pregnant wife so severely that she died along with their unborn twins. He was tried, found guilty, and sentenced to be hanged at the foot of the Capitol, where an ardent crowd gathered to watch the spectacle.[53] However, after the executioner tied the rope around his neck, but before the hood could be drawn over his head, McGirk suddenly leaped off the platform. With his body swaying and the crowd looking on in horror, the authorities tried to pull him back to the platform to prevent the suicide, but it was too late. After McGirk was cut down, the crowd swooped in and eagerly cut the noose into pieces (said to be helpful in curing headaches, toothaches, and other maladies).[54] They showed rather less respect to his corpse: first buried in a local cemetery, then dug up by living relatives of the dead in nearby plots and dumped into a ravine, retrieved from the ravine by the murderer's friends, reburied in the cemetery, and finally dug up again and deposited in a quagmire under thorn bushes.

This wasn't surprising—topographically, that is—since Washington City's physical landscape could be just as forbidding as its social counterpart, teeming with ravines, quagmires, and other undeveloped land. Magnificent houses stood next to rude shacks,[55] decent housing was hard to find under what some called "pioneer conditions,"[56] and the analogy to a patchwork quilt—pockets of random buildings separated by huge stretches of empty land—was so common that it was taken for granted.[57] In an unexpected twist, the one place where a decent number of buildings had sprouted, Greenleaf's Point, took its name from the charlatan who had done so much to impede the city's development.[58] (The area's previous name had been Turkey Buzzard Point, a fitting description of the Washington speculator.)

Without any guidance from the federal government, capital development proceeded on a pell-mell path led, once again, by the greed of the original landowners. Amazingly, even after the first speculative bubble popped and few buyers could be found, these men still possessed the ludicrous idea of selling their land for obscene prices. Each vied with the others to turn his own thinly populated sliver into the focus of development. This competition had the counterintuitive effect of ensuring that much of the region remained countryside and what settlement took place in the capital remained mired in "village conditions."[59] In Benjamin Latrobe's words, "The proprietors of the soil, on which the town is to be spread, are rivals and enemies, and each opposes every project which appears more advantageous to his neighbor than to himself. Speculators, of all degrees of honesty and of desperation, made a game of hazard of the scheme."[60]

Critics saw these problems as an embarrassment not only to the region but to the nation as a whole and called for the relocation of the seat of government to a more sensible spot like New York or Philadelphia. Fearful of being stripped of their would-be urban showpiece, the leaders of Virginia and Maryland stepped in to offer loans for capital improvements.[61] Their unexpected largesse improved prospects for growth in certain pockets, but overall the District remained, according to John Reps, "a kind of archipelago of neighborhoods separated from one another almost as if divided by water instead of expanses of undeveloped land."[62]

But Pierre L'Enfant hadn't designed the city as an island chain.

L'Enfant's Tattered Plan

The French architect had instead imagined the capital as an ideal metropolis, enlivened with triumphal arches, gardens, theaters, museums, a victory column, a national pantheon, a massive central fountain, and a shopping arcade to rival the Palais Royale in Paris.[63] It was a fantastic vision, but though politicians were satisfied with the utopia on paper, they had no effective means of executing it. By its nature, L'Enfant's glorious blueprint couldn't address the boring nuts and bolts of urban planning:

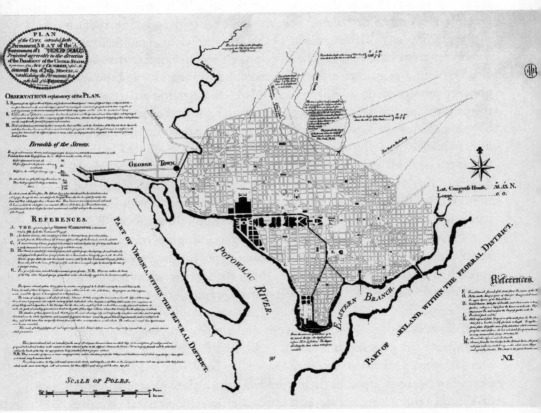

Pierre L'Enfant's idealized plan for the city, before Andrew Ellicott reimagined it.

adequate investment capital, a broad tax base, reliable funding for infra-structure, and a leadership committed to solving civic problems. Struggles with these issues, along with speculative madness and political haymak-ing, wrenched the plan away from its charming baroque assumptions and grounded it firmly in the mud of urban reality.

Quite literally, a lot of real mud lay in the new center of town. Instead of the Capitol and Jenkins Hill acting as the nexus of commerce and housing, a boggy tract of mediocre farmland, once owned by America's angriest farmer, would be the place where the center would rise. As other new pockets of growth emerged, they spread the town's points of interest across even wider distances, making Washington City, for all its preten-sions to centralized authority, a strangely decentralized place.

In what's now Foggy Bottom, German immigrant Jacob Funk had created Hamburgh, aka Funkstown, in 1765, subdividing it into lots from 19th to 24th Streets within a few blocks of the Potomac. Even from the beginning, Funk had designed it with speculation in mind.[64] But aside from a brewery and a glassblower, it offered little in the way of business, and few people wanted to live in a place where swamps and mudflats bred mosquitoes that spread malaria and yellow fever and the summertime weather created a tropical sauna of nearly unbearable heat and humidity.[65] Even by the 1840s the area had only sixty households.[66]

Several miles south of the town center, the Navy Yard hosted Ameri-ca's seminal military fleet. In 1799 George Washington had sited the yard two miles up from the confluence of the Potomac on the Eastern Branch, and by 1806 the yard was thriving by building, equipping, and repairing warships. Employees received the unheard-of perk of daily "refreshments" drawn from hundred-barrel lots of whiskey.[67] These refreshments made it a popular place to work, and the yard soon became the chief manufac-turing site in the District. Another business thrived there too: whoring. According to Charles Janson, the yard densely featured "Tippling shops and houses of rendezvous for sailors and their doxies, with a number of the lowest order of traders."[68]

To the west, Charles Carroll intended Carrollsburg, near the junc-tion of the Potomac and the Eastern Branch, to be a budding townsite, but it ended up more a potential settlement than an actual one. Nearby, on land at the tip of the rivers' confluence, Greenleaf's Point still had

occupants during the early nineteenth century. However, as a fitting tribute to the speculator who gave it his name, the fifty or so houses there
were mostly ill-kempt, a handful occupied by squatters, and the warehouse and wharf that offered a few outward signs of industry were disused
if not abandoned.[69]

North of the point and south of the Capitol, the neighborhood
now known as Southwest was called The Island starting in the 1810s on
account of the Washington City Canal acting as a moat between it and
the rest of the city. Spec houses clustered here, but mostly The Island
offered a ragtag assortment of workers' shanties, industrial facilities, and
grand plantations slowly being sold and subdivided, just as their owners
were selling their slaves and subdividing their families (about which more
is covered in chapter four).[70]

Farther north, and due west of the Capitol, L'Enfant had planned
the Mall as a central feature of the city, a "grand and majestic avenue"
stretching for a mile and standing four hundred feet wide, bounded by
the expansive lawns of ambassadors' residences, peppered with gardens,
a pond, groves of trees, a luxury shopping district, arcades, and triumphal arches.[71] Sadly, it looked nothing like that. Other than storage sheds,
hardly any buildings rose on it at all, and swamps choked most of the
terrain.[72] The rest remained a mishmash of private garden plots, lumber
and firewood yards, and dumps for "rubbish of an offensive and unsightly
kind."[73] As the cofounder of the National Institute (predecessor to the
Smithsonian) put it, the Mall was "a magnificent Sahara of solitude and
waste—appropriated as a cow pasture and frog pond, and decorated with
a stone-cutter's yard, a slaughter-house and pig-pens."[74]

Practically the only major sites on the L'Enfant map that developed
as planned were the Capitol and the Executive Mansion, still the focus of
the town's energies and funding. Although the president's house increased
in esteem over the years, at the time it provoked divergent views. Some
lauded the "pleasing" and "captivating" qualities of the Georgian manor,
while others dismissed it as too big and unfurnished, or too "cold and
damp in winter."[75] The house of the legislature, by contrast, earned much
high praise. Frances Trollope—mother of Anthony, a novelist in her own
right and otherwise a bitter critic of America—recalled her "admira-
tion and surprise" at seeing a building of such "beauty and majesty."[76]

Other writers, also otherwise hostile, used terms such as "dazzling whiteness," "a creation of fairy-land," and "the eighth wonder of the world" to describe it.[77]

Apart from these well-financed federal structures—which also included the departments of State and Treasury, Post Office, and Patent Office—the rest of the capital continued to languish, its infrastructure and civic amenities either dilapidated or simply nonexistent. As Charles Dickens later wrote in *American Notes*, to create such a city as this required a perverse sort of inspiration:

> *plant a great deal of coarse turf in every place where it ought not to be; erect three handsome buildings in stone and marble, anywhere, but the more entirely out of everybody's way the better . . . make it scorching hot in the morning, and freezing cold in the afternoon, with an occasional tornado of wind and dust; leave a brick-field without the bricks, in all central places where a street may naturally be expected; and that's Washington.*[78]

Road Rage

Nothing symbolized the sorry state of the capital better than its streets. What looked so elegant on L'Enfant's blueprint—a web of radial baroque avenues overlapping a rectangular street grid—in practice became a confusing network of ragged and rutted strips of mud. Historian Constance Green wrote of the challenges of traversing the roads: "At night the journey was utterly dangerous; pot-holes and tree stumps threatened to overturn carriages; most of the thoroughfares lay in utter darkness."[79] For politicians heading home from the Capitol in the dark, walking presented an occupational hazard: "At times they slipped into the gutter or stumbled against a bank of earth. But even when with care they kept their feet from straying, they fell over barrels or a pile of bricks."[80] In one case, the deplorable condition of the District's roads almost changed the course of history, when the carriage of James A. Bayard Sr. of Delaware nearly overturned in the cratered muck.[81] He survived, though, and cast the key vote in the 1801 House decision that made Thomas Jefferson the president in 1801 after an electoral college tie. Otherwise, Aaron Burr—future killer of Alexander Hamilton and alleged treasonist—might have won.

Pennsylvania Avenue, the most important road in town, was among the worst thoroughfares. Tasteful drawings that promoted the District depicted the avenue as a lovely promenade lined with poplars—which Jefferson ordered planted in neat rows as in Paris—but in reality it was barely more than a quagmire.[82] This "deep morass covered with elder brushes" was, for most of its length, a muddy concourse cutting through the forest. In spring it often flooded, and the rest of the time street children scampered about in search of handouts for sweeping dust from the crossings.[83] It was ridiculously expensive to maintain because, at 160 feet wide, "To pave it was like attempting to pave a field."[84] Not until 1834 did the avenue finally get a decent roadbed to provide for a minimal level of usability.

However, just about the time that macadam covered Pennsylvania Avenue, the few dozen whale-oil lamps lighting it went dark due to high fuel prices, and they wouldn't be turned back on until the next decade.[85] Thus, as the District's two glittering monuments, the White House and Capitol, rose proudly at either end, the main drag connecting them was a pothole-choked mire littered with bricks and tree stumps, unwise to cross during the day and unsafe to cross at night.

The Tap Runs Dry

As with its battered system of thoroughfares, the basic services and amenities that other cities took for granted either came late to the District or didn't come at all. Buildings were designed poorly and then left to stand empty until they fell apart. Farmers still were seeding crops near major roads and impeding traffic. Most roads didn't have sidewalks. Livestock wandered freely. No sewer system served the city. Flu and other diseases broke out with disturbing regularity.[86] The minimal population had settled largely around the old Burnes tract and a few far-flung locations, but most travel took place across wide distances on foot or by horseback.[87]

Like many cities of the era, the District couldn't afford a modern waterworks, so a "pump mender" got the water out of the ground in lieu of an actual engineer or water department.[88] This arrangement proved searingly inadequate when fires erupted[89] and consumed the mostly wood-framed structures with ease ... usually while volunteer firefighters—in the absence of a commissioned department—watched helplessly.

Major crimes were uncommon, but petty crimes ran rampant.[90] Along with fending off low-rent thieves and burglars, the few law enforcement officers (basically a marshal and a sheriff) checked volunteer fire companies' fire buckets and issued health regulations to prevent the spread of infectious diseases, all the more challenging in a place littered with swampland and pools of stagnant water.[91]

All in all, Washington's "grand capital city" resembled a dysfunctional village. The president's and the legislature's houses loomed formidably, to be sure, along with a few other stately federal buildings, but everything else was crumbling or absent. According to Charles Hurd, two things existed in abundance: "ample space to disperse the slops and garbage thrown into the streets, and plenty of mud to absorb the droppings of horses, cattle and hogs that had the run of the streets."[92]

For most cities, then or now, such decrepit conditions would have led to a mayoral recall, voter revolt, political conflict, or at least a few protest marches. But the dismal state of civic amenities didn't lead to any of these outcomes. Without being able to vote for their national leaders, hold their government accountable, or challenge it in any way, the voters of Washington City had no choice but to take what scraps the members of Congress deigned to give them, which most of the time was very little.

Politics in Extremis

Visitors could tell the town was in bad shape even before they arrived, because it was so hard to get there. A network of turnpikes—wide, graded roads allowing for the interstate transport of goods and material such as crops, livestock, alcohol, and fuel—was interlacing much of the Northeast and the mid-Atlantic region. But Washington City remained virtually stranded, again like an island chain. The District had faced problems with constructing turnpikes to tie the region to the western frontier since its founding.[93] Functional roads went only to Maryland and the South, and the "western route proved impossible to develop in the face of undisguised hostility from Baltimore,"[94] which had little interest in a new economic competitor springing up practically in its backyard.

Maryland's biggest city served as the source of other painful contrasts too. Baltimore streets glowed with gas lighting around 1820, while Washington City's denizens still were fumbling around in the dark, lurching from one distant corner lit by whale oil to another. The District didn't see gas light until 1848, long after the new technology had become widespread in other cities. Earlier attempts to establish a municipal gas company also failed because local government "had no desire to encourage an innovation so dangerous, so offensive and one likely to injure the business of candle makers and oil dealers."[95]

In the same parochial fashion, Washington's hackmen fought against the development of sidewalks for fear that, if it were easier to walk down the road, fewer people would pay for horse-drawn transit. On account of their lobbying efforts, along with the usual mix of political cowardice and civic apathy, no omnibus line or other regular public transport existed in the District's first three decades.[96]

The town also offered limited or no means of education to its residents. Although the inglorious rise of the capital took place before the large-scale development of government-run schools, the District largely ignored the expansion of public schooling in other major cities of the time. Even as late as 1839, one study showed that, of the 5,200 children in the capital, around a thousand went either to private or "pauper" schools, but the rest—80 percent—had no means of education beyond what they could learn on their own.[97] Higher education didn't fare much better. The creation of a national university, which some had proposed at the same time as the formation of the District itself, foundered when Congress couldn't find the funds to build one but stubbornly refused offers of private assistance. The desperate solution of a lottery to raise funds also flopped when the lottery operator ended up in jail.[98]

Financial Mud Pit

The fiscal problems were manifold: Local government revenue came mostly from property taxes and license fees, but federal property—the only kind worth anything—was off-limits. A justice of the peace appointed by the president, not a local official, assessed real estate values. Redundant city and county taxes exposed residents to double taxation, and half of the entire budget went to road and bridge maintenance.[99]

That last point was the core problem. With a few exceptions, Congress left the full cost of grading and leveling roads to the local government, which couldn't afford it. In the first twenty years of the capital's life, Congress provided a pittance of $15,000 for work on Pennsylvania Avenue and the roads around the White House. Road maintenance in 1821 alone ran to $43,000. Local leaders had no choice but to take the town further into debt to pay for it.[100]

Fiscal challenges led to fiscal emergencies, and these, combined with national recessions and the "panics" of bank runs, left the District starving for cash. Money shortages prompted banks to offer paper not backed by specie and prompted local officials to issue the equivalent of IOUs, sometimes down to a penny.[101]

Throughout these decades the attitude that congressmen took was curious. They represented their own, often distant constituencies, but they had to live and work in Washington City for part of the year. Only a deep-seated and rabid antigovernment hostility or a serious case of masochism could explain how they could tolerate a place so often on the verge of fiscal collapse or why they kept funding to a minimum even as they "floundered through oceans of mud to reach the Capitol from lodgings jammed to the eaves."[102] In 1822, Senator John Eaton of Tennessee called for the federal government to take a larger share of maintaining Pennsylvania Avenue since it was unusable by humans or horses. The burden had been falling on taxpayers already being taxed at wartime levels, and the critical roadway was still a wreck. Congress responded by dribbling some money into the District's common fund, but the meager show of support had little effect.[103]

Requiem for a Dreamer

Meanwhile, L'Enfant was faring even worse than the city he had planned. Instead of leaving the place that had done so much to make his reputation, then forever broke him, he hung around, increasingly miserable, living off friends and sometimes lodging at Rhodes Tavern. Latrobe described the "picture of famine, L'Enfant and his dog ... He is too proud to receive any assistance, and it is very doubtful in what manner he subsists."[104] L'Enfant claimed that the federal government owed him up to $100,000,[105] and, while occasional offers would have provided a fraction of that amount, he refused all recompense until he was paid in full. That never happened, of course, and he cut a bleak figure in Washington City, where people might recognize this "quiet, harmless, and unoffending ... Old Major," then in his sixties, whose "broken shoes [and] rent pantaloons" made him more suitable for a Greek tragedy than a revolutionary epic.[106]

By the time he died in 1825, the capital L'Enfant had designed also looked moribund. Along with a crumbling infrastructure, few civic amenities, and a feeble transit network, the town lacked any significant mercantile house or means of profitable commerce except for the keeping of boardinghouses, many of which ended up as brothels (about which more later).[107] The only commodity it had in abundance was politicians.

The aggregation of numerous factors—economic, fiscal, political, psychological—meant that, however much its creators, promoters, and residents wished otherwise, Washington City still hadn't become a real city. Not only did it lag far behind other nearby urban areas such as Baltimore and Philadelphia, it even trailed the other towns in the District, Georgetown and Alexandria, which its founders expected it to eclipse quickly. Every year of decline brought louder calls to move the national capital elsewhere.

The numbers told the tale. Even as the rest of America was exploding with dynamic growth, the capital remained its own little island chain, and could barely hold back the tide or keep from drowning in a sea of apathy and red ink. Its population rarely grew by more than a thousand people a year from 1800 until the Civil War,[108] and from 1800 to 1830 the country's four most urbanized counties outpaced it by 115 to 300 percent. Even the mostly rural nation as a whole grew 12 percent more.[109]

Visiting Washington City in 1804, Irish poet Thomas Moore gazed upon the condition of the town and, like so many critics, summed it up mordantly:

> *This embryo capital, where Fancy sees*
> *Squares in morasses, obelisks in trees;*
> *Where second-sighted seers e'en now adorn*
> *With shrines unbuilt and heroes yet unborn*
> *Though now but woods—and Jefferson—they see*
> *Where streets should run and sages ought to be.*[110]

TWO

A PLAGUE OF WATERS

If Washington had formed a metaphorical island chain spread across vast distances, it was becoming in some places a literal one too. The unexpected focus of downtown development on the Burnes tract meant that Washington City was rising on one of the marshiest and swampiest tracts in the region—and the lowest point of a huge drainage basin stretching miles north of the city[1]—with much of downtown having a high water table that made it damp and prone to flooding. Even the president's house sat in an unhealthy location prone to pollution and disease. It comes as no surprise, then, that the lowest-lying tracts ultimately came to be occupied by the poor and transient while more well-to-do Washingtonians fled northward to drier land.[2]

Of course, one person's failed city is another person's arcadia. Thanks to city leaders' maladroit attempts at development, much of this sodden land remained rustic and unexploited—or to some, sylvan and idyllic. Just after the Civil War, eighty-five-year-old Christian Hines wrote a series of reminiscences of his youth, published as the book *Early Recollections of Washington City*. In these evocative anecdotes from the early 1800s, in stories "we had treasured up in memory from our youthful days," he describes a place barely cut from the wilderness, hardly a village let alone a city.

The City of Hines

At the time, the western half of what we know today as the Mall didn't yet exist. Instead, submerging the area was the sizable Tiber Creek, "a large sheet of water clear from Burnes' old farm-house to the Seventh-street bridge above the market-house" where "a great many sycamore and other trees" grew and Hines often walked "in search of turtle nests."[3] Near the

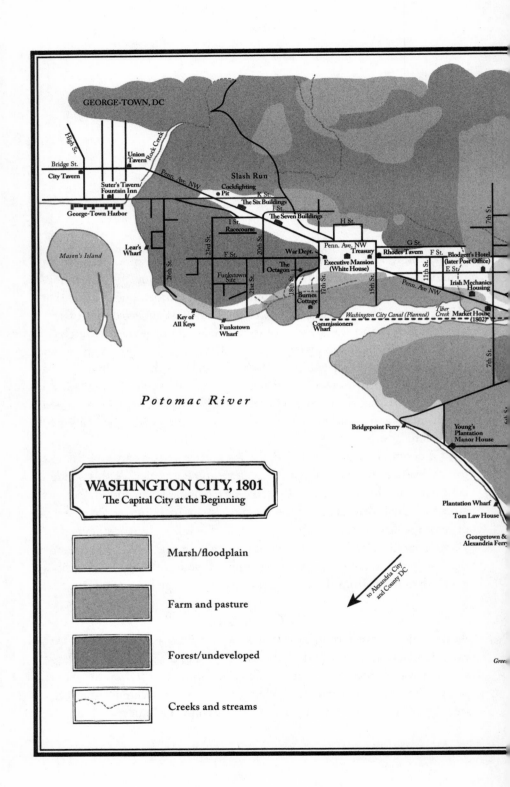

GEORGE-TOWN, DC

High St.

Bridge St.
City Tavern

Union
Tavern

Rock Creek

Penn. Ave. NW

Slash Run

Suter's Tavern/
Fountain Inn

Cockfighting
Pit

K St.

The Six Buildings

I St.

The Seven Buildings

George-Town Harbor

I St.
Racecourse

H St.

Lear's
Wharf

23rd St.

20th St.

Mason's Island

26th St.

F St.

21st St.

Penn. Ave. NW
War Dept.

G St.

Treasury

Rhodes Tavern

F St.

Blodgett's Hotel
(later Post Office)

E St.

7th St.

The
Octagon

Funkstown
Site

18th St.

12th St.

Executive Mansion
(White House)

11th St.

Irish Mechanics
Housing

Burnes
Cottage

15th St.

Penn. Ave. NW

Key of
All Keys

Funkstown
Wharf

Commissioners
Wharf

Washington City Canal (Planned)

Tiber
Creek

Market House
(1802)

7th St.

Potomac River

Bridgepoint Ferry

Young's
Plantation
Manor House

WASHINGTON CITY, 1801
The Capital City at the Beginning

Plantation Wharf

Tom Law House

Georgetown &
Alexandria Ferry

Marsh/floodplain

Farm and pasture

to Alexandria City
and County DC

Forest/undeveloped

Gree...

Creeks and streams

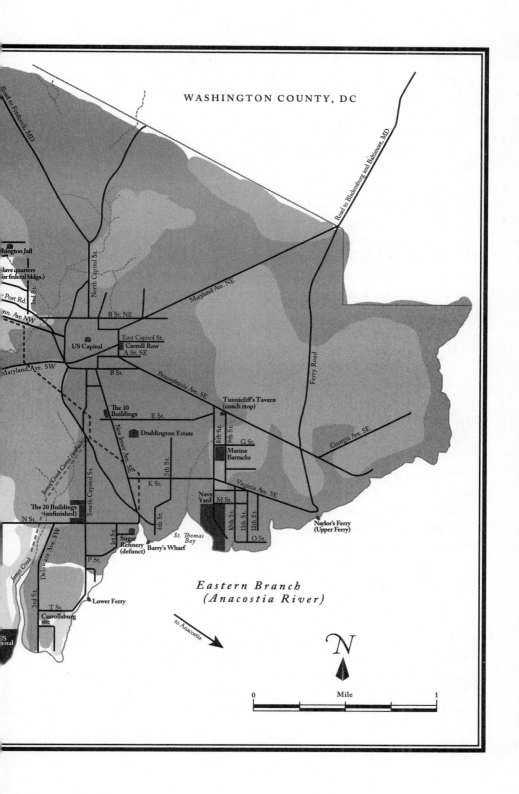

WASHINGTON COUNTY, DC

Road to Frederick, MD

Road to Bladensburg and Baltimore, MD

Washington Jail
Slave quarters
(for federal bldgs.)

Post Rd.

Penn. Ave. NW

North Capitol St.

3rd St.

B St. NE

Maryland Ave. NE

US Capitol

East Capitol St.
Carroll Row
A St. SE

Maryland Ave. SW

B St.

Pennsylvania Ave. SE

Tunnicliff's Tavern
(coach stop)

Ferry Road

The 10
Buildings

E St.

New Jersey Ave. SE

Duddington Estate

8th St.

9th St.

G St.

Marine
Barracks

Georgia Ave. SE

James Creek Canal (towpath)

South Capitol St.

5th St.

K St.

Virginia Ave. SE

The 20 Buildings
(unfinished)

N St.

4th St.

Navy
Yard

M St.

Naylor's Ferry
(Upper Ferry)

1st St.

Sugar
Refinery
(defunct)

Barry's Wharf

St. Thomas
Bay

10th St.

11th St.

12th St.

O St.

Delaware Ave. SW

P St.

James Creek

3rd St.

T St.

Lower Ferry

Carrollsburg
site

US
Arsenal

Eastern Branch
(Anacostia River)

to Anacostia

N

0   Mile   1

bridge "was a considerable swamp, overgrown with bushes, briars, thorns, &c. . . . At times, when the tides were high, the fish would come up the little stream as high as E street, especially the smaller kind, such as perch, smelts, eels &c."[4] The land was rich and verdant, thick with thorn bushes and grape vines, as well as hickory, oak and chestnut trees, making for "a complete little wilderness."[5]

Not surprising for a place littered with swamps and marshes, the region was one of the most well-watered landscapes on the East Coast, featuring no fewer than thirty-eight individual springs,[6] a convenient and accessible source of drinking water in the first half of the nineteenth century, much of it drawn by pumps and wells from the groundwater just below the surface. Some of the springs fed creeks of varying size. These included Rock Creek, cascading in from the north and forming the border between Georgetown and Washington City; its tributary, Slash Run, just east of it; and James Creek, leading from the Capitol south to the Eastern Branch near Greenleaf's Point.[7]

The largest and most important creek, the Tiber, didn't quite live up to the grandeur of its namesake, but at least it was a lot cleaner than its Roman counterpart. It began three and a half miles north of the Capitol, its main branch taking a westward turn near what became downtown—past the complete wilderness from Hines's youth—then widening around 17th Street before dumping into the Potomac.[8] Together, the Tiber and the tidal marshes near its mouth gave the appearance of a lake, stretching a thousand feet across, thronged with swans, ducks, and geese.[9] (Tiber Creek was better and perhaps more accurately known as Goose Creek.) The creek and its marshlands formed the center of the city, which sat in a broad natural amphitheater surrounded by a series of river terraces with bluffs up to thirty feet high and peppered with countless bogs, ponds, and swamps.[10] Farther north lay an even steeper escarpment, where Boundary Avenue marked the curving northern edge of Washington City.[11]

Where the Tiber met the Potomac, along its northern bank, stood the so-called Key of All Keys, a huge rocky outcrop where British general Edward Braddock reputedly landed in 1755 during the French and Indian War, before enemy forces ambushed him at Fort Duquesne. A landmark of sorts, also known as Braddock's Rock, it later became a quarry, and its stone helped form the foundations of the White House and Capitol until what remained of it was blasted away in the 1830s.[12] (A fragment of it remains, hidden deep in a rocky shaft just off an approach ramp to Highway 50 and covered by several feet of groundwater.) Among General Braddock's men was a lieutenant colonel named George Washington, whose subsequent acquaintance with this part of the Potomac in no small measure encouraged him to site the new American capital here thirty-five years later.

Washington's Potomac Logic

Well before he became president, Washington had developed a theory on why the inland Potomac region would make an ideal spot for settlement. For one, the site lay at the nexus of future commerce, near the primary north-south coastal road along the eastern seaboard, yet it also could capture its share of maritime trade on Chesapeake Bay. It lay inland enough to have access to the American heartland, in the mountains and valleys of which lay deposits for mining, forests for lumber, and wheat and cattle for farming. The area had a great historical pedigree: Captain John Smith had explored this part of the bay in 1608, his party dining on venison and bear while trading with the Natives for beaver and otter skins. Smith remarked that the fish were "lying so thicke with their heads aboue the water, as for want of nets . . . we attempted to catch them with a frying pan."[13]

Georgetown already had shown what opportunities the area offered, its deepwater port accommodating vessels for overseas trade, carrying a variety of goods from tobacco, leather, and candles to soap, flour, and beer, as well as river craft hauling shad and herring to neighboring colonies.[14] Just down the river sat Alexandria, which dominated the Virginia trade in wheat, flour, and tobacco and boasted plantation manors owned by some of the biggest names in the Tidewater.[15] However, above all this stood the most important geographic reason for the new capital to be sited here: the Fall Line.

At the Fall Line, the harder, erosion-resistant rocks of the Piedmont plateau meet the softer sediments of the Atlantic coastal plain. In the topography of the region, a series of waterfalls or rapids typically marks this boundary, of which Great Falls, with its "wild and romantic scenery," is the most prominent near Washington.[16] Most major East Coast cities sprang up along this line to give them access to the river-borne trade of the interior, as well as saltwater commerce overseas, and to use the water power to operate mills and other industrial enterprises.[17] Washington City was no different. But navigating past the Fall Line presented challenges: Strong currents capsized boats and dumped commercial loads overboard, especially during floods, and in low water rocks and snags transformed rivers into obstacle courses.[18] For practical purposes, the Fall Line marked the "head of navigation," the farthest point upriver where boats could travel without locks or portage as well as the most inland reach of the tidewater. On the Potomac, the head of navigation lay at Little Falls, and the modest whitewater of these falls spilled out over the northwest border of the District.[19] For these reasons, Washington was sold on the river, thanking "the goodness of that Providence which has dealt its favors to us with so profuse a hand. Would to God we had the wisdom enough to improve them."[20]

Improving on nature in this case meant building canals, which would breach the Fall Line and open the western interior as far as Cumberland, Maryland, and beyond—perhaps even to the Great Lakes. Washington saw it as a great opportunity for anyone "who wants land to cultivate [and] may repair thither and abound, as in the Land of Promise, with milk and honey: the ways are preparing, and the road will be made easy thro' the channels of the Potomac."[21]

To that end, in 1785 he became the first president of the Pawtomack Company, also known as the Potomack Canal Company, its stated goal to link the Tidewater region to the interior West. The plan first called for removing obstructions in the river and then constructing five canals to skirt the various falls that made upstream travel so difficult.[22] With this auspicious beginning, the people of the nation would come together in common purpose as they developed the resources of the heartland, thereby building the country into a peerless commercial and industrial juggernaut.[23]

That was the theory, anyway.

The Trouble with Canals, Part One

George Washington was many things: skillful surveyor, stalwart general, supreme president. But a successful entrepreneur he wasn't. His political

skills and those of his fellow directors helped the company receive charters from the state legislatures of Maryland and Virginia in 1784 and
1785, respectively, and the initial capital seemed sufficient to start constructing the canals. But stockholders funded the Pawtomack Company
on a pay-as-you-go basis, and this financing method proved disastrous
when construction costs doubled and the original investors could pay
no more. Faced with the prospect of their operation going under, the
directors resorted to the desperate solution of lotteries to raise capital.
When that didn't raise enough money, the company went into debt to
pay its bills and kept borrowing.[24] In the end, the Pawtomack Company
devolved into a financial disaster. By the time the tidewater states finally
revoked its charter, it had lost half a million dollars.[25]

From an engineering standpoint, however, the company's bypass
canals were an amazing feat. Untrained builders with almost no formal
technical knowledge constructed them, and they succeeded in allowing passage for rafts and keelboats through 218 upstream miles of the
Potomac. Unfortunately, the canals took a long time to build—the last
one, at Great Falls, was completed in 1802 after Washington's death—
and low water levels meant that they operated only for about six weeks of
the year.[26] Instead of shaping the Potomac into an essential commercial
artery through the heart of America, the canals offered little more than
a scenic curiosity. Their failure hardly dampened the desire of Washingtonians to develop the region's resources, however, and that desire would
only increase in coming decades.

Diamond on the Potomac

Washington's insistence on squeezing Alexandria, Georgetown, and sites
like Little Falls into the diamond-shaped boundary of the new federal
district ensured that the enclave would be huge: one hundred square miles
that needed roads, buildings, canals, wharves, and all manner of improvements. Encouraging citizens to relocate to the capital and building adequate housing and infrastructure for them posed an obvious challenge.
But an even bigger question was the water—and what to do with all of it.

As with all of its early problems, the District had to look to its own
sopping backyard for a solution. As historian Frederick Gutheim says,
"the city was literally built out of the natural resources" of the region, from

the timber and stone for its buildings and streets, to the marble for its monuments, to the canals cut from its creek beds.[27] Those who worked the rivers had a head start on exploiting their potential. Shippers in Georgetown and Alexandria offered prices comparable to or even lower than the costs for transporting goods overland; the Navy Yard manufactured vessels and ordnance to defend the nation (albeit increasingly underfunded by the Jeffersonians); and an array of maritime facilities lined the Eastern Branch.[28] The region's fishermen made a good catch in shad, gar, eels, pike, sturgeon, perch, and smelt, with herring being especially abundant in the waters of the mid-Atlantic.[29]

Elsewhere, shipping facilities operated at Lear's Wharf, Barry's Wharf, and Commissioners Wharf, and riverside links connected Virginia to the Georgetown and Alexandria and Bridgepoint ferry landings (soon the site of the Long Bridge) and to the small settlements in Anacostia at the Upper and Lower Ferry sites.[30] All that needed to happen was for the leaders of Washington, like those of Baltimore and other ports, to develop their city's docks, yards, and other maritime infrastructure, thus giving the District a real commercial vigor and making it a valid threat to its Atlantic competitors.

But the city's planners didn't just envision an economically viable city. They wanted a place with grand aesthetic appeal and visual harmony, a majestic landscape to serve as a testament to republican strength and virtue and to rival any of the creaky old cities of Europe. So why not start the District's rise to greatness with a bold stroke by channeling its waterways into beautiful fountains and canals, both functional and attractive?

Artful Designs

Pierre L'Enfant envisioned a magnificent canal in the French style flowing through the center of the capital. At Versailles, the Grand Canal and copious fountains not only offered visual delight but also drained the area's lowlands. So too would those of the federal city, according to his plan. Tiber Creek would become a grand canal in the American style, and fountains would cascade forth from Jenkins Hill below the Capitol, in a colossal show of engineering skill and invention.[31] The new canal would link the Potomac near old Funkstown (now Foggy Bottom), run between downtown and the Mall, take a great turn southward at the Capitol, and finally split into two branches terminating respectively near the mouth of James Creek and New Jersey Avenue SE.*[32]

The canal also would open nautical traffic, and thus trade and industry, between the Potomac and the Eastern Branch, conveniently passing the capital's major civil and commercial centers along the way.[33] George Washington quickly saw the benefits of L'Enfant's vision, endorsing it in a letter to Jefferson in August 1791 as essential to the prosperity of the city.[34] But the following February, Washington fired the prickly city surveyor, and in a huff L'Enfant took his capital plans with him.

The setback was serious but not insurmountable. Into L'Enfant's place stepped Andrew Ellicott, and the map he created bore many of the hallmarks of L'Enfant's baroque design, including the much-vaunted canal. A few twists and turns had changed, but in many respects it was the same waterway that the peevish Frenchman had designed.[35] All the capital's canal needed was capital.

At the time, private companies funded most urban improvement ventures, whether through pay-as-you-go investments or devices like lotteries. Usually with the blessing of a municipal or federal charter, such companies constructed bridges, turnpikes, and canals, their work overseen by a board of directors that included a host of prominent citizens. In the case of the Washington City Canal, one of them was a certain Mr. Law.

Tom Law, Canal Builder

When we last encountered him, Tom Law was wading neck deep into property speculation, letting James Greenleaf take him for a ride through the turbulent waters of Washington real estate. But along with property development, Tom Law had another great interest: public works projects. In 1796 the Maryland legislature authorized Law and Daniel Carroll to raise $52,000 for the creation of the Washington City Canal.[36] In the District's logrolling environment, it made sense: The two men obviously wanted to enhance the value of their property, and a lovely watercourse nearby wouldn't hurt. They were banking on it, literally and figuratively, to

---

* Many early maps of the District depict both canal branches. However, the James Creek canal never existed at the same time as the New Jersey Avenue canal. It took seventy-five years for the former to be built, and then only after the latter had been converted into a sewer, making maps from the era more aspirational than factual.

provide a profitable link between their waterside lots in Southeast Washington and the riches of the Georgetown market.

Progress on raising capital for the canal had come slowly ever since it had appeared so tantalizingly on the maps of L'Enfant and Ellicott half a decade earlier. So Law and Carroll, along with a few other directors of the enterprise, opted for lotteries to provide investment capital. But they soon found it rough going, as the lotteries failed to provide significant funds.[37] So they shelved the idea for several more years.

But Law didn't give up. His speculative energies may have fizzled and his fortune may have vanished into the black hole of the Greenleaf syndicate, but he entered the nineteenth century more committed than ever to see his projects through. In 1802 Congress granted him and his partners—including two different Daniel Carrolls—a charter to dig the Washington City Canal as long as they could raise the money.[38] Ever industrious, Law already had a plan to run packet boats between Tiber Creek and the Navy Yard as a means of transport to compete with hackney cabs.[39] Two years later, he anonymously wrote a pamphlet claiming "the salubrity of the city will be benefited by the canal," while adding the caveat that "few will be induced to become subscribers, unless it can be demonstrated by calculation, that it will yield an immediate and constantly increasing profit."[40] He should have listened to his own advice.

The Washington Canal Company failed to raise the funds by 1809, when the company's charter ran out. Congress reauthorized the company the same year to seek out $100,000 for construction, and it held a groundbreaking ceremony the following year, digging a few trenches before running out of money again in 1812.[41] Congress once more came to the company's aid and declared that the old Maryland lotteries remained intact to raise capital, but these too failed. Two years later, during the War of 1812, the British invaded and burned down the capital.

By this point it should have become clear that it wasn't easy or simple to fund a canal by private means in the early nineteenth century. The construction required too much labor and capital for the tastes of fickle pay-as-you-go investors or lottery-ticket buyers, and not enough well-heeled investors wanted to risk their fortunes on speculative building schemes—enough of those already existed on dry land. Civic leaders didn't help matters either since they took more interest in envisioning grand plans than finding the practical means of executing them. But in the end it didn't matter—the canal got built anyway.

With its reauthorization from Congress, the canal company was *supposed* to raise $100,000 in capital stock. However, according to Frederick May, the president of the company, it actually began "with permission to go into operation when 40,000 Dollars should be subscribed. Stock in the amount of 47,000 Dollars was taken and the work commenced."[42] It was a clever tactic, and it got work on the canal started. (It's worth noting, however, that, in the letter from May to the secretary of the treasury, the original script says "without permission." Someone later went back and struck through "out," raising the question of whether initial work had ever actually—and legally—been authorized.)

The Trouble with Canals, Part Two

Thanks largely to the labor of Irish immigrants (about which more in chapter three) the canal had opened for business by the end of 1815.[43] The November celebration commenced with proud Tom Law and the other company directors, along with prominent citizens and city council members, floating through it on a barge followed by the Marine Band in another boat.[44] It was all very lively and inspiring, just as it had been five years earlier when work had begun, but the company's financial state didn't stand in much better shape than it had then, and the canal itself left much to be desired.

With a few wharves and bridges already in place, the canal accommodated some barges and rafts carrying firewood, food, stone, and, of course, whiskey.[45] But most larger boats couldn't travel on it because of a lack of drawbridges at critical downtown crossings at 12th and 14th Streets. Any boat that drew more than a foot or two of water wouldn't make it either because the canal had been cut to a depth of just three feet. In a slightly ridiculous touch, builders even lined the canal with stone to accommodate the wash of steamboats somehow expected to crowd the waterway. It all added up to a sorry sight: "Business was lacking, but even if that had come, the canal was useless."[46]

What made the canal worse than useless, though, were the tides. At high tide, water rushed in and inundated the canal, sending some boats out of control and grounding others along its banks. At low tide, hardly any water filled the middle section of the canal, which resembled little more than a muddy trench. No one had accounted for these fluctuations, and the situation worsened. By 1818 the channel was usable only at high tide because of the buildup of silt deposited by the river, and cargo had to be scowed in to the wharves downtown.[47] (The silt resulted from the felling of area trees, which promoted erosion as the Potomac and Eastern Branch sent unrooted earth downriver, plugging up river channels as well as the outlets of the city canal.[48]) The canal's center section soon turned stagnant, and garbage began to collect there.

Nevertheless, canal promoters, Tom Law among them, refused to consider their project a failure.[49] If the canal could be deepened and improved, they argued, the District would have its economic lifeline in working order. That may have been true, but there wasn't enough money in the canal company's coffers to do anything about it. Maintenance and repair work were lacking, and the company had barely enough money to exist: as little as $5,402 in 1822 to cover its annual costs.[50] Even though the federal government stood to gain from the success of the canal, it refused to help until the company effectively foundered and the canal had become a financial disaster.

The stagnant city canal created a moat around Southwest Washington City, which became known as The Island.

That didn't happen until 1831, but in the meantime came another, much more serious bout of canal fever.

Canal Fever

To most in the country, public works glory reached its pinnacle with the Erie Canal, "the greatest water resource project of the nineteenth century."[51] That legendary concourse of commerce connected New York City with the Great Lakes and gave it access to all the riches of America's heartland and the Midwest. Completed in 1825, the Erie Canal helped New York usurp what should have been the glory of New Orleans and secure its place as the country's greatest port, commercial entrepôt, financial capital, and population nexus. With good reason historians use the phrase "canal fever" to refer to the heady promise of the Erie Canal for many American cities, which then built other channels in its wake, a phenomenon that "almost reached the proportions of a mania."[52] Washington's leaders gave into the fever as well—even as their earlier attempt at creating a municipal canal sat pungent and moldering under ever-deeper layers of mud and silt, a dirty open scar of civic failure that couldn't be wished or washed away.

Perhaps not surprisingly, one of the promoters of the brand-new canal was Tom Law. While still a director of the failed city canal, Law put his remaining energy, at seventy years old, into the freshly devised Chesapeake and Ohio Canal. A member of the promotions committee for the canal, he had been working since 1823 to help create a new watercourse to unite the mid-Atlantic with the Midwest politically and commercially. Four years later, Law testified before Congress about the glories of the proposed channel, and a year after that, on the Fourth of July, toasted the alliance of "the River of Swans with *la belle Riviere*"—a fancy French way of saying that the Potomac would link up to the Ohio Valley and the growing city of Pittsburgh.[53] It was the District's last, best chance to develop a canal that worked.

The Next Wonder of the World

The Chesapeake and Ohio Canal still exists. You can visit this national historical park on a tour of Georgetown, enjoy a boat ride through some of its locks, hike along its banks, take pictures of its industrial technology, and try to imagine the picaresque days of canal men piloting their barges in view of the Potomac while mules did most of the work on the towpath. In fact, if you didn't know better, you might never suspect that this 184.5-mile watercourse nearly ruined the city of Washington, plunged the region into a fiscal crisis, and caused the nineteenth-century federal government to take that rarest of actions—bailing out a failed corporation—all to prevent foreign creditors from calling in their debts and forcing the nation's capital into bankruptcy and liquidation. Such are the ironies of the C&O Canal.

But at least the C&O wasn't as ill-considered as its Washington City counterpart. The C&O did have a useful aim in paralleling the Potomac and getting around its obstructions, and the old Pawtomack Company's assets and infrastructure transferred into the new enterprise too. Reaching the Monongahela River would give the region a lifeline into the agricultural and industrial riches of the Ohio Valley, and Washington City surely would make a reasonable outlet for that commerce (which, after all, couldn't *all* go to New York City). Even better, the brilliant Benjamin

A leisurely boat ride along the Chesapeake and Ohio Canal in later years.

Wright would serve as head engineer for the new canal, as he had for the Erie Canal. With business and public enthusiasm to spare and count-less newspaper editorials hailing the inevitable greatness of the canal, the groundbreaking ceremony took place on Independence Day in 1828, with President John Quincy Adams himself holding the shovel. He proclaimed the C&O would be a "conquest over physical nature such as never yet been achieved by man. . . . The wonders of the ancient world, the Pyramids of Egypt, the Colossus of Rhodes, the Temple of Ephesus, the Mauso-leum of Artemisia, the Wall of China, sink into significance before it."[54]

Inspired by his own hyperbole at the groundbreaking, President Adams plunged in his shovel—and immediately hit the root of a hickory tree (an ominous portent, since Old Hickory himself, Andrew Jackson, beat him in the November election). Taking off his jacket, President Adams hacked at it for a while until it gave way and the first chunk of soil could be cut from the earth.[55] It was an obvious warning sign, but the problems had begun well before the president struck that pesky root.

The earliest red flag had been an 1826 report by the Army Board of Engineers that estimated the project to cost more than twenty-two mil-lion dollars, four times its original budget. After an outcry, another report deftly reduced the required sum to four million dollars, with the capital to be raised from corporate subscription. Lower Potomac cities would bor-row money and raise taxes to pay the interest on their new public debt, which of course would be retired when the canal began paying dividends.[56] The new report made another change: It halved the canal's path, which now would run only to Cumberland, Maryland, stopping well short of the Monongahela River and making its name a misnomer. The C&O Canal had lost its "O" and arguably its reason for being. As you might expect, however, this twist didn't halt work on the canal. Instead, canal fever raged.

In 1828 Congress passed a bill allowing municipalities in the District to triple their public debt to help fund the canal. Instead of public alarm or even debate ensuing, Washington's mayor hoisted the flag, and a can-non sounded a peal of fiery joy.[57] Business owners in Georgetown took note of the frenzy and dramatically raised the sale prices of their land and easements to allow the canal to pass through. Among them, Charles Car-roll, like his relative Daniel, couldn't resist a bit of speculation when he had the chance.[58] Everyone wanted to cash in.

Potomac Valley Blues

The area's desperation for a link to the C&O stemmed from more than
just canal fever, though. The District's commercial and industrial development was languishing, banks were closing, and the mood was growing
dire. Washington City's mayor rued his town's "almost total absence" of
commerce, and even those in Georgetown took a bleak outlook: "Our
town, notwithstanding its local and natural advantages for trade, has been
gradually declining, our population is deminished; our houses unten-
anted; and the people earnestly pleading that the avenues of commerce
may be opened."[59]

Residents and leaders of the cities saw the waterway almost as a mag-
ical talisman, hoping and expecting it to bring them relief from their dol-
drums. Alexandria created an aqueduct that carried C&O barges across
the Potomac from Georgetown and fed into a branch of the canal that
traveled seven miles south before reaching the city. The cost ran to $1.25
million, an amount difficult to raise by private subscription, which meant
that the Virginia channel took until 1843 to complete.[60] Washington City,
however, as the seat of federal power, had more clout than Alexandria. It
just blackmailed Georgetown to get what it wanted.

Georgetown had the gall to propose terminating the C&O at Little
Falls, well north of the capital city's border. But Washington City's trump
card was simple: It too was an investor in the C&O, but it hadn't yet paid
its million-dollar subscription. Nor would it unless the canal's directors
approved a linkage to the Washington City Canal. Already short of funds,
the C&O directors had no choice but to pay for an extension and locks to
connect it to the city canal.[61] But by then, in 1833, the bill for canal fever
was coming due.

The Trouble with Canals, Part Three

The problems this time had started in 1831 when Washington City bought
out the Washington City Canal Company for fifty thousand dollars and
then contributed more money to widening the dysfunctional waterway,
with the notion that such improvements would be needed for the linkup
to the C&O.[62] In reality, the buyout did little to stimulate commerce and
only pulled the city further into debt, made worse by its capital contribu-
tions to getting the C&O finished and losses from lotteries to pay for

the city canal. The debt level reached $1.7 million, which Washington City tried to offset by raising its municipal tax rate to the highest in the nation.[63]

It's worth remembering that at this time most of Washington's roads were unlit, unpaved, rutted, and dangerous. Garbage lined the streets, and feral hogs scavenged the filth.[64] Pockets of unfinished, derelict houses gave the place the look of a village instead of a city. In short, the place was commercially and industrially stunted. Yet despite such a clear need for major civic improvements, the city's leaders funneled money foolishly and profligately into the canal business and made the town suffer for it. As Senator Samuel Southard, chairman of a committee overseeing the District, put it: The city had such colossal debt that "it is *utterly impossible* that it can be relieved by any means within its own control" and "it will very probably in a short time be driven to the surrender of its charter"[65]— meaning an abrupt end to Washington City itself.

In their zeal to find funding, the District's cities had borrowed lustily from bankers overseas, in this case from Holland, long a favored source of foreign investment. Now that the debt was maturing and the cities scarcely could pay the interest, let alone the principal, panic bloomed. Southard saw, at a minimum, that bankers would "become the owners of a great proportion of the property within the capital of the Union" and other politicians worried that "the agents of the foreign creditors are here ready to purchase the property of these citizens of Washington [the canal shareholders] under the hammer, so that there is danger emphatically that this city may be sold to the Dutch."[66] It wasn't an empty threat, either. As one observer wrote, "it may be safely affirmed, that unless Congress pays the debt . . . the whole city of Washington must soon be for sale, and be the property of the Dutch bankers."[67] Indeed, the foreign investors had already arrived in the District and stood at the ready to get their money back by laying claim to the collateral.[68]

Facing the absurd possibility of the capital of American democracy legally falling into the hands of Europeans, Congress finally stepped in and paid $1.5 million to settle the cities' debts in exchange for control of their canal stock.[69] In 1836 the nation thereby took ownership of the watery white elephants created by the cities of the District of Columbia. It wasn't much of a bargain for the federal government.

The Alexandria and Washington City Canals never lived up to their promise, and the C&O Canal took another fourteen years to complete. While that canal did prove useful during the Civil War for ferrying troops into Maryland and for hauling great loads of coal downstream from Cumberland, this $11 million watercourse for the most part failed to deliver on its promise and became increasingly antiquated as the years passed.[70]

As a telling coincidence, ground broke on the C&O Canal and the Baltimore and Ohio (B&O) Railroad on the same day, July 4, 1828.[71] But the rail line struck much more successfully into the heart of the Midwest, often paralleling the canal itself and reaching Cumberland in 1842, eight full years before the canal did. The railroad even extended a branch to Washington City in 1835 (though Congress perversely forbade steam engines from entering the capital itself for another seventeen years), ending the stagecoach monopoly over land transit and halving the travel time between Baltimore and Washington City.[72] Even more than the railroad, the Panic of 1837 delivered the ultimate cure for canal fever, thrusting America into a six-year economic tailspin and scuttling most of the major waterway projects not already under way.

The battle for American transportation supremacy had ended, and canals had lost.

The Pride of Waters

Natural waterways continued to fare better than their man-made counterparts. Lined with facilities for making or storing beer, guns, rope, sugar, and tobacco, the Eastern Branch hummed with activity.[73] On that river, the Navy Yard wasn't just the local military powerhouse, it also offered one of the few bright spots in the District for manufacturing, its forges and furnaces churning out everything from anchors and anvils to copper nails and lead pumps.[74] Around the Navy Yard, a thriving working-class neighborhood developed. To the west, the Potomac River continued its profitable commerce in bar iron, flour, grain, sugar, timber, and whiskey,[75] providing an economic pulse to the struggling cities of the District and showing how much more valuable the workaday river trade was to the capital than the chimera of canal trade. Area rivers boasted some 150 fisheries that hauled in so much fish—including 400,000 barrels of herring, according to one report—that the surplus catch was used for fertilizer.[76]

In the shadow of a domeless Capitol, the dismal Washington City Canal
flows through the Mall in 1860.

In the end, the rivers greatly advantaged the District, and the tidewater served as an essential economic outlet. But civic planners continued to look the wrong way with their ill-fated schemes to reach the interior of the country by channeling upriver and forcibly imposing an urban waterscape on a region that naturally resisted it.

Arcadia Lost

In his reminiscences, Christian Hines focused on the years of his youth, around 1800, with good reason. Shortly after that, the city slowly emerged, and his little wilderness began to disappear. The old streams that once funneled freshwater through the terraces vanished first, replaced by drains and culverts starting in 1810. Some thirty years later, spring and well water began to flow into private residences, and sewage was pumped out and into those same drains and culverts. By the eve of the Civil War, most waterborne waste poured directly into the rivers.[77] Washington City accordingly became as dirty as any other city, its freshwater springs and wells increasingly polluted or drying up.[78] Even the grounds south of the White House transformed into a filthy marsh choked with sewage and wastewater from urban runoff.[79]

But worst of all, the "Great Tiber Freshet" became the Washington City Canal. While its northern reach fed into a system of drains and culverts, the part running along downtown was channeled, graded, walled, and streamlined to become the city's most notorious public works disaster. Unlike the C&O Canal—which functioned to some extent—the city canal posed an active and worsening public health threat. Even in the mid-nineteenth century, it served as an ongoing and unavoidable reminder of the poor decisions and political ineptitude that had marked the District from the moment it became the capital.

THREE

A MECHANIC'S GUIDE TO WASHINGTON CITY

Aside from gaining access to inland rivers, George Washington had another key reason for locating the capital so far upstream: wartime defense. In his view, the city would be much safer nestled upstream between the dicey shoals and bars of its rivers. Only a foolhardy attacker would risk sailing into the treacherous waters in sight of the guns of the Navy Yard and the eighty-nine-acre US Arsenal at Greenleaf's Point.[1] The theory was reasonably sound; to date, no foreign power has made a successful attack on Washington, DC, by sea. But in the end it didn't matter. The British burned it to the ground anyway.

In August 1814, in one of the last acts of the futile and misnamed War of 1812, British forces dropped anchor at Benedict, Maryland, some forty-five miles southeast of the District. Avenging the American army's devastation of the Canadian city of York, the British marched to Bladensburg, where they routed a force of capital militia. From there they attacked Washington City from the north, only to find it abandoned by its defenders. The British torched the Capitol, the Library of Congress, and other public buildings before finding a fully prepared meal laid out for guests at the Executive Mansion, which they gobbled down before burning that building too.[2]

As an act of political vengeance, it was a bold stroke; as a strategic maneuver, it was pointless. The British lost a much more important battle at Baltimore the next month, denting the reputation of the king's navy and leading Francis Scott Key to write a dramatic poem that became a stirring though nearly unsingable anthem for the American cause.

The Capitol stood in wartime ruin in 1814.

The burning of Washington City had important repercussions. As author Margaret Bayard Smith wrote at the time, "The district certainly was not in a state of preparation . . . [but] The city was capable of defence and ought to have been defended."[3] Some blamed the disorderly militia retreat from the initial battle, which soon became known as the Bladensburg Races.[4] Others saw treason in the behavior of those who chose to stay and bargain with the enemy. (In one case, instead of receiving praise for talking the British out of burning the Patent Office, Dr. William Thornton faced questions about his patriotism from the mayor.)[5] Still others criticized the executive branch and the president, who chose to scuttle away rather than stand and fight. Whatever the case, nature itself did more to save Washington City than any human defender, sending down a timely rainstorm just as flames threatened to immolate the entire town.

Phantom Rome

Following the war, the city was a carbonized shell of its former self. Some critics—mostly representing rival claimants to the capital site—demanded that the seat of government should be moved away from the lowly, marshy village and all its problems. In response to the threat, Congress authorized funds to rebuild key public structures, and private companies raised fresh capital for construction projects. A heroic legend even emerged to give the capital the luster of preordained, classical glory. Author D. B. Warden wrote in 1816 that one mythical farmer, in naming his creek the Tiber and his place of residence Rome, was "endowed with prophetical powers [and] foresaw the destinies of the Columbia territory."[6] As Ms. Smith put it, "May a Roman spirit animate our people, and the Roman example be followed by the Americans."[7] Similarly, later writers couldn't resist describing the capital as such a shining city, "an emporium that should vie with the noblest cities of the ancient world," among other hosannas.[8]

Needless to say, Washington City had little in common with ancient Rome—other than that most of its citizens couldn't vote. The gilded rhetoric of politicians and promoters didn't fool everyone, of course. Visiting British authors were the most obvious critics, but their critiques often met with hostility, the inevitable insults of monarch-worshipping foreigners.

But one American writer had a more potent effect, seeing the capital as it was, without illusion:

Washington city is repeated with a sort of holy enthusiasm; nothing evil or low mingles with the sound; it conveys sentiments at once the most pleasing, the most elevated. But how are we disappointed upon coming to this Idol of America! . . . I will venture to say that no city of the same age has kept pace with it in vice and dissolute manners.[9]

Anne Royall—a trenchant, thought-provoking, frequently infuriating critic of the town and its denizens—has contributed much to our knowledge of how Washington City actually looked, who lived there, what they did, and why the place had so many problems. Moreover, unlike many writers and critics at the time, she looked past the grand public buildings and the political rhetoric to take stock of the lives of the common residents of Washington City, the "mechanics" who made up much of its working class and the poor who composed the class below them.

Royall Style

Anne developed an interest in writing during her marriage to Captain William Royall, who had raised a Virginia company and served under Lafayette during the revolution. He introduced her to several entities that would prove influential, including Masonry, Shakespeare, and Voltaire,[10] and it was the writing of that groundbreaking French iconoclast that most shaped the style and invective of her later work. Although writing represented an uncommon career for women of the era, some like Royall pursued it vigorously, describing more than just the doings of politicians and the elite (as later stereotypes had it).[11] Indeed, her voice had no limits, no matter how unseemly or contrary to the national mood. In five years she wrote ten volumes of *Travels in the United States* and "tramped around all day, in all weathers, taking notes, holding interviews and acting as her own soliciting and delivery agent."[12] In the capital, she took a keen interest in dissecting the class structure:

> *The population of Washington may be said to consist of four classes of people, whose pursuits, interests, and manners differ as widely as though they lived on opposite sides of the globe, viz. those who keep congress boarders and their mutual friends, the subordinate officers of government . . . secondly, the labouring class; thirdly, what may be called the better sort; and fourthly, the free negroes.*[13]

To her, the ruling caste of politicians was "proud, ignorant, and many of them insolent," while the workers were "mostly very dissipated," all too ready to spend their wages as quickly as they earned them.[14] It was a punchy counterargument to the notion that America had no class system, an idea that made plain the barriers to social advancement that existed and highlighted the struggles of those without wealth or status.

Scavengers and Sweepmasters

Workers didn't make much money: only half or three-quarters of a dollar per day, with female servants and seamstresses making as little as two to four dollars a month.[15] This was at a time when the average national wage was around a dollar per day.[16] Competition with slave labor no doubt depressed the average wage in the District, but so too did the lack of jobs stemming from the moribund commercial and industrial state of Washington City. What jobs there were, outside the government, tended to involve small-scale merchandising, skilled and unskilled labor, and perilous grunt work. Judah Delano's comprehensive 1822 *Washington Directory* lists each head of household in Washington City along with his or her occupation and address. Some of the names and jobs include:

John L. Brightwell, sexton of eastern burial ground
Mary Cook, widow
Mrs. Corbett, school mistress
Hugh Dawson, ornamental plasterer
Mrs. E. Fonde, ladies' fancy wareroom
Thomas Green, huckster
Henry Guegan, foreign bookseller and teacher of French language
Alice Hepburn, midwife
Jacob Hilbus, organ builder
Mary Hughes, milliner
Henry Kurtz, foreman anchor smith at navy yard
Vincent Massi, dancing master
Joshua Millard, keeper of the tollhouse at the Washington Bridge
Elizabeth Queen, boarding house
John Smith, sweepmaster
John Tucker, whitesmith and bell hanger
Alexander Ward, tinman
Thomas Wheat, teacher Hamiltonian school
Thomas White, ship carpenter
John Wilson, scavenger
Samuel Wimsatt, wood corder and coal measurer [17]

A talented historian could write a book about the information contained in Delano's directory, but a few key points stand out: It includes few women other than widows. Free blacks are identified as "col'd," while other residents are assumed to be white. Most of the jobs belong to tradesmen and laborers, and some of the job titles provide only a hint of the challenges involved with low-paying, sometimes dangerous work.

A scavenger had to "remove nuisances and all offensive substances" from privies, receiving half a dollar per every seven cubic feet emptied. A sweepmaster shimmied down chimneys and cleaned them for a fee of ten cents per building story. A huckster sold cheap, sometimes shoddy wares from a street wagon. A tinman worked tin, of course, while a whitesmith finished iron, and a burial-ground sexton and his deputies were the only people allowed by law to dig and fill graves. Along with these jobs came the full range of familiar antebellum occupations: bricklayer, carpenter, carter, cooper, hatter, miller, saddler, shoemaker, stone cutter, and tailor. The directory also lists a few prominent names and occupations, such as Charles Bulfinch, "architect of capitol, e side 6w btw D and En near Unitarian church," and James Monroe, "president of the United States, at the president's house."[18]

In the Trenches

Although the directory doesn't specifically mention canal workers, plenty lived and worked in the District too—many of them Irish immigrants. As early as the 1780s, a notable Irish presence had formed there. An initial group of two hundred built the ill-fated Pawtomack Canal, with later waves of Irish immigrants contributing labor for the building trades and various public works projects.[19] D. B. Warden even claimed, with some embellishment: "Nearly one half of the population of Washington is of Irish origin. The labouring class is chiefly Irish, and many of them have no acquaintance with the English language. They have cut the canal, made, and repaired the streets, and executed most of the manual labour of the city."[20]

It's no exaggeration, however, to say that aside from slave labor the Irish did some of the toughest, dirtiest, riskiest jobs in the District. On the Washington City Canal, regardless of weather or temperature, they used picks, shovels, and wheelbarrows to carve a ditch into the sodden earth, suffering a reduced chance of survival in "the hot and humid District with its canals . . . swamps, and mosquitos."[21] Margaret Bayard Smith took pause from detailing the lifestyles of the elite to remark that the Irish had to board with the poorest citizens in town, crowded into rude shacks, and worked "in the midst of disease," much of it fatal.[22]

Not all immigrants had to do trench work. Some skilled artisans, such as bricklayers and stone cutters, did well enough to have other men working for them, establishing their own companies and contracting for work with the federal or city government or private businesses. Young men could apprentice for several years with well-established master artisans and learn a trade in exchange for room and board, and when the contract was fulfilled, receive a set amount of money and a "freedom suit" of new clothing. It could be a useful system to someone committed to starting a career, but it came with a lot of strings. All of the following could be forbidden: revealing the master's secrets; wasting the master's goods; leaving work without permission; playing cards, dice, or other games of chance; visiting alehouses, taverns, or theaters; or getting married.[23]

Regardless of their skill level, mechanics had to contend with an uncertain economic environment, unexpected layoffs, a high cost of living, and stagnating wages.[24] For the Irish and other Roman Catholics, their practicing of a religion contrary to that of the majority in town didn't help matters, either. As Anne Royall wrote, "I have heard them stigmatized by every harsh name, and accounted little better than heretics."[25]

However, some political groups, such as Andrew Jackson's Democrats, had better ideas. Instead of insulting the mechanics, they made them the bulwark of their electoral power.

Laborers' Levees

This newfound embrace of the white working classes, no matter their heritage, made for some rousing scenes. President Jackson threw a lively "levee" at the White House that included a large contingent of Irish. For visiting English critics such as Thomas Hamilton, these "great unwashed" represented "the very lowest sort of people." Despite his prejudice, though, Hamilton detailed a growing, albeit chaotic, democratic spirit that came to animate the politics of the District, along with the rest of the country:

> *There were present at this levee, men begrimed with all the sweat and filth accumulated in their day's—perhaps their week's—labours . . . There were majors in broad cloth and corduroys, redolent of gin and tobacco, and majors' ladies in chintz or russet, with huge Paris earrings, and tawny necks, profusely decorated with beads of colored glass. There were tailors from the board, and judges from the bench; lawyers who opened their mouths at one bar, and the tapster who closed them at another;—in short, every trade, craft, calling, and profession, appeared to have sent its delegates to this extraordinary convention.[26]*

Nor was this the first time that common folk had enjoyed a party at the seat of the government. In 1802 Thomas Jefferson had welcomed the public to the White House to feast their eyes on a 1,200-pound block of Massachusetts cheese and take a hearty bite of it. (Two years later,

Jefferson was still snacking on the once-colossal, now pungent remnants of the cheese.)[27] Also during Jefferson's administration, a crowd of laborers burst into the Capitol bearing a loaf of bread, some beef sirloin, and casks of wine, cider, and whiskey, throwing an impromptu barbecue for all: rich and poor, black and white, free and enslaved. Never one to miss a public display of food, the president strolled in and cut off a chunk of meat with his pocketknife before irate senators shut down the drunken proceedings.[28]

Indeed, no matter how much power they wielded, presidents couldn't overlook the interests of the mechanics, especially as property requirements for voting were disappearing and the franchise was opening to more people than ever before. As Thomas Hamilton wrote, the president's only hope of staying in power was by "conciliating the favour of the lowest—and, therefore, most numerous—order of his constituents," despite having to "shake hands with men whose very appearance suggested the precaution of a glove."[29] Even in a town where the locals couldn't vote for their federal leaders, mingling with the commoners made for good practice.

Uncertain Arrivals

The Irish weren't the only new arrivals to change the social and cultural makeup of the capital. The Germans had a presence that started small, hampered no doubt by the failure of Jacob Funk's Funkstown to draw property buyers. But their number slowly increased in size and influence in the first half of the nineteenth century, topping three thousand by the Civil War. They found employment as brewers, butchers, jewelers, machinists, printers, tailors, and woodworkers.[30] The English and Scottish continued to arrive, along with Swiss and French immigrants and a broad range of other Europeans, including a handful of Italians who worked as music teachers and dancing masters and played in ensembles like the Marine Band.[31] All of them came to town with high hopes of finding suitable jobs. Some did, but many found a scarcity of steady work and were soon cast adrift in an inhospitable place that offered few social bonds for help when times got tough.[32]

The lack of work made for a lot of poverty in town. Yet most of the tracts and pamphlets about the District—so vivid in their descriptions of the public buildings, so eager to promote the capital to audiences domestic and foreign—said very little about its economic failures or the growing numbers of the destitute. Anne Royall stood out as the exception.

Asylum Records

Royall carefully observed the poor because she herself had once been penniless. Her husband, William Royall, died in 1813 a wealthy man and dictated that the bulk of his estate go to Anne. But his relatives had other ideas, contesting the will and beginning one of those legal sagas that seems more at home in the pages of Dickens than in early nineteenth-century America. It took ten years for the case to be decided, and she lost. Now impoverished, dodging debt collectors, her health failing, and "without a cent in my pocket or change of raiment, badly dressed," she petitioned Congress in 1824 to receive her husband's pension as the widow of a Revolutionary War officer.[33] So began an even longer legal saga. In the meantime, she still needed money, so she devoted herself to writing, beginning her work in earnest at the age of fifty-four.[34]

Her own struggles gave her considerably more insight into the lives of the underprivileged than other writers at a time when poverty was considered more a moral nuisance than a public outrage: "In every other country, in every other town or city, some semblance is maintained in that attention which is due to the poor and the rich. But if you are poor, you have no business in Washington, and unless you are well dressed, you will have good luck if you be not kicked out of doors by the servants, should you attempt to enter a house."[35]

On Pennsylvania Avenue, orphaned and homeless children begged for money, sometimes picking up spare change by sweeping the giant road or by shining the shoes of passersby.[36] Other of the town's destitute received penance at the local poorhouse, the Washington Asylum. Founded in the early days of the District, the Washington Asylum was becoming increasingly overcrowded, disease-ridden, and dangerous. It wasn't just an almshouse but a workhouse that confined vagrants and minor lawbreakers. It also took in the overflow from the Washington County Jail, which had too little space and too many criminals.[37] The Washington Infirmary, the town's first hospital, functioned as a de facto poorhouse as well, though with little means to fight poverty and the illnesses that accompanied it.[38] Public money available for the relief of the poor was paltry and also balkanized by city ward. The central districts got the lion's share, while the outlying areas northeast of the center and along the riverfront received much less, setting a geographic pattern for poverty that persists to this day.[39]

For Anne Royall, the Washington Asylum was abysmal. "This wretched establishment only exists to disgrace Washington. I found several wretched children in this dreary and comfortless asylum, without one cheering voice, or hand of kindness to comfort or cherish them." It was a "place replete with human wo[e]" run by a man "wholly unfit for the place, and his wife a perfect she dragon. . . . Death would be mercy compared to the situation of the unfortunate inmates." By contrast, she voiced her support of the orphan asylum and the women who ran it—"the glory of Washington" that "reflects the highest honor upon its promoters"— noting the vigorous spirit of charity for children that elsewhere proved all too absent for adults.[40]

The era she described was a transitional one for poor relief. In 1802 Washington City had allocated 42 percent of its fiscal budget for purchasing housing and clothing for the underprivileged, but that figure plunged to just 6 percent by the Civil War.[41] Like other Southern cities, the District of Columbia relied on a mix of middle-class philanthropists and charitable groups to provide assistance. They did what they could to fight destitution but still had a limited effect on it. Anne Royall saw how poverty washed over the District: "Daily and hourly . . . you see some woman or child begging a mouthful of victuals at our doors," as the local government stood largely indifferent, merely offering to "throw a few cents to the poor wretches."[42]

Churches of course had their own charitable entities, such as the Roman Catholic Orphan Asylum, run by the Sisters of Charity of St. Joseph, which included a day school that cared for up to two hundred indigent girls.[43] It was a noble effort—if something of a bandage over a bullet wound. Nonetheless, many religious organizations saw helping the poor as an opportunity to fulfill the gospel mission, establish a greater social presence in town, and perhaps make a few converts along the way. Their efforts took place during the Second Great Awakening, a time when new forms of worship were sprouting almost overnight and the clergy were assuming a greater public and political role than before.

Black Book versus Black Book

The denominations in the District were mostly Protestant, consisting of thirty-eight churches by midcentury: around one-third Methodist, half other mainline Protestant groups, and most of the rest Roman Catholic, with one synagogue and one Quaker meetinghouse.[44] But Anne Royall wasn't comfortable with any of them. The bulk of her ire fell on the rapidly growing evangelical sects, which she saw not only as a threat to rationality and humanist endeavor but to the republic itself. She made it her mission "with a full determination to keep my eye on priests and missionaries, determined to strip the mask from hypocrisy, expose evil, patronize virtue, and side with no sect or party."[45]

But America in the throes of the Second Great Awakening was no place for a Voltaire in training. Though she was far from an atheist and if anything believed strongly in the ecumenical tenets of her beloved Masonry, the charges that Anne Royall levied against clergymen sound caustic even today: "Their visage is long, their complexion a dirty wan; they are generally tall, gaunt and supple! Distant and vulgar in their manners, the gloom of their countenance is never interrupted with a smile. They usually have a train of women after them with the same lowering looks." She counted their worst offense eroding the separation between church and state and advocating for laws that tried to ban public and private activity on Sunday. In her *Black Book* of travel writing and commentary, she laid out her view of evangelical churchmen and missionaries in bracing style, positing her view of the Bible against theirs:

> *A Christian is one thing, they another. A Christian honors his country and respects its rulers. They disgrace their country, and call their rulers a lawless set of men, that must be put down. A Christian is meek and merciful. They are turbulent and cruel. . . . A Christian loves his neighbor and honors God. They hate their neighbor; call him a heretic, an infidel; and make God no better than a usurer.*[46]

In one chapter alone, she rails for more than eighty pages against the evils of missionaries, going into hair-splitting detail about their severe and inhuman philosophy, their insidious methods of conversion, and their subversive methods of undermining the body politic. Needless to say, the churchmen took notice.

Sacred versus Profane

For her strong opinions, the clergymen made Anne Royall a pariah and inveighed against her brand of anticlericalism. They cast her as a godless harpy and a threat to moral order. A man she called a "missionary" even attacked her in Vermont in 1827, dislocating her ankle and keeping her off her feet for six months.[47] But her foremost nemesis was the Reverend Ezra Stiles Ely of Philadelphia, a champion of melding church and state through the election of avowedly Christian candidates for office.

A skillful polemicist—through his American Tract Society, which widely distributed his pamphlets in the 1820s[48]—Ely and his associate in the District, John Coyle, hatched a plan to bait Royall into trouble. First, a group of children on their way to Sunday school threw rocks at her house and broke her windows. She told their parents, but they took no action to stop the little miscreants. Instead, groups of churchgoers prayed and chanted below her broken windows around the clock. After several days of religious racket, she had had enough and called one prayer leader, Coyle himself, a "damned old bald headed son of a bitch." This rare example of her using profanity lit the fuse, and soon a group of young boys and church leaders came "to shower the house with stones, yell and blow horns."[49] A grand jury convened—but instead of going after the rock-throwers, it indicted Anne Royall herself.

The clergymen got what they wanted. The local district attorney accused her of being "a public nuisance, a common brawler, and a common scold."[50] Those were the official charges, but the unofficial charge was just as damning: Anne Royall was a menace to the natural ideal of womanhood. Instead of being demure, unthreatening, and docile, she was proud, acerbic, and fierce. Had she been a man, she never would have faced the same legal complaint, particularly in the vigorous culture of dispute that prevailed then in which pro- and anticlerical activists used all manner of rhetoric and sometimes violence against one another.[51] A frail sixty-year-old widow couldn't use physical force to her advantage, but her words got her into more than enough trouble.

The idea of the "common scold" had a long and dubious history, going all the way back to the medieval era. Originally it amounted to little more than a woman disturbing the peace, but it evolved into an all-purpose charge to contain the behavior of "disorderly" women. With a growing number of such women in the frenzied, increasingly democratic culture of the 1820s and 1830s, the list of charges expanded for female offenders, including such "crimes" as "lewd and lascivious carriage, stubbornness and disorderly conduct, to adultery and fornication."[52] To those in charge, Anne Royall seemed as good a test case as any.

Virago on Trial

The trial that followed owed less to tragedy and more to farce. Instead of sober testimony, Royall offered up an impressive display of wit and sarcasm that had the galleries laughing. She labeled her accusers "Satan's walking-stick" and "a good natured simpleton." She described one of them this way: "His hair is macaroni, his arms over five feet extended, his face pale, his nose hooked, with a gray goggle eye, and Shakespeare's smile." She facetiously suggested the trial was a great event to be "painted and put in the rotunda of the Capitol with our national paintings, reserving a conspicuous place for myself."[53] The opposing side offered up the usual ponderous arguments, depicting her as a vulgar harridan, a threat to public order, and a "virago"—that is, a woman who broke established gender boundaries and behaved like a man.[54] (More ambivalently, John Quincy Adams had once pronounced her "a virago errant in enchanted armor.") In the end, the US Circuit Court found her guilty. Then the real absurdity began.

The traditional punishment for a common scold was "ducking," in which the offender was lowered by chair into a body of cold water. The time spent underwater could last a few seconds or, as one wag put it, "in Mrs. Royall's case, perhaps from two to four hours."[55] Marines at the Navy Yard duly constructed the ducking stool in short order and showed it off to interested crowds.[56] Its rope coil turned a lever that could deposit a chair into, say, the Eastern Branch of the Potomac, with the common scold buckled in for her chilly plunge and public shaming. It was one of the most ingenious and ridiculous disciplinary devices ever created in America, and luckily it never got to "duck" anyone. Anne Royall got off with a ten-dollar fine, the equivalent of a modern speeding ticket.[57]

Although embarrassed by the episode, Royall had become a public figure. People were now seeking out and buying her writing, and she made some surprising friends in influential places, namely at such newspapers as the *National Intelligencer*—whose reporters paid the fine in her honor—and in the Andrew Jackson wing of the Democratic Party, which she generally supported.[58] (In one famous legend, upon arriving in town, Ms. Royall encountered Jackson's nemesis, John Quincy Adams, skinny-dipping in the river. Finding a captive audience, she sat down on his clothes while lecturing the naked president on various issues of the day.)

Understandably the whole episode only fired her up more to write about corruption and injustice where she saw it, to root out malefactors where she found them, and to add to her growing ranks of friends and enemies—all of which made her a fitting symbol of an adversarial age.

Unsteady State

These events occurred at a time when Jackson's policies were sending his admirers into a lather of excitement and his detractors into a stew of contempt, whether he set his targets on opposition senators, New York bankers, or Native tribes. Regardless of their effect, Jackson's policies did help secure the votes and loyalty of much of the white working class, turning the party into an electoral force that dominated American politics until the Civil War.

Still, while they had attained a newfound political importance, the mechanics remained economically vulnerable. No matter how many hands Jackson shook at his levees, his political ethos didn't do much for laborers struggling to make ends meet. Skilled tradesmen still eked out a meager existence, sometimes sufficient for survival but more often hampered by the lack of commerce and industry in the District. Unskilled laborers had to make do with seasonal work that depended on whether congressional funds, private capital, or lotteries could get a construction project started or keep one going for more than a few months. Everyone lived under the constant threat of the next economic bubble or "panic" that could put workers out of work and into the poorhouse. This unsteady state was most apparent in how and where people lived.

Capital Enclaves

The houses of Washington City were scattered widely over the terrain, making for a crazy quilt of farmland, log cabins, simple frame houses, and planter estates more akin to a rural landscape than anything urban.[59]

In 1800 the city had only 372 houses, most wooden but a good number brick, and this number increased to 2,346 by 1823.[60] Many workers lodged at taverns or boardinghouses, with multiple men and sometimes entire families jammed into spaces meant for far fewer people. The lack of affordable housing caused the construction grounds around the Capitol and President's House to mushroom with dumpy wooden huts, giving a dismal cast to even the finest landscapes of the District.[61] Even "permanent" structures looked ramshackle and temporary, including an array of one- and two-story frame houses and tiny wooden hovels that resembled booths at English country fairs, stuffed with up to eight people inside.[62]

As the years progressed, the larger houses were subdivided and their yards filled in with smaller, often dark and cramped back-buildings that lined the interior streets and alleys. This created a neo-medieval but characteristically Washingtonian housing pattern that bred disease and claustrophobia during the next century. In more established cities like Georgetown, housing conditions for workers and the poor didn't rate much better. Some single-story wooden houses contained as little as

The Patent Office looming over the chockablock buildings of downtown Washington City in 1846.

two hundred square feet lit by two small windows. Some of the crudest structures had walls of planks or logs, the smallest no more than ten feet square.[63]

Amid this landscape of scattershot development, a few pockets of dwellings made for what some called neighborhoods, but they were really more like tiny enclaves where ethnic groups crowded together, rudimentary gangs established hangouts, and feral children roamed in packs. Samuel Busey's nostalgic *Pictures of the City of Washington in the Past* and Constance Green's urban history provide a glimpse into some of the more colorful redoubts:

- Camp Hill, near the US Observatory, the local lovers' lane
- Chicken Cock Hill, part of the former Carroll estate that became contested turf for rival groups of stone-throwing children
- Chronic Row, north of Foggy Bottom, home to "chronic drinkers and fighters"
- English Hill, northeast of downtown, small weedy area with its own street gang
- Frogtown, south of the Capitol, known less for amphibians than for its street gangs
- The Island, mostly downtrodden area southwest of the city canal, which acted as a moat between it and the rest of town
- Night Hawk Hill, northeast of the White House, a favorite place for hunters to shoot the eponymous birds
- Northern Liberties, north of downtown, known for its market, firehouse company, and street gang
- Paddy Mageetown, north of Foggy Bottom, named for a mythical Irish tavern keeper and home to "good drinkers and a jolly set"
- School House Hill, between Georgetown and Washington City, where children battled and "the weapons were stones, and cut heads were the usual casualties"
- Shinar's Lake, southeast of Capitol Hill, one of many disease-breeding swamps
- Swampoodle, half a mile north of the Capitol, notorious Irish slum built over the Tiber Creek marsh[64]

Traveling from one of these areas to another—to go to work, visit a favorite tavern, or hunt down a rival group of schoolchildren—was no easy task in Washington City. The distances were ridiculously long, the streets uniformly terrible, and the landscape littered with swamps, gullies, and rocky outcrops. You could get around, though, if you had a few cents.

Taking the Low Roads

Coming in to Washington City from the Potomac shoreline, Anne Royall rode in a "carry-all," a sort of stagecoach that could hold up to twenty people[65] and conveyed its passengers under the power of a pair of draft horses.[66] Several irregularly scheduled omnibus lines operated around town, and on a typical trip, for twelve and a half cents, a rider could expect to be jostled to the point of nausea in a cramped wooden box at the mercy of a driver going much too fast for the capital's miserable, mire-choked roads.[67] Smaller hackney cabs cost a little more, between twelve and twenty-five cents, and, though the city established exact rates, unscrupulous drivers often hid the official rate sheet and charged up to four times as much.[68]

If you wanted to get out of town and away from the heat and dust of the capital, taking a stagecoach was a more expensive proposition. During the early nineteenth century, it cost three dollars (almost a week's wages) to take a trip from, say, Georgetown to Annapolis.[69] But riding in a stagecoach over any distance amounted to slow-moving torture, as Thomas Twining recounts in his *Travels in America 100 Years Ago*. Not only was the road itself "in a very rude state," full of stumps and mud, but the passengers were mashed together in the wagon to prevent it from overturning, and the "obscurity and suffocation" of the vehicle's interior was "very dark and oppressively hot, there being no aperture for light and air excepting the front."[70]

Mechanic Gastronomy

If a coach ride lay beyond the means of the mechanics of the District, so too did a good meal. Taverns commonly offered sustenance for all classes, as we'll see, but workers had fewer options at home. They could put soup and vegetables on the table, but hardly any of them had more than spoons with which to eat; knives and forks were uncommon. Most people had plenty of chairs on which to seat their guests around mahogany tables, but the majority didn't have tablecloths to cover them. The food served on those tables was bland and monotonous—bread, bacon, sweet potatoes, and cabbage—but diners did have the option of nineteenth-century takeout: One Alexandria business sold hot mutton, beef, veal, and chicken pies for those who didn't feel like cooking.[71]

Of course, dining out anywhere was a luxury, and gourmands typically had to make do at one of the markets in town. By the 1840s the District had four of them, one on Capitol Hill, one at the Navy Yard, and two downtown.[72] At the better markets and certain groceries you could find a variety of meat and fish, fruits and vegetables, nuts and spices, wine and pastries, and even oysters and wild mushrooms.[73] Despite the variety of options on site, buyers often griped about prices, which could exceed the budgets of many laborers. In the summer of 1820, for example, a bushel of potatoes cost between fifty and seventy-five cents, as much as a daily wage for some.[74]

The largest emporium, the legendary Centre Market, bordered the city canal on 7th Street and began at the turn of the nineteenth century. Known as the "Marsh Market," it was built on Tiber Creek swampland

Centre Market, the famed meat and produce emporium, stood for nearly 130 years in various forms.

at one of the lowest points in the District, and as it grew it expanded over the reclaimed mire. Charged an annual fee of just ten dollars for renting a market stall, sellers flocked to the popular market and brought a bounty of goods.[75] Librarian of Congress George Watterston claimed "the quality and abundance of the commodities brought there for sale, is not excelled by any market in the United States"—an exaggeration, but it was one of the biggest in the Chesapeake region.[76] Jefferson even maintained a seasonality chart that showed which of the market's thirty-seven different vegetables were available when. It directed him to buy sprouts from February to May, asparagus from April to June, and radishes from September to December.[77] Less appealingly, in a live-fish market at the back of the complex, fishmongers kept their selection "fresh" in baskets lowered into the fetid waters of the city canal.[78]

The market sat at one of the liveliest corners in town, adjacent to an energetic street scene where Washingtonians gambled, ate and drank, caroused, and sometimes fought. Theaters, saloons, and restaurants lined Pennsylvania Avenue here, along with messier butcheries, tanneries, and woolen mills. Area undertakers announced their services with wooden coffins propped up on the sidewalk.[79] The market's popularity made it the center of chaos: An array of tumbledown huts and shacks littered the street; sellers hawked their wares from rickety frame sheds; and produce wagons backed up traffic to 11th Street.[80] But the market offered chaos with a purpose: By paying rent to the town, the vendors provided one of the few reliable sources of municipal income. After the Civil War, the site grew into the largest and most modern food market in the country.[81]

Popular Distractions

Also along this busy stretch of avenue, a goodly number of amusements gave the mechanics a break from their toil and bland diets. Although violent forms of "entertainment" like fistfights and blood sport were well established by the mid-nineteenth century (as we'll see later), less aggressive pursuits were also on offer.

In the 1790s, for between twenty-five and seventy-five cents, a Georgetowner or Alexandrian could drop by a local tavern like Suter's or Ward's and catch an itinerant theater troupe performing a recent play, with musical interludes for those who wanted to stretch their legs and dance. On view might be a stirring drama such as *The Roman Father; or, He Saved All Who Saved the State*, a farce such as *The Devil to Pay*, or a rousing selection of "Republican Songs of Mount Vernon and the Land of Freedom." The shows often included material from British authors, with various Shakespearean plays, comedies of manners, tear-jerking melodramas, and a "historical pantomime" of *Robinson Crusoe* making appearances.[82]

A more permanent theater came into being just after the capital did. On its opening night in 1804, the Washington Theatre, a major draw, promised to delight crowds with a "Grand Medley Entertainment" of assorted "songs, magic, dancing and acting automatons, mechanical pictures, and spectacular effects." That theater lasted until 1836, when the National Theatre, founded the year before, put it out of business and became a theatrical institution. The National Theatre offered a similar repertoire and a shifting seating design. At first the lower classes occupied the parterre (floor seating), with the elites in boxes above, as in Elizabethan England. But once the theater owners realized that some of the best seats were down below, they redesigned it, moving working-class folk to the upper balcony—where there was a convenient saloon—and putting black theatergoers even farther back on the most distant, third level, a segregation policy that lasted until 1952.[83]

The theater business was a rough trade. Actors were paid minimal sums and had to travel by crude wagons or on foot between venues. Newspapers largely ignored theatrical performances, except for displaying their ads.[84] Most of the venues, though well attended, left a lot to be desired. When the National opened, Frances Trollope complained it was "astonishingly dirty and void of decoration, considering that it is the only place of amusement the city affords."[85] Audiences were rowdy at best, disdainful at worst, prone to "loud talking, whooping, hee-hawing, swearing" and yelling "Hats off in front!"[86] As Trollope reports:

> *One man in the pit was seized with a violent fit of vomiting, which appeared not in the least to annoy or surprise his neighbours. . . . The spitting was incessant; and not one in ten of the male part of the illustrious legislative audiences sat according to the usual custom of human beings; the legs were thrown sometimes over the front of the*

*box, sometimes over the side of it. . . . In many instances the front rail
was preferred as a seat.*[87]

The crowd knew what it liked, and it particularly liked theater legend Edwin Forrest, who made triumphant appearances in Washington
City in the 1830s in an assortment of Shakespearean roles, delighting
theatergoers with his punchy, emphatic style.[88] He wasn't what you'd call
naturalistic, but he did send the crowd into a frenzy with his "explosions
of physical action" as he showcased "the vital, burly, aggressive American-
ism of his age"[89] —which of course reflected the behavior of much of the
audience.

Related Diversions

Theater wasn't the only amusement in town for mechanics with a little
spare cash. One of the first circuses appeared in the 1790s, featuring rope
dancing and "comic feats on horseback" by a husband-and-wife team
with a "Polander Dwarf too and a trained horse known as Cornplanter."
George Washington even made an honorary appearance in the audience.[90] Traveling circuses also came to town, with names such as "The
Grand Caravan of Most Rare and Interesting Animals," which advertised
their exotic beasts and charged visitors a quarter to see leopards, monkeys,
tigers, and zebras. The National Theatre itself briefly became a circus in
1844, "the pit becoming an amphitheatre for clowns, trained horses, and
educated dogs."[91]

Just a few years later, panoramas—huge sheets of painted canvas—
provided the first "moving pictures" long before the invention of cinema.
For fifty cents, viewers could watch exotic foreign scenes or heroic conti-
nental landscapes unwind across giant cylinders in dramatically lit rooms.
On tour in Washington City in April 1850, Henry Lewis's panorama
depicted Mississippi River scenes on a colossal scroll a mile long, among
the largest in America or Europe. In the crowd sat President Zachary
Taylor, who gazed at evocative scenes that included his own Cypress
Grove estate, one of the last times he "saw" his plantation before dying
two months later.[92]

For less enlightened pursuits, the District had a number of race-
courses that drew a wide mix of gamblers. Christian Hines recalls several

popular tracks where bettors could watch stock horses compete in the heat and dust of graded farmland near cornfields and apple orchards.[93] As one reverend who attended a race in 1803 recalled, the spectators were "three and four thousand, black, white and yellow; of all conditions from the President of the United States to the beggar in his rags, of all ages and of both sexes, for I should judge one-third were females."[94]

Wagering offered a great amusement for all corners of society, whether that meant senators playing whist, merchants betting on cards in a tavern, or laborers speculating on which rooster would hack the other to pieces. In most American cities in the early nineteenth century, the most popular games included Hazard, which involved slamming boxes of dice on a well-worn tavern table; Brag, a card game like poker; and Faro, a table game with intricate rules.[95] The District had harsh laws against gambling, but the authorities usually ignored them unless someone needed to go to court to get his money back from a swindler. The pastime was so visible throughout the District that the most prominent stretch of Pennsylvania Avenue was "lined with faro banks, where good suppers were served and well-supplied sideboards were free to all comers."[96] As Anne Royall wrote, "Gambling, and play of almost every description, is almost wholly exploded in Washington at present, and (I am sorry to add) I wish I could say the same of other vices.[97]

Crank for the Ages

With her trenchant commentary, Anne Royall continued to play a notable role in the District in the 1830s, tormenting her enemies with her gadfly prose and acting as a keen, sardonic observer of the changes taking place. She soured on the Jacksonians by the later part of the decade, using her publications *Paul Pry* and *The Huntress*—arguably the first muckraking papers in the country—to inveigh against corruption and fight against atrocities like "Post Office frauds," "Indian land frauds," and "the abandonment of Reform by General Jackson." For her uniquely abrasive style and scabrous opinions, her rivals called her a "public nuisance," an "old hag," and a "crank."[98] Insults escalated to violence when a crazed bookstore clerk in Pittsburgh whipped her bloody with a cowskin, and she barely escaped an angry mob in Charlottesville, Virginia.[99]

Undaunted, this small, elderly woman continued to stir the pot, exploring and writing about the various regions of the expanding nation. She provided detailed descriptions of the best and worst of the American character, including the myriad run-ins she had with any number of people. Although not the most even-tempered witness to her times, she gives a clear picture of the violent, ragged world of Washington City in the antebellum years, imparting details of the social and cultural life of the capital that might otherwise have been lost to history or obscured by more reverent writers. That's one reason, among many, that her work seems so engaging and lively today, while the writing of her contemporaries often feels so dry, musty, and dead. Not surprisingly, thanks to her vitality, she outlasted many of her adversaries and the obstacles they put in her path, and finally received her husband's pension in 1848—at the age of seventy-nine.[100]

FOUR

DRIVING SOULS

Perceptive as she was, Anne Royall couldn't overcome the great moral blind spot of her age: slavery. She firmly opposed the institution in print, but she held slaves at various points in her life along with a wary view of abolition.[1] Like her, many intellectuals of the era ought to have known better, but they instead chose to rationalize a practice that even casual visitors to America knew caused limitless human suffering and terror. Washington City served as one of the nation's most prominent depots of slave trading, but the town's guidebook writers barely mentioned it. In this respect, Anne Royall fell squarely in line with the shameless civic boosters she despised.

Slavery came to the English colonies in 1619 when a Dutch trading ship brought twenty slaves to Jamestown, Virginia. Tobacco planters favored forced human labor to cultivate their cash crop,[2] but by the end of the eighteenth century, tobacco cultivation had largely become a dead letter along the Potomac. Farmers had exhausted the soil on many of the old plantations, and the agricultural infrastructure was collapsing. Slavery, however, persisted.

In 1800 African Americans made up 29 percent of the District's roughly 14,000 people, with 80 percent of their number enslaved. Few free blacks owned property in the capital or held prominent occupations. (Benjamin Banneker, Andrew Ellicott's surveyor assistant in 1791, had been a rare exception.) The laws of Maryland and Virginia, which held sway in DC until the 1830s, severely limited them with a broad range of codes and restrictions. In Virginia, freed slaves couldn't even remain in the state, which gave them six months to leave after their manumission or risk being sold back into slavery.[3]

Forced labor was common enough in Washington City that contractors used slaves to build the Capitol. This fact went unremarked in histories of the District throughout the nineteenth century, but in more recent decades the weight of evidence has made the conclusion unavoidable. Even Congress itself had to recognize the truth when in 2009 it produced a formal resolution that included the following introductory clauses:

> *Whereas enslaved African-Americans provided labor essential to the construction of the United States Capitol;*
>
> *Whereas enslaved African-Americans performed the back-breaking work of quarrying the stone which comprised many of the floors, walls, and columns of the Capitol;*
>
> *Whereas enslaved African-Americans also participated in other facets of the construction of the Capitol, including carpentry, masonry, carting, rafting, roofing, plastering, glazing, painting, and sawing;*
>
> *Whereas the marble columns in the Old Senate Chamber and the sandstone walls of the East Front corridor remain as the lasting legacies of the enslaved African-Americans who worked the quarries. . .*
>
> . . . therefore a plaque would be placed in the visitor center.[4]

As admissions of guilt go, it wasn't much. But at least it put an official imprimatur on our understanding of just how fundamental slavery was to the District. Indeed, the very presence of the "peculiar institution" in the capital served as a symbol for all the contradictions of a place where the defenders of human bondage and the champions of personal liberty not only coexisted but bizarrely were often one in the same.

Slavery Calculus

American slavery didn't belong exclusively to the province of white-suit-wearing, mint-julep-swilling plantation masters in Greek Revival mansions on the banks of the Mississippi. Instead, it was an endemic transnational phenomenon that connected the "slave supply in Virginia, credit availability from New York, cotton prices on the Liverpool market, and the prices and demand for slaves at New Orleans and Natchez."[5]

Numerous corporations took part in this complex financial web of buying and selling human beings. Modern descendants of those companies include investment banks such as Lehman Brothers; railroads Norfolk Southern and CSX (which took over the B&O Railroad); publishers Knight Ridder, Gannett, and Tribune Company; and insurance carriers Aetna and AIG[6]—and that doesn't take into account the many institutions, including the nation's oldest and most prestigious universities, that invested in and therefore profited from the companies doing the dirty work.

With the mortality rate for humans used as chattel as high as it was, a range of insurance companies issued policies to slaveholders to protect their "property," including one in 1856 that cost $2.00 to insure a ten-year-old domestic worker and another that cost $5.50 for a middle-aged adult slave.[7] Carrying the calculus of human bondage further, D. B. Warden notes in his 1816 Washington City guide that the daily expense of a slave, which took into account food, drink, clothing, and insurance, totaled "nearly twenty-seven cents." Washington City taxed the owners of male slaves aged fifteen to forty-five $1.50 each and comparable females a dollar.[8]

Once established, slavery inevitably required a fully integrated network to support it: Owners had title to fellow humans; traders trafficked in such "commodities"; companies created infrastructure to support that economy; local governments regulated the trade with laws and taxes; and the national government tied domestic slavery to foreign trade, principally with Britain. All these aspects of the slave trade united in one place: the American capital itself.

The Architecture of Confinement

In 1800 slaves were visible on area plantations and at occasional slave auctions, but not to the degree that came after Congress banned the transatlantic slave trade in 1808.[9] That ban wasn't as high-minded as it sounded: It had less to do with abolishing the barbaric practice than with increasing the value of slaves already present in North America and fostering an increasingly lucrative domestic trade.

By the middle of the next decade, a boom in cotton sales and production in the Deep South created a yawning demand for slaves nationwide, with Alexandria and Washington City quickly taking advantage.[10] Within two decades the region had transformed itself from a sleepy backwater with a scattering of slaves on shambling farmsteads into a fearsome juggernaut of slave trading, the "great Man-market of the nation," according to a famous broadside.[11]

Abolitionist broadsides decried the sale of human beings in "the land of the free." See next page for detail images.

Even free blacks could be sold into slavery.

The Alexandria prison where slaves were held until being sold to plantations in the Deep South.

The port of Alexandria in particular became a hub for the delivery of slaves from Philadelphia, Baltimore, and other American locations. The Virginia port also shipped out men, women, and children born and raised in the capital area as captives to plantations and other sites around the country. Ship manifests from the late eighteenth and early nineteenth centuries provide physical descriptions of their human cargo with elliptical yet revealing notes. Along with age, height, and skin tone—"dark," "brown," "light," "fair"—slaves are identified by the scars on their bodies. In one case, sixteen-year-old Alexandria native Jonathan Horne had a lump on his lower lip, a smallpox mark on his chin, a mark of unknown origin on his left arm, and a "crossmark by the bite of a dog on his left cheek." Other slaves exhibited telltale burns, cuts, pricks, scars and "red marks" across their bodies.[12]

One of the largest landowners was Notley Young, his acreage occupying almost all of Southwest Washington City in a sprawling estate worked by sixty bondsmen housed in eleven buildings marked "Negro quarters." A typical slave quarter might contain "pens" made of rough logs, with walls, fireplace, a roof, and little else. Only fourteen by sixteen feet in size, such a cramped wooden box may have held up to ten people.[13] Bondsmen planted and harvested crops of various kinds and brought them to market. They assisted in the operation of the estate houses by cooking, sewing, cleaning, and undertaking other household chores. They built new outbuildings and fixed old ones and generally performed the labors necessary to make the farm profitable.

More numerous than the planters, though, were common slaveholders, who usually had only a few slaves they used as domestic workers. Some stayed in their masters' attics, stables, or carriage houses, but in other cases the middle-class house itself served as a sort of prison. Back yards essentially became slave spaces, often with a two-story outbuilding with kitchens, laundries, and other service rooms on the ground floor and sleeping quarters above.[14] Confined by high brick walls up to a foot thick, forced laborers found themselves trapped away from public view, in isolated rooms without windows, and corridors without exits. Inside this harsh, inhuman space, "the bondsman could see only a maze of brick and stone, the forbidding reminders of his servile confinement."[15]

Newer urban houses for the elite replaced the old plantations with stylish architecture in front and hidden slave quarters in back. One of the most prominent examples, John Tayloe's Octagon—which had six sides instead of eight—was among the most famous private houses in Washington City. Designed by Capitol architect William Thornton in the Federal style, it hosted ambassadors and treaty signings and served as the residence of the president after the British burned the White House. Its high walls enclosed a two-story structure for slaves and outbuildings, which included a stable, smokehouse, and cowshed.[16] It also had a basement with a kitchen and a warren of narrow little rooms and work spaces. While slaves labored in the hot, choking confines belowground, "men in their picturesque costumes [and] ladies in their Empire dresses of soft silk" danced "graceful minuets" on the floors above.[17]

Rise of the Slavemongers

But slaves who had the misfortune to pass through the District, instead of living there, had it worse. Everyone knew what awaited bondsmen sold to the Deep South, say, to a mosquito-infested Louisiana sugar cane plantation or, more likely, an industrial cotton operation in the wilds of Alabama and Mississippi: isolation on a remote farmstead, the violence of the lash, years of crushing labor, and often an early death. Masters in the capital used their slaves' knowledge of the terror of being sold to the Deep South as leverage beyond the whip, or shipped them away without a second thought if there wasn't enough work available.[18]

Isaac Franklin, one of the District's upstarts, founded his slaving operation in the capital with his nephew John Armfield (along with partner Rice Ballard outside DC) in 1828. It was the first and most notorious of five successive slave-trading firms to operate from the same headquarters in Alexandria, the last operating until the Civil War.[19] The Franklin and Armfield business initially acquired capital from a range of national banks to buy slaves from the decaying plantations of Maryland and Virginia. From there, they sent their human cargo to New Orleans and Natchez, then routed their profits back through banks in New York and Philadelphia. They fiendishly converted human beings into commodities, whether "packed onto slavers' brigs like cordwood, imprisoned in cholera-infested Natchez pens like cattle, or displayed on the market like wool and ivory."

They used that last phrase, "wool and ivory," as shorthand for blacks in general and developed a range of euphemisms to describe both their business operations and those whom they shipped into bondage. One such term was "fancy maid," which, despite its winsome connotations, referred to a woman sold for carnal exploitation, to be kept as a sex slave for planters or otherwise raped by the traders themselves. To this end, the slavers impudently called themselves "one-eyed men," in crude reference to their genitals.[20]

The traders didn't open their prison to the general public, but they weren't exactly discreet, either. One of their advertisements in an Alexandria newspaper promised CASH FOR 500 NEGROES:

Including both sexes, from 12 to 25 years of age. Persons having likely servants to dispose of, will find it to their interest to give us a call, as we will give higher prices, in cash, than any other purchaser who is now, or may hereafter come into this market.[21]

Professor E. A. Andrews, a fervent critic of slavery, received a rare private tour of Franklin and Armfield's slave pen. It was the early American equivalent of a publicity tour for a prison, with inmates lined up for inspection, "the most studied attention paid to cleanliness" of the facility, and the slave traders acting as witty, gracious hosts. But Andrews saw the great lie for what it was, a testament to the "countless evils occasioned in this world of sin and misery."[22]

The slavemongers couldn't fully conceal their horrors from the general public, and more than a few residents found it contradictory at the very least that those operations should spring up in a town that billed itself as a paragon of liberty. One man, Solomon Northup, whose story of being kidnapped into Southern slavery, *Twelve Years a Slave*, has become quite well known recently, recalls looking out from the windows of a holding cell to see a familiar building: "Strange as it may seem, within plain sight of this same house, looking down from its commanding height upon it, was the Capitol. The voices of patriotic representatives boasting of freedom and equality, and the rattling of the poor slave's chains, almost commingled. A slave pen within the very shadow of the Capitol!"[23]

Even more conspicuous was the sight of slave drivers forcing their gangs through the street with "the whip of the slave-driver and the

Slaves in leg irons being marched off to auction were a common sight in prewar DC.

clanking of chains" providing the soundtrack as "the gangs were kept together and driven like sheep under the watchful eyes of their brutal guards."[24] In regular public human auctions, slavers broke up families and parceled them out to different parts of the country, stripped and revealed the naked bodies of their captives before the eyes of eager buyers, and even forced them to dance to showcase their "liveliness."[25] Such inhumanity composed a typical day's work for the men known as "soul-drivers."[26]

Private Prisons

The drivers held their captives in notorious slave warrens in cellars and basements of houses, hotels, and taverns, carefully confined away from the public view. The Williams Slave Pen sat across from the Smithsonian grounds, a three-story, "pleasant looking" brick house in which slaves were tightly shackled in a holding room next to the kitchen.[27] The pen at Robey's Tavern was a "wretched hovel" near the Capitol with no air circulation, oppressively hot in summer and frigid in winter, its conditions worse than regular jail cells.[28] The St. Charles Hotel contained subterranean rooms with six thirty-foot-long barrel-vaulted cells with iron rings attached to the walls to secure the captives.[29] It even advertised its services: "The Proprietor of this hotel has roomy underground cells for confining slaves for safe keeping, and patrons are notified that their slaves will be well cared for. In case of escape, full value of the Negro will be paid for by the Proprietor."[30]

"Well cared for" is an audacious euphemism—most accounts of these prisons describe people forced to sleep on cold floors, chained to walls, whipped and beaten by overseers, stuffed into gloomy cells, and unprotected from vermin or disease. During an 1832 cholera epidemic, the number of deaths at one slave pen reached such a number "that both coffins and undertakers were insufficient to fill the demand, and they were obliged to send to other cities for help."[31]

The Picture of Cruelty

As the slave trade became more visible, some began calling for change. One event in particular crystallized many opinions against the practice. In 1815 a black woman, name unknown, jumped from the third-story window of a downtown tavern where she was being held and broke her back and both arms in the fall. She was desperately trying to escape the men who had confined her and to keep from being separated from her husband and children—to no avail.[32] The story spread widely thanks to Jesse Torrey's seminal book *A Portraiture of Domestic Slavery, in the United States*, which not only brought attention to the cruelties meted out to slaves but also to the kidnapping of free black citizens.

Torrey had spoken to two such individuals, Delaware residents, whom the slavers had kidnapped and held in the same tavern from which the woman had leapt. He then went a step further and raised funds for their legal defense, and a few months later a court freed them.[33] This episode wasn't isolated. Critics of slavery claimed the traders' primary goal was to "kidnap every colored stranger they could lay their hands on,"[34] and the burden of proof lay on black citizens to prove they were free. If they didn't have the right papers, they could be arrested and sold at auction. Even if they did have proof but were arrested mistakenly, they could still be sold as slaves if they couldn't pay for their room and board while wrongly imprisoned.[35]

The sight of captives manacled and dragged through the streets, the horrific conditions of the slave pens, the division of families at auction, the kidnapping of free blacks—these atrocities led many to call for the end of slave trafficking in the capital. One of the most vocal was John Randolph, House member from Virginia, an active slaveholder and ardent states' rights champion, who nevertheless saw slave trading as "a crying shame before God and man, not surpassed in abomination in any part of the earth; for in no part of it, not even excepting the rivers on the coast of Africa, is there so great, so infamous a slave market as in the metropolis, in the seat of government of this nation which prides itself on freedom."[36]

Judge James Morsell of the Circuit Court conducted a judicial investigation on the legality of "manacled captives" being driven through the streets, seeing it as "repugnant" to the spirit of the republic and the rights of humanity.[37] Jesse Torrey called for Congress, as "guardians of the public liberty," to ensure that free blacks were not kidnapped or otherwise abused by the traffickers.[38] Washington City citizens, including a number of slaveholders, presented a petition to Congress in 1819 demanding an end to the transport of slaves through the city and their shipment from it.[39] To these carefully worded calls, petitions, and entreaties, members of the national legislature considered this great moral question, took stock of the weighty issues—and did nothing.

The Colonial Gambit

In the absence of congressional action, it appeared that the nation's leading politicians might find a different way to end slave trafficking. Just before Torrey's polemic against the trade appeared, figures such as John Randolph, Henry Clay, and Daniel Webster staged the first meeting of the American Colonization Society.[40] With Torrey himself claiming credit for the idea behind the group, the society stated its goal as bringing about the demise of slave trading and similar practices by founding an African colony that would take in blacks from America and develop a sort of model society of freedmen.[41] In 1820 the first waves of expatriated blacks began arriving on the western coast of Africa, and two years after that they founded the new country of Liberia. They named their capital Monrovia in honor of then-president James Monroe, author of the political doctrine that forbade European colonization of or interference in the Western Hemisphere but helpfully said nothing about American colonization of or interference in the Eastern Hemisphere.

Leading opponents of slavery supported the society, as did leading slaveholders, but the group favored getting rid of the public eyesore of slave trading rather than eradicating the institution itself. It never wanted to free slaves but to ship free blacks to Africa.[42] Thus the group's dual purpose, according to critics, was salving the conscience of whites troubled by signs of the slave economy and reducing the number of free blacks in America who might threaten that economy. Which explains why major slaveholders such as Randolph, who owned hundreds of people, supported and belonged to the group.

Fighting the Plague

By contrast, the District's first real abolition movement took as much of a stance against colonization as it did slavery. Activists in the movement suspected the society of trying to ship the most ardent black opponents of slavery out of the country in order to strengthen the business of human bondage. Educator John Prout denounced moves to remove blacks from the only country most had ever known—the native country of many—and leading black figures from Baltimore, including teacher Jacob Greener and minister William Watkins, attacked the society in print and in public forums.[43] They advocated a branch of abolition called "immediatism" to counter the gradualism that wasn't making much progress against the moral scourge.

Among the most famous abolitionists in the Chesapeake region were Benjamin Lundy and William Lloyd Garrison. Lundy, a white Quaker, published his weekly *Genius of Universal Emancipation* in the Midwest before moving to Baltimore in 1824. There he worked with Greener and Watkins to print the newspaper and got into all manner of altercations with local slaveholders. He denounced one who brutally beat him in return; in court the judge called the beating a "merited chastisement" and

let the slaver off with a dollar fine.[44] Lundy left Baltimore soon after, finding Maryland's "spirit of tyranny . . . too strong and malignant for me."[45]

Garrison wrote for Lundy's paper before he famously began his
own antislavery newspaper, *The Liberator*, on January 1, 1831. In it he
denounced both African colonization and gradual abolition as wrong-
headed and counterproductive ideas. In that first issue, he didn't mince
words about the capital:

> *That District is rotten with the plague, and stinks in the nostrils of the*
> *world . . . a fouler spot scarcely exists on earth. In it the worst features of*
> *slavery are exhibited; and as a mart for slave-traders, it is unequalled.*
> *These facts are well known to our two or three hundred representatives,*
> *but no remedy is proposed; they are known, if not minutely at least*
> *generally, to our whole population,—but who calls for redress?[46]*

The answer of course was Garrison himself. However, while the
columnist activist had a huge impact on the nation, he did most of his
pioneering work from New England, and many of his opinions—which
favored women's rights and nonviolent protest and condemned American
politics and organized religion—lay so far ahead of their time that many
abolitionists, both black and white, kept their distance, seeing him as a
distraction from their primary goal.[47]

These abolitionists had more important matters to worry about than
Garrison, though. They operated in a place hostile to their goals at best,
at worst malicious and violent. Their protests often met with fists, bricks,
knives, or guns. One of their prime enemies was slave trader Hope Slatter,
notorious for separating black families at the auction block, abusing slaves
and their rescuers, and inciting mobs to attack abolitionists and blacks
in general. The threat that Slatter and many like him presented had the
paradoxical effect of binding black and white activists together, whether
"as victors over slaveholders or victims of their wrath."[48]

Mob Mentality

By the 1830s racial violence spread beyond those with a direct economic
interest in slavery to larger sections of the white public, who took alarm
at the competition that black emancipation might introduce to the white

working classes. Throughout the North, mobs attacked abolitionists and free blacks in churches and their homes, with conflicts in 1834 in New York City and Philadelphia turning especially fierce.[49]

The next summer in Washington City, the simmering climate of racial hostility increased as rumors flew of a slave attacking his master after being caught stealing. It worsened when officers arrested Reuben Crandall, a botanist and physician, for possession of abolitionist literature. District Attorney Francis Scott Key—composer of "The Star Spangled Banner," promoter of African colonization, and enemy of abolitionists— charged him with sedition and threw him in jail. In response, a mob of four hundred mechanics, including many striking laborers from the Navy Yard, converged on the jail to "take the damned rascal and hang him up on one of the trees."[50]

Finding him well guarded and inaccessible, the mob moved on to Beverly Snow, a black restaurateur, who allegedly had insulted the wives of white mechanics. Again not finding their intended victim, they settled for ransacking Snow's restaurant and destroying several black homes, schools, and churches.[51] Before the mob could march on the city's public buildings and destroy them too, soldiers were called out to be "posted at their doors, and their windows barricaded, to defend them against the citizens of Washington."[52] When the tumult subsided, the city council took quick action, not by enforcing laws against mob violence but by cracking down on business licenses issued to free blacks and by imposing other sanctions on them.[53]

Gag Reflex

Amid the chaos, some abolitionists continued to hold out hope that Congress would see the damage wrought by this social crisis and end slavery in the capital for good. In the mid-1830s they sent the government 100,000 petitions arguing for the abolition of slavery in DC, and by the end of the decade another half-million signatures arrived. Again, the gridlocked legislature failed to take action. Southern members vowed to defend slavery at all costs and even threatened the dissolution of the Union if they didn't get their way.[54] One measure that did break the gridlock and pass the House was the infamous gag rule, which prevented any petition related to slavery in the District to be read or discussed.[55]

Around the same time, William Lloyd Garrison's American Anti-Slavery Society mailed one million pamphlets to Southern editors, businessmen, and others to illuminate them on the topic of slavery. The pamphlets had their intended effect: The Southerners held great public bonfires with the mailers as fuel. The South saw the elimination of slave trading in terms of domino theory: Abolishing that institution would cause other established social traditions to tumble in an unbroken path that would lead invariably to the demise of the plantation system and of white supremacy.

Antislavery politicians of the North countered with a more immediate issue: They wanted to get rid of DC slavery because Northern tax dollars were financing the capital prisons where slave traffickers kept their captives,[56] a business of which they obviously wanted no part. But the most powerful Northerner, President Martin Van Buren, had a different view. In 1837 he promised to be "the inflexible and uncompromising opponent of every attempt on the part of Congress to abolish slavery in the District of Columbia against the wishes of the slaveholding states."[57] (This exercise in political cowardice didn't win him any friends in the North. In his failed reelection attempt, he lost 158 of the region's 170 electoral votes.)

The federal government was proving to be feckless. No matter the legal violation, the violent event, the moral outrage, Congress and the president chose inertia over action, and when they did act it usually made matters worse for the capital's black residents. In turn, many abolitionists gave up on legal paths to achieve an end to slavery, seeing the law as an impediment—instead of an avenue—to their goals.

Tales from the Underground

The Underground Railroad—a vast, awe-inspiring institution—had a formidable reach into the South. To white Southerners, it represented a conspiracy to deprive them of their property; for Northerners, it gave proof positive of the nightmarish conditions that slaves endured and their determination to escape it. The District of Columbia had one of the earliest and most well-established lines, which years later Frederick Douglass recalled as stretching from the capital to Philadelphia, New York, Albany, Rochester, and finally Canada, the true land of freedom.[58] Before escaped slaves reached any of those destinations, though, they traveled through a shadowy network of safe houses, many of them in destitute areas of Southern cities where they could find shelter and seclusion but police rarely ventured.[59]

The South fought back by limiting slaves' knowledge of local geography, levying steep and violent penalties on escapees, and fostering a counternetwork of professional slave catchers. The Washington Auxiliary Guard, which employed eighteen such men in the District, arrested free blacks for curfew violations and hunted down runaway slaves.[60] As the official history of the police department explains it: "The ringing of the [signal] bell at 10 p.m. was of special importance to the colored people, as after that hour if out without a pass they were subject to arrest, fine, and flogging. The last was administered sometimes at the guard-house and sometimes at the whipping-post of the jail, on the northeast corner of Judiciary Square."[61]

The Railroad needed daring and clever figures to counteract these measures, and two of the most adept were Thomas Smallwood, a

For violating the Black Code, countless blacks faced grim conditions
at the city jail.

middle-class shoemaker and former slave, and the Reverend Charles Torrey, whom some called "the regular Rob Roy MacGregor of dare-devil philanthropy."[62] Together the two worked to free Southern captives, establishing a wide network that included black and white abolitionists, among them a dentist, a minister, a boardinghouse owner, and an Ohio congressman. In 1842 alone they freed between 150 and 400 slaves in groups of ten to fifteen at a time. Individuals escaped singly or in pairs from bondage and converged at prearranged "places of deposit" around the Washington region, from where teamsters in wagons conveyed them northward.[63] The journey wasn't cheap to arrange; Smallwood and Torrey initially paid teamsters between eight and twenty-five dollars per escapee, later deciding to purchase their own wagon and horses instead.[64]

Slaveholders offered handsome rewards for the return of their "property," so those running the Underground Railroad took care not to trust people unknown to them.[65] Skirting the law and avoiding capture proved hard and dangerous work, yet it didn't stop Smallwood from taunting slaveholders in the pages of abolitionist newspapers that Torrey edited. Using the pen name Samivel Weller Jr. (after a character in *The Pickwick Papers* by Charles Dickens), Smallwood baited his enemies and mocked them as "poor puppies," among other jabs.[66] Taking care not to be identified, he successfully eluded capture over the years. If people did discover his name, authorities had difficulty finding him amid all the other Smallwoods in Washington City.[67]

Eventually his luck and Torrey's ran out, though. In November 1843 the police came upon their wagon, horses, and fourteen runaways and took possession of all of them. (Torrey brazenly filed suit to recover the wagon and horses seized from their illegal mission.)[68] The police raid ended Smallwood's activities in the capital, after which he relocated to Canada. Later in a memoir he condemned his former country as "hypocritical, guileful, and arrogant" and worse than any other nation in its treatment of black people.[69]

In his own writings Torrey offered an open threat to those holding slaves, saying "God judgeth the *heart* of each man. I do not. I only affirm the guilt of the sin, and its inconsistency with piety, and warn men to leave it off."[70] He continued his clandestine if increasingly daring liberation of slaves until late 1844, when Hope Slatter arranged for his arrest by Baltimore authorities. From a jail cell Torrey wrote: "The question of my prudence, I must adjourn to Judgement Day. I *have* done, many things in the South, that prudent men *dared* not do . . . I am *bold & decided*. God made me so. He did not make me *cautious*."[71]

Torrey may have been a zealot, but his zealotry did more to weaken the bonds of slavery in the Chesapeake than all the well-meaning words of politicians or the impassioned editorials of newspaper writers. It came at a cost, though. The reward for Torrey's lack of caution was death from tuberculosis in a Maryland prison in 1846.

The Freedmen's Progress

The Underground Railroad offered the most prominent local means of undermining slavery, but another force had just as great an impact. Its effects were subtle and took many years to accumulate, but in the end they proved unstoppable in undermining human bondage in the District. It was a small but fatal flaw in the mechanism of slavery itself.

From the beginning of the capital's history, Washington City constantly needed laborers to construct public buildings as well as its mansions and other structures. Contractors routinely ran short of workers, and the easiest, most expedient way of finding them was to hire slaves from their masters.[72] In the most visible example, from 1795 to 1801 contractors constructing the Capitol paid slaveholders sixty dollars per month per slave for all manner of manual labor, from carting and carpentry to plastering and painting. Most of the money went to the master of course, but slaves received allowances for working nights, Sundays, and holidays.[73] (This was notably the case for black sawyers on the project; for other trades and unskilled labor, the recompense may have been less.) Around the same time, city commissioners developed a plan for building projects that would pay slaves thirteen cents a day beyond what was owed the master. The commissioners offered this small sum not out of any sense of charity, but because they believed the amount would provide an incentive for bondsmen to work even harder at their backbreaking labors.[74]

From this arrangement, the system broadened beyond the construction trades and increased dramatically in the capital in decades to come, reaching the point at which most waiters, private servants, and many artisans were hired-out slaves.[75] Other Southern cities employed this system as well, if to a lesser degree, and Washington was much more open to it than neighboring Baltimore, which had the least slave hiring of any urban area in the South.[76]

From a purely financial angle, this form of hiring reallocated the labor supply to jobs where demand was highest, and parties to the contracts specified price, length of service, working conditions, and work to be performed.[77] Hired-out slaves often lived on the premises of their temporary employer, whether a ropewalk, tavern, mill, or bakery.[78] But in some cases, to lessen the financial cost of the employer, they found independent housing of their own, often in neighborhoods with many free black residents.[79] It made economic sense to all parties: The slave owner made money hiring out the bondsman, the temporary employer didn't have to pay for housing, and the slave caught a break from the employer's constant watch. While out on their own, slaves could sell homegrown vegetables in the market for small amounts of money, and in certain cases could make a bit more money by hiring their own time—namely, finding their own work, paying their master a certain percentage, and keeping the rest.[80] Richard Wade, in his pioneering study *Slavery in the Cities*, explains it this way:

> *Under this arrangement, masters told their Negroes to locate a job, make their own agreement on wages, and simply bring back a certain sum every week or month. The slave, moreover, could pocket any profit he made. . . . Often the owner did not know where his blacks worked; no contract bound master and employer; and no special public supervision governed the arrangement.*[81]

Frederick Douglass took part in this system, writing in his autobiography that as a slave he learned to caulk, and then "I sought my own employment . . . made my own contracts, and collected my own earnings."[82] If a slave salted away enough earnings, he might purchase his own freedom and, in less common cases, that of family members. Althea Tanner remains one of the most notable examples of this phenomenon. She sold enough of her garden produce to such customers as Thomas Jefferson that she eventually raised $1,400 for her own freedom and that of twenty-two friends and relatives.[83]

Jonathan Martin, in his key recent study of slave hiring in antebellum America, posits that the will of enslaved peoples was fundamental to
this economic system. Specifically, slaves did what they could to control
their hiring and used their capacity for work as a means of leverage with
their employer.[84] Of course, they took a real risk in standing up for their
labor, and they were still subject to physical violence and punishment if
they came into conflict with their masters. Nonetheless, in Washington
City at least, the economic incentive for slave hiring became too great for
slaveholders and employers to resist, and a chain reaction began—well
beyond anyone's expectations.

As slaves were hired out, they earned small sums of money above
the wages paid to masters; as they gained extra money from that and
side jobs like gardening, they could live on their own; as they lived on
their own, they developed a sense of autonomy; and when they developed
enough autonomy, they bought their freedom. Slave hiring—combined
with bondsmen's escapes from captivity and the ongoing sale of slaves
from cities to plantations—dramatically reduced the presence of urban
slavery as a percentage of the labor force. The census for Washington City
told the story:

Year	1800	1820	1840	1860
Free blacks	123	1,796	4,808	9,209
Slaves	623	1,945	1,713	1,774[85]

Even as the capital's population grew, the number of slaves remained
static after 1820, while the number of free blacks increased dramatically. To
put it another way: In 1800, one of every five residents of Washington City
was enslaved, and by 1860 that ratio had dropped to one in thirty-five.[86]

That said, the long-term effect of slave hiring in reducing the number
of bondsmen had nothing to do with the development of a conscience
among slaveholders, who still benefited greatly from the arrangement.
Masters who freed their slaves had benefited from years of unpaid labor
that never was reimbursed. Masters who manumitted slaves in their wills
still received the full benefit of slaves' forced labor and merely prevented
their heirs from receiving that same benefit. Masters who hired out their
slaves received the benefit of years of (mostly) unpaid labor and received a
substantial capital gain when slaves paid for their freedom.

But the experience of slavery gave newly freed blacks a commitment to abolishing the system entirely. Many of them lived among current slaves and heard their stories and struggles. In many cases, slaves and free blacks didn't exist as separate, distinct classes but instead overlapped in countless ways in their jobs, families, churches, and neighborhoods. Marriage between free and enslaved blacks was common, making up half the black marriages in the District by midcentury, and churches supported and extended community ties by helping to provide assistance to children if a parent was sold at auction or died.[87]

The Chesapeake had the nation's largest concentration of free blacks even before the capital was built,[88] and as they became a greater percentage of the population they became more active in the abolition movement and the Underground Railroad, which included many important figures who had once been enslaved, such as Jacob Greener, Thomas Smallwood, and of course Frederick Douglass. Slaves hiring out their time not only opened the door to more autonomy, they also helped marshal the forces fighting their oppression nationwide.

Internal Immigrants

Whether formerly enslaved or not, free blacks in the District increased in number as they abandoned the tobacco farmsteads of Maryland and Virginia, where work was hard to find, and came to Washington City in search of jobs.[89] Often these rural areas imposed such harsh limitations on free blacks that relocation was their only choice.[90] Maryland slaveholders even considered them "a standing incitement to servile disorder" and made it a priority to drive them out of the state.[91]

The capital, by contrast, even though it had its own stringent racial codes, as we'll see, became one of the Southern cities most open to black immigration. This distinction alone elevated Washington City above other Southern towns and drew more blacks to the District, which cemented an even stronger community.[92] Most of the work they found when they arrived fell into a few occupations: carter, coach driver, cook, domestic servant, manual laborer, seamstress, waiter, or washwoman.[93] The income from such jobs didn't amount to much—less than 2 percent of total income in the District, though they were 16 percent of the population[94]—but at least it was theirs and not going into the pocket of someone who claimed to own them. Some even became entrepreneurs, selling perfume, baked goods, or seafood, or opening their own oyster houses or restaurants, like Beverly Snow's.

If an antebellum African American saved up enough money, he or she might purchase property in one of the neighborhoods of the District. Particular concentrations of black homeowners cropped up in the southeast District from Capitol Hill to the Navy Yard, the more down-at-heel "Island" southwest of the Capitol, and the slowly expanding reaches of northwest and northeast DC.[95] But poorer blacks lived in alleys with such names as Willow Tree, Goat Alley, and Tin Cup Alley, within tiny rooms in "flimsy frame shacks or converted carriage houses and horse stables behind the more respectable homes of the whites."[96] In this way, the geography of poverty still followed the contours established by the slave quarters behind the old mansions.

The Rock of Abolition

As more blacks gained their freedom and the community expanded, churches played an enormous role in the bonding and cohesion of that community. The first, Mount Zion Negro Church, established in 1814, was integrated, but later churches separated from their white counterparts due to parishioner disgust at segregated seating or at ministers owning slaves. Many of the breakaway institutions and their preachers took overtly antislavery stances, including Daniel Alexander Payne and John F. Cook, both enslaved once and happy to work with Northern and local abolitionists to eradicate the institution for good.[97] Cook's aunt Althea—the same vegetable seller who paid for her freedom and that of nearly two dozen others—freed him as a child, and he became a shoemaker and messenger as well as a minister at Fifteenth Street Presbyterian Church.[98]

Perhaps the most important denomination in the District was Methodism. Wesley Zion Church and African Methodist Episcopal, like the Fifteenth Street church, went well beyond spiritual centers and took part in all aspects of the lives of freedmen as well as slaves. Wesley Zion in particular provided a broad range of help: information on jobs and social services to established free blacks; food, housing, and work for newly freed slaves; Sunday schools and community forums; plus shelter for runaway slaves, training for active abolitionist ministers, and fund-raising for the Underground Railroad.[99]

Education proved especially critical for blacks in Washington City. Slaveholders had tried to deny their captives any sort of enlightenment and prevented them from joining together to transmit information, communicate with the outside world, find ways to escape, or otherwise rebel. But any sort of education for the lower classes, white or black, was inadequate in the District. Numerous private schools existed in the early capital, as did underfunded "pauper schools" for indigent children, but both excluded black children. It took until nearly the middle of the century for the city to fund a few taxpayer-supported public schools, but only about four hundred students enrolled, and unfortunately, again, black children were mostly kept out.[100]

Instead, an array of privately funded schools for blacks arose, and they started even before Washington City itself existed. In the 1790s, Quaker abolitionists funded both childhood and adult education, and the undertaking increased in the 1820s and 1830s as abolitionists fostered a range of schools with biracial instructors.[101] By the Civil War, African Americans funded fifty-two schools in the District, and some of them, such as the Columbian Institute, were quite well regarded.[102] School benefactors put a strong focus on antislavery teaching, and students soon learned from opponents of slavery the importance and methods of eliminating that system.

A frail white New Yorker, Myrtilla Miner ran the most prominent school and received funding from such notable abolitionists as Henry Ward Beecher, Wendell Phillips, and Lucretia Mott. She referred to her institution as "a genteel school for missus of color," but the lessons proved anything but quiet and conventional. She provided her pupils with a potent mix of abolitionism and feminism, tying together the fate of all women and blacks and charging that women were "left to the same degraded position in regard to liberty as the degraded African."[103] She strove to train a new class of black women to become effective, well-trained opponents of slavery south of the Mason-Dixon Line, and to that end the quality of instruction at her school often exceeded the education offered by schools for white students.[104]

Her plan was daring, direct, determined, and doomed. As progressive as he was, Frederick Douglass considered her strategy "reckless, almost to the point of madness," considering the growing hostility from whites in Washington of the 1850s. Sure enough, she and her students soon faced threats and intimidation from racists, legal disputes from landlords, and the deterioration of Miner's health, which she described as "that stage of nervousness and irritability which ends in insanity." Hostility from official Washington and an arson attack forced the school to close in 1860.[105]

The Black Code

The struggles that free blacks faced in education formed a microcosm of their challenges in the District as a whole. Those started with the law itself. In 1808 the capital passed its first "Black Code," which it updated and tightened periodically in later decades, usually after a race riot or major slave escape or rebellion.[106] Many of these criminal regulations derived from archaic Maryland and Virginia laws, while Congress passed additional overlapping laws that only confused the issue. By midcentury the District had such a tangle of racial regulations that it was hard to keep track of them all. Some of the major provisions held as follows:

- Masters were prohibited from allowing slaves to be hired by contract, and employers from entering into such contracts.
- Persons undertaking any economic transaction with a slave, but without a license from the slave's owner, were fined two thousand pounds of tobacco.
- Slaves found away from their homes could be punished with up to thirty-nine lashes.
- No black person could testify in court against a white person, but he or she could against a fellow black person.
- Free blacks had to post a bond with the city with testimony from five white witnesses who could vouch for their good behavior.
- A white woman bearing a black man's child became enslaved for seven years.
- A white man siring a black woman's child became enslaved for seven years.
- Slaves, and in some cases all blacks, couldn't bathe in the river, be drunk in public, beg, break the Sabbath, carry weapons, gamble, go out in public after 10:00 p.m., go to church after 10:00 p.m., hold

private meetings after 10:00 p.m., hold dances without a license, join "disorderly or tumultuous assemblages," keep barnyard animals, kill game, "ramble," ride horses, run horses in the street, sell "old metals," sell liquor, set off firecrackers, or travel without a pass.[107]

Arbitrary, mean-spirited, and draconian, the District's Black Code represented the accumulated pathology of Washington's fear and paranoia about what a quarter of its residents might be doing at any given time. At fifty-seven single-spaced pages by the middle of the century, it covered just about every possibility.

In the end, such laws proved futile. The same financial logic that created a fully functioning network to support slavery also crippled it. Despite all the restrictions on it, slave hiring prevailed in the District of Columbia as an economic necessity.[108] Even the behavior code for free blacks was only "periodically enforced, usually when whites were anxious over the threat of a slave riot or the protests of abolitionists."[109] Likewise, a prohibition on black-owned and black-run businesses was never effective, put to use only in a climate of fear or retribution.[110] Indeed, no matter how many rigid, punitive clauses the city and Congress added after a riot or revolt, the needs of business owners combined with black determination trumped each edition of the code before it took effect.

Decline of Slave Power

By the mid-1840s slavery was collapsing in Washington City. Virginia planters and others with an economic interest in slavery took the first step, pushing a bill through Congress in 1846 to return to their state its share of the District of Columbia: one-third of the capital's total square miles. Although disgruntled at the capital's weak economy, they really wanted to add more pro-slavery members to the Virginia legislature against antislavery adversaries on the western side of the state (a clever strategy for sixteen years, at which point those westerners, tired of being pushed around, created their own state: West Virginia).[111] Virginia law mandated forcing out freed slaves after their manumission, which of course only encouraged them to migrate to Washington City, dramatically increasing its free black population, which jumped almost 70 percent from 1840 to 1850.[112] The District developed an even stronger black community, while

Interior of the slave prison in Alexandria, one of several throughout
the capital area.

Virginia slithered further into the slavery camp. The Potomac River had
become as much a racial and social divide as a geographic one.

Two years later, in 1848, the schooner *Pearl* ran adrift outside the capital on a Potomac shoal. A ship owned by a Georgetown tobacco merchant
intercepted it, and authorities discovered seventy-seven slaves aboard, who
were trying to escape. One of the men who had arranged their failed journey, Paul Jennings, was a free black servant of US Senator Daniel Webster.
Riots ensued, in which white mobs attacked the Centre Market, where
many blacks worked; destroyed the offices of an abolitionist newspaper;
and assaulted Congressman Joshua Giddings, who had defended members

of the *Pearl*'s crew publicly.[113] The recaptured slaves were put into slave pens in Alexandria and then sold into the Deep South, and the terrible public spectacle played out in the capital and on the pages of national newspapers. Northerners reacted in horror; Southerners called for increased legislation and vigilance against all blacks. In Washington City, abolitionists may have lost the *Pearl* fight, but they helped cement antislavery feeling in the North and, through changing public opinion, won "a strategic victory that further weakened slavery in the nation's capital."[114]

In 1850, perhaps sensing the shifting tide of opinion, Congress finally passed a measure to control slavery in the District—or at least that's what some of its members claimed. Technically the bill prohibited the importation of slaves and their transportation elsewhere. But in practice, those movements could continue in Alexandria, no longer a part of DC, and nothing in the bill stopped people from owning slaves in Washington City, slave pens from operating in its jails and taverns, or chain gangs of slaves from traveling through its streets.[115] It was a paper victory, a feel-good attempt to remove some of the ugliness of human trafficking in the capital while doing little to affect the practice itself. More than anything else, the congressional rear-guard action showed how much the debate over slavery had reshaped public opinion.

The policies of the federal and local government clearly inhibited blacks instead of helping them, but despite such baleful efforts, Washington City was becoming more hospitable, or at least less intolerable, to blacks than almost anywhere else in the South. As with so many endeavors the authorities undertook—from selling houses at auction to creating canals, from providing for the poor to building a functional economy—they demonstrated once again their ineptitude in running a capital. But in this case, their heavy-handed attempts at racial and social control positively, mercifully, failed.

The rising class of free blacks stood as the rare positive result from official neglect, inertia, and incompetence, and it proved critical in years to come. For when a new administration came to town in 1861, it found not just planters and slave traders as sworn enemies but also abolitionists and free blacks as potential allies, providing a firm if fragile base for the prosecution of the Civil War, the fight to protect the Union, and the ultimate demise of slavery.

FIVE

THE COMPANY THEY KEPT

In the hardscrabble landscape of Washington City, as slaves, free blacks, and white mechanics toiled at their respective labors, the capital elite were busy enjoying the fruits of their leisure. At one memorable party in 1820, miles from town at a hillside villa, the views evoked "a Tivoli grandeur of atmosphere and Roman landscape . . . like the sybil's rhapsodies to the eye and the soul." A splendid array of the highest echelons of society held court: Maryland planters, country gentlemen, and the District gentry.[1] The guests drank punch by a woodside spring then feasted and sang songs. President Monroe himself laughed with delight, "beating time with his fork" to the lively tunes. Amid the revels, the lord of the house arrived by carriage, his white horse charging through the clover like a thunderbolt. Out stepped the master of ceremonies—Tom Law.[2]

But appearances deceived. The man throwing the resplendent party was anything but rich. Nearly broke, he couldn't even pay his wife alimony. Luckily, the spectacle so delighted and mesmerized his guests that they couldn't help but offer "ready money" to the star-crossed Mr. Law to help him stay afloat—as a gift, of course, not charity.[3]

Law's troubles began with the Greenleaf syndicate and the city canal project, and he remained financially unstable for the rest of his life. But he *seemed* as though he should be wealthy, and that's what counted. In that respect, he had plenty of company, for most upper-class Washingtonians were well practiced in the arts of guile and deception, developing elaborate codes, etiquette, and manners to create a rigid social pecking order that hid behind a veil of grace and whimsy. Seemingly inconsequential details—from the kind of forks on the dinner table to the method of inviting someone to a party—teemed with meaning and purpose, showing how the elite sorted and ranked themselves. The company they kept, from their elegant soirees to their secret societies, said a lot about how Washington City really operated inside its grand public buildings and palatial mansions. Here, a flair for wit and charm could wield more power than a flush bank account, and a well-deployed smile could conceal the most baleful thoughts or ruthless ambition.

Edge of the Vortex

The guests at Tom Law's party provided a good microcosm of Washington City's upper caste. Its nucleus was the rich planters who owned land and slaves in the District, along with established countryside families who held property dating from the days of Lord Baltimore (and who intermarried like European royalty to preserve their dynasties) and old-time Georgetown landowners and merchants who formed the core of the local elite before the capital was built.[4] But there were other, less expected figures too, including British critics and authors, smartly dressed foreign diplomats, and journalists in favor with the ruling class.

The town's biggest names included Robert Brent, who served as the town's first mayor; Thomas Peter, who built the elegant Tudor Place mansion; William Seaton, who ran the *National Intelligencer* and served as mayor in the 1820s; John Tayloe, whose slaves tarried underground in his Octagon house; and Elisha Riggs, who set up the eponymous Georgetown bank.[5] But the women of Washington City's elite society were arguably its most important operators, planning its functions, arranging its liaisons, enforcing its codes, and recording its history. Indeed, Mary Bagot, Margaret Bayard Smith, Mary Boardman Crowninshield, and Harriet Martineau stood as some of the District's most incisive writers, chronicling social life in their often voluminous journals and letters.

Martineau in particular—an English intellectual who wrote books on politics, economics, and sociology—proved herself a fine and thoughtful critic of America and a bold supporter of women's rights, secularism, and abolition. (She even traveled south to inform the locals their support for slavery was "inconsistent with the law of God." The Southerners offered a quick response: "They would hang me: they would cut my tongue out, and cast it on a dunghill.")[6] What attracted her to the provincial aristocracy of the District of Columbia is anyone's guess, but the considerable time she spent in Washington City gave her work perspective and insight lacking in the more superficial dismissals of the capital from the likes of Charles Dickens and Anthony Trollope. Her overview of DC society was especially acute. It was

> *singularly compounded from the largest variety of elements—foreign ambassadors, the American government, members of Congress . . . flippant young belles, "pious" wives . . . grave judges, saucy travellers, pert newspaper reporters, melancholy Indian chiefs, and timid New England ladies, trembling on the edge of the vortex,—all this was wholly unlike any thing that is to be seen in any other city in the world; for all these are mixed up together in daily intercourse, like the higher circle of a little village, and there is nothing else. You have this or nothing; you pass your days among these people, or you spend them alone.*[7]

Not overly fond of the capital, Martineau saw it as a place for those "who love dissipation . . . It is dreary to those whose pursuits and affections are domestic."[8] Despite this view, a lot of the high-society action took place in salons and drawing rooms—the few spaces in the early republic that provided women with domains in which they could exercise social power and influence. By contrast, in the public eye, young ladies of distinction couldn't walk through town without a male escort, and precise codes of gender segregation held sway at prominent events like balls and banquets.[9] An independent figure such as Anne Royall obviously broke the mold, but she never belonged to the social set—especially when she revealed secrets like purebred ladies' affection for drinking wine every day, often to excess.[10] Gender conventions began to change in the 1830s, as women became more involved in American politics, especially with the Whig Party, but most elite women still focused much of their attention on private affairs.[11]

The queen of her class was undoubtedly Marcia Burnes, who reigned over her own segment of blue-blooded society . . . despite her embarrassing origin as the daughter of the District's angriest farmer, Davy Burnes. Many in the elite conveniently forgot this fact when she became the wife of John Peter Van Ness, a House representative, general of the city militia, and mayor of Washington City in the 1830s. As Marcia Van Ness, she

Gilbert Stuart's portrait of David Burnes's daughter at
age twenty-three, the future socialite and philanthropist
Marcia Van Ness.

combined her husband's ties to the District's political brass with her own
substantial real estate holdings to become the socialite par excellence. At
her parties, ladies and gentlemen commingled with a sense of "freedom
and equality,"[12] and the Van Ness mansion became the focal point for
top-shelf amusements. Its social functions attracted presidents, politicians, and diplomats; its rose gardens featured secluded "lovers' walks" for
venturesome paramours; and its elaborate Spanish tile decor, Turkish carpets, and woodwork and tapestries "were the wonder and gossip of their
day."[13] Even Anne Royall, a severe critic as any, compared Mrs. Van Ness
favorably to John Milton's Eve.[14]

Visual Discord

The Van Nesses' peers also built great mansions throughout town, many of them next to the modest dwellings of the poor and working class,[15] regardless of the visual or moral contradictions. Such structures included anything from modest Federal-style houses to such grand estates as Commodore David Porter's Meridian Hill, which was "set in a hundred and ten acres of grounds and required the employment of enough servants, grooms and gardeners to people a small village."[16] (Despite its grandeur, Porter didn't long enjoy it: He was court-martialed seven years after he built the estate and fled to become the commander of the Mexican Navy.)

Plantation tracts and colossal estates like Porter's obviously wouldn't last long in a modern city, but Washington City wasn't anything like a real city in its early days. The rural landholders of Virginia and Maryland stamped their provincial character all over the capital, from the large houses built with stables, gardens, carriage houses, kitchens, and slave quarters, to the style of their hospitality and the fashion of their parties, to their rigid emphasis on class order and place-holding in society.[17] These phenomena only added to the visual mishmash of Washington City: plantations suitable for Chesapeake tobacco farming, public buildings echoing ancient Rome, a street layout in the style of Baroque France, shambling log cabins like those on the western frontier, and wretched shacks and hovels as bad as any urban slum in America.

Reign of the Gourmands

Other contrasts emerged as well. Common folk had to content themselves with diets consisting mostly of bread, cabbage, and sweet potatoes, but upper-crusters had a cornucopia of delights with which to stuff themselves. Attorney General William Wirt mentions in one letter to his wife how he gorged on a range of delights: a small ham, a goose, two chickens, various vegetables, beans, sweetmeats, cheeses, peaches, and pears, crowning the feast with a fine glass of claret.[18] Society banquets featured all kinds of game, side dishes, and desserts, with particular attention to one local delicacy: the canvasback duck. English diplomat Sir Augustus John Foster gushed wildly over this waterfowl in his book on America, hailing them as "the most delicious eating, and I have frequently seen four dishes of them served up at the same time on the same table."[19] Mary Bagot described another favorite, turtle, as being served "in the shell steamed with a little pepper & butter"—which might sound appetizing until you consider that her companion sourced the creature from a roadside ditch.[20]

To eat the likes of turtle (roadkill or otherwise), guests were provided with glittering silver forks, which were as much a status symbol as a fine wardrobe or handsome carriage. Although presidents such as John Adams and Thomas Jefferson dined with these refined "French forks," other bluebloods such as Charles Carroll saw them as an improper indulgence and Mary Crowninshield complained about how heavy and clumsy they were.[21] More humble Americans had a darker view, as some feared the new republic would be "stuck to death with four-prong'd forks" and others vowed never to cast a ballot for a presidential candidate who ate with such fancy utensils.[22]

The Jam and Squeeze

Thomas Jefferson, master of the fork and other things French, ironically proved much more democratic when it came to entertaining. He invited small groups of no more than fourteen to the White House and seated them without regard to rank or custom, breaking up cliques to force people to mingle with one another in lively conversations.[23] But Jefferson was an anomaly, and in later years presidents and their congressional counterparts refined and tightened social codes to the point where rank became paramount and White House dinners became dreary rituals, thick with rigid etiquette.[24]

Private affairs were a bit more animated but still required a lengthy, formal process of invitation, acceptance, and scheduling as precise as it was inflexible. Librarian of Congress George Watterston provides this overview to the rather elaborate procedure:

> *The cards of invitation to those parties are sent out about nine days before they are to be given, and if the invitation be to dinner, the person invited must return a written acceptance of the invitation, or an apology for declining. . . . The guest appears at the hour designated, generally about six o'clock, P.M.; for it is deemed uncivil to attend too early or too late on such an occasion. At soirees, or evening parties, the*

*company usually assemble at from nine to eleven o'clock, and retire at
from twelve to two o'clock.*[25]

At these large nighttime parties, known as "jams" or "squeezes,"[26]
plenty of elegant gentlemen and ladies knew how to make a fine
impression—even as others just wanted to make a splash with personal
style bordering on the ridiculous. Men might wear ballooning "Cossack"
trousers with "Hessian" boots adorned with gold tassels, or dress coats
with "enormous collars and short waists" or "tight-fitting pantaloons, silk
stockings and pumps." Women with a flair for "scantiness" might wear
dresses that stopped at the ankle and sport silk stockings with slippers
ornamented with rosettes and tiny buckles.[27]

At the fashionable balls, they all stepped lively to country dances,
quadrilles, minuets, and the basket dance, a forerunner to the modern
square dance. The musicians were usually black, both free and enslaved, as
were most of the servants. They doled out ice cream, lemonade, port wine,
and desserts to the ravenous gourmands, who in their gluttony might
appear "with one hand bearing well-filled glasses, and in the other sustaining a plate heaped up with cake."[28]

The cream of society's crop made an even greater effort to entertain
their cronies. George Custis—son of Martha Washington by her first
husband and adopted by George Washington—built a dancing pavilion
at his estate at Arlington and held elaborate picnics on the grounds. At
one event he presented a full-dress performance of a play he wrote, *Poca-
hontas; or, the First Settlers of Virginia*, with dresses, props, and scenery
provided by the federal Indian Bureau, "to aid the aboriginal effect."[29]
With its elaborate manor house, gardens, and hundreds of slaves, the
massive estate also hosted the 1831 wedding of his daughter, Mary. It was
a grand social affair in which she wed a lieutenant in the US Army who
happened to be one of her third cousins: Robert E. Lee.

"The Natural Best"

The capital elite didn't just eat canvasback ducks and dress up for fancy
balls and weddings. Some joined secret societies, establishing fraternal,
business, and sometimes political connections with those deemed worthy.
The most famous group were the Freemasons. They claimed their secret

heritage dated back millennia to Biblical times, but Masonry really took off in America only during and after the revolutionary era, when such figures as Benjamin Franklin and George Washington associated themselves with it. The group stated its aim as spreading republican ideals and serving as "priests, teachers, and missionaries of liberty, virtue, and true religion." They claimed to be meritocratic, elevating the so-called "natural *aristoi*" to positions of prominence without regard to birth and wealth.[30] In practice, though, membership amounted to an effective way to establish credentials within the tight circle of the wealthy and powerful.[31] Some well-heeled artisans joined, but the lower orders were excluded because admitting them would "inevitably bring the Craft into the greatest Disgrace imaginable."[32]

Masons favored public spectacle and acknowledgment in splashy parades and honorary processions through town, but they also favored privacy and countless arcane codes, systems, and rituals—including, for the higher levels, forcing initiates to crawl over a pile of garbage or drink wine from a skull.[33] Nonetheless, for the first few American decades, they did well, providing education, charity, and funerals for their members[34]— and for their proponents, such as Anne Royall, who would have had a tough time surviving the lean years without such charity. At the same time they dampened potentially noxious strains of religious conflict and tribalism that had weakened many failed republics. Their proudest public display came in 1793, when President Washington laid the cornerstone of the US Capitol in a ceremony thick with Masonic ritual, followed by chanting, prayers, and an artillery volley.[35]

In theory, Freemasonry tried to limit partisan strife and bridge political, ethnic, and religious divides between gentlemen. That it failed and itself became a political issue represented just one of the bitter little ironies that animated the tumultuous 1820s and 1830s. During that time, with the rise of Jacksonian democracy, the Masons' secretive rituals and bizarre symbolism invited a backlash, even though Jackson himself belonged to the order. The group already had a dangerous reputation for being cosmopolitan, elitist, and potentially irreligious, but when a handful of its members decided to kidnap New Yorker William Morgan, who had threatened to expose their secrets, and he was later found dead, the masses revolted. Freemasonry became a "hydra-headed monster," an enemy of

Christians and republicans everywhere, and the Anti-Masonic Party formed.[36] The party attacked social privilege and decried the secret order as evil, murderous, monarchical, antirepublican, elitist, and barbaric; and "We aim, therefore, at its annihilation."[37]

Such a potentially revolutionary (or reactionary) group should have made the Washington City elites quake in their Hessian boots, and no doubt many of the town's top citizens did—but not all. The first and only presidential candidate of the Anti-Masons was William Wirt, the insatiable attorney general who had stuffed himself with that lengthy grocery list of dishes among elite company. But his candidacy made for dish of a different sort: Wirt, once a Mason, now had to justify all those inconvenient social bonds in accepting the party's nomination. He tried to ride the democratic wave as best he could, calling Freemasonry a "noxious institution" that would "sacrifice its victims with pleasure and with impunity" by silencing the opposition with "mysterious terrors"[38]—which of course he knew only too well but wasn't at liberty to reveal since, of course, he had taken the Masonic oath.

Wirt told the Anti-Masonic convention what it wanted to hear, but really he was maneuvering to become the anti-Jackson candidate. When Henry Clay got the nod instead, Wirt had doubts about remaining with the Anti-Masons and tried to reject the nomination several times, but his new radical friends wouldn't hear of it. "I cannot think of a rational or patriotic motive they can have for continuing me in the field," he complained in a private letter.[39] But he was stuck . . . and running for president, like it or not. In the 1832 election, he won a single state: Vermont.*

Society Improvements

If we take Wirt as an example, the District elite had a hard time navigating the new political landscape of the 1830s. Nothing about their lifestyle—acres of land, great mansions, legions of slaves, indulgent dining, Cossack trousers, silk stockings—related even remotely to the common man or woman. Their secret societies, incantations, and mysticism only proved

---

* He made a more ghoulish appearance in 2005 when his skull turned up in the office of a District councilman. Apparently, in the 1970s a grave robber had rifled through the coffins of the family vault, stolen Wirt's cranium, and then presumably sold it to a dealer in macabre relics. It has since returned to the Wirt vault at Congressional Cemetery. (Mark W. Grabowski, et al., "Cemetery Vandalism: The Strange Case of William Wirt," *Washington History* 22 (2010): 57–68)

how they had removed themselves from the day-to-day existence of those who labored in the trenches, scraped by in the poorhouse, or stood on the auction block. But the top shelf had to display some sympathy to those below them in rank. The French Revolution, inspired by the American one, had long before showed them that. Many remained indifferent to the plight of less wealthy citizens, but some participated in charitable societies that counterbalanced private societies like the Masons that were causing so much trouble. The more notable organizations included:

- American Historical Society (old papers and artifacts)
- Columbia Horticultural Society (flowers and gardens)
- Columbian Institute (art and science)
- Female Union Benevolent Society (poor women)
- Howard Society (job training for the poor)
- Navy Yard Beneficial Society (sailors' families)
- Temperance societies (alcohol prohibition)
- Union Literary Debating Society (public speaking)
- Washington City Benevolent Society (poverty relief)
- Washington Relief Society (aiding poor immigrants)[40]

Perhaps the most well-regarded philanthropist was Marcia Van Ness, who was as devoted to public service as she was to her private social world, if not more so. She cofounded and directed the Washington Female Orphan Asylum after the 1814 British invasion to care for the town's many destitute children,[41] offering the land for the asylum's building and donating food, clothing, furniture, and other supplies. She continued her good works until 1832, when cholera hit Washington City and killed many of its citizens. One of them was Van Ness herself, who died from the plague while nursing its victims.[42]

Phoenix in Brick

The most community-minded figure among the elite, however, had the least claim to be there. Cash-poor from the real estate bubble and facing constant struggles with the city canal, Tom Law remained only a nominal member of the upper class in the early nineteenth century. But he persevered and found himself in the right place at the right time when the capital needed help.

It never needed more help than after it burned in 1814. With many of the federal buildings in ruin, politicians from Pennsylvania and other states tried to use the District's sorry condition as an excuse to move the national capital elsewhere. "The appearance of our public buildings is enough to make one cut his throat," said one Virginian.[43] While Congress was debating what to do, Law took the lead in raising $500,000 in loans for the construction of a temporary building to house the legislature, which had been laying down the law in Blodgett's Hotel while its chambers were in ruins.[44] Some later claimed Law's efforts for this new "Brick Capitol" kept the seat of government in Washington City, but in practice Congress had already decided to rebuild the Capitol when the brick version opened for business.[45] Still, a rosy halo formed over him as one of the saviors of the capital, and he imagined the future growth and glory of the rebuilt city:

At this methought a peal of victory rung
And a new edifice in splendor sprung,
Like phoenix from its ashes, and a sound
Of triumph and rejoicing rose around.[46]

It wasn't the first time he waxed poetic, nor was it the last time he tried to help his adopted city. But who was this failed real estate baron, struggling canal builder, legendary partier, and would-be poet, and why did he care so much about Washington City?

The Poetical Ludubrian

Law came to America with an impeccable English pedigree and legacy. His father, Edmund Law, bishop of Carlisle, had written the trailblazing *Theory of Religion*, which excited many ecclesiastical debates in the old country. His most famous brother was Edmund Law, later attorney general and speaker of the House of Lords.[47] Unlike his relatives, Law found his calling overseas, alighting for India at age seventeen and remaining in the employ of the East India Company for nearly two decades. As

THOS. LAW

The ever-optimistic, often financially
troubled Thomas Law.

revenue collector for the state of Bihar, he transformed an onerous system
of taxation and introduced the concept of private property rights independent of lands owned by the crown. As newspaper editor William Duane
said of him, "Mr. Law's revolution without bloodshed eventually changed
the whole moral and social condition of Hindostan."[48] Law returned to
England in 1791, fighting the East India Company over a claim against
a paymaster in his employ and for whom he had vouched. In the first of

many financial twists of fate, Law was held responsible for the £10,000 claim, a fifth of his total fortune. He filed suit against the company and left for America in 1794 to start over.

Arriving in the new republic, he immediately discovered the potential riches on offer. Oddly, for someone who already had plenty of money and never showed a weakness for greed during the rest of his life, Law swooned at the prospect of speculation, with the capital itself his drug: "I shall certainly go to Washington City & my heart & my mind are full of it—You may say that I had rather sell my horses or books or any thing rather than part with a foot at present of Washington City."[49]

In town only a year, the socially adept thirty-seven-year-old wed the first lady's nineteen-year-old granddaughter, Eliza Parke Custis. A few years later, a young Thomas Twining visited from Britain and observed Law hard at work building spec houses: "The clearing of ground and building of small houses, amongst the woods of the Potomac, seemed an uncongenial occupation for a man of so accomplished a mind. . . . America, of all countries, seemed the least suited to the activity or leisure of such a person." Twining had a foreboding about his friend, thinking that "his inexperience in commercial affairs, amidst rivals so experienced and intelligent, might expose him to litigation and disappointment, and involve a considerable diminution of his fortune."[50] The young man's prophecy proved true.

Even as Law was busy losing money on real estate, he was investing even more of it elsewhere. In 1797, near the Eastern Branch, he helped create the first and largest manufacturing operation in Washington City, a sugar refinery.[51] Law planned to import sugar from India using non-slave labor to establish a thriving business in America while encouraging India to free the bondsmen who worked the sugar plantations there.[52] Sadly, that noble idea resulted four years later in "a very large but perfectly empty warehouse, and a wharf graced by not a single vessel."[53]

But Law kept trying. In 1798 he became a director of the District's first bank, then designed and advocated a plan for a national currency, which fell on deaf congressional ears.[54] For decades after, he wrote a column in the *National Intelligencer*, under the pseudonym "Homo," pushing for a national banking system, publicly financed debt, and an agricultural society, among other points.[55] In 1814 he wrote to President Madison recommending the establishment of a university and military college, since Congress was treating the District with an "opprobrium of neglect."[56]

Three years later, Law helped found the Columbian Institute, which Congress chartered in 1818 to promote math, science, literature, and art. He summoned all the top names in town, including Benjamin Latrobe, William Seaton, and William Thornton to help him run the institution, a forerunner to the modern museums in the District today, which collected an array of books, minerals, shrubs, and trees.[57] The institute also built at the foot of the Capitol a fine botanical garden, which collected specimens of plants, fossils, and minerals from around the world—perhaps its greatest endeavor. The Columbian Institute closed its doors in 1838, but its collection formed the core of the National Institute, which later became part of the Smithsonian.

Any good philanthropist might have pursued the founding of institutions or the funding of civic improvements, but Law, despite his tenuous status as a "rich man," followed all manner of whims and curiosities too. He had a flair for what he called "poetical ludubria" and indulged it when the short-lived United States Theatre opened in Washington City in 1800 by writing a prologue to the main play with a gentle poke at his audience:

> *Those ruddy cheeks evince the air is fine,*
> *And those fat sides show on the best you dine.*
> *Well faith, we've form'd a tolerable stage;*
> *Here's room for comic glee or tragic rage;*
> *But there [pointing at the crowd] the city populates so quick,*
> *I fear you've stowed yourselves away too thick!*[58]

Wordsworth it wasn't, but Law cut a charming figure as a patron of the theater, both in verse and purse, and helped fund other arty endeavors, such as the Washington Dancing Assembly. Law's charisma was substantial enough that even his respected biographer Allen Clark abandoned objectivity and wildly praised him as "the scion of Britsh aristocracy, a lord of India, bright in speech, elegant in manner, and handsome . . . Tom Law, paragon of manly perfection"![59]

More unusual, considering the circles in which he moved, was his association with freethinkers and the Unitarian Church. He generously funded the latter and commented that people should "seek salvation according to the dictates of their own conscience," thereby denying the authority of established churches.[60] Defying the racist attitudes of the era, this associate of wealthy planters called presciently in his newspaper column for the abolition of slavery as a way to prevent civil war. He publicly acknowledged and supported his three mixed-race sons from a previous marriage in India, who became prominent figures in the District and, like their father, were "generous, kind-hearted, and most intelligent . . . free from all aristocratic pride."[61]

Needless to say, many of Law's peers didn't know what to make of him. Margaret Bayard Smith saw him as generous to a fault, "connected with the most respectable people," always raising money for some good cause or other, but still—"it is impossible to describe this man; he is one of the strangest I ever met with."[62] She was right: He was a true oddball. Not only did he declaim in verse whatever random subject crossed his mind, but he impulsively went skinny-dipping and strutted around in the nude afterward.[63] He had a curious knack for kneading bread in his hands while lost in deep thought on a walk and had such a terrible memory that when a random notion hit, he would "wildly rush about, exclaiming, 'Pen and ink, pen and ink, an idea, I have an idea, quick!'"[64] He read and spoke Persian and encouraged his guests to smoke a hookah with him by the riverside.[65] Yet despite all his eccentricities, his top-shelf friends, perhaps amused by him, helped him fund his lifestyle and his civic projects—if only because at his grand picnics he made sure to indulge them in "cold meat, bread & cheese & oceans of wine, punch & brandy."[66]

Whether using his own cash or his friends', Law funded or helped start a great many projects that otherwise would have died in Congress. His own returns from those projects were usually quite meager, and he managed to lose money on many of them. Ultimately, apart from the District's major public buildings, Law invested more in the capital than the federal government did throughout the course of thirty years, a fact both remarkable and depressing.[67]

The Great Castle

Holding a core collection derived from the institutions that Law and his peers helped fund, the greatest emblem of private philanthropy in the

capital was and still is the Smithsonian Institution. In 1826 English sci-
entist James Smithson left a bequest for an institution to be founded
in America for "the increase and diffusion of knowledge among men."[68]
Smithson never visited the United States, yet to the new country he left
his fortune (though it took a dozen years for the will to be settled). The
$500,000 bequest arrived in the United States in 1838 in the form of 105
bags of gold bullion coins sent by packet boat. Leading politicians had all
kinds of ideas about what the money should fund, so Congress dithered
for eight years trying to figure out what to do with it. In 1846 the legislature accepted the money to fund a facility that would include a museum
with art and science displays, a library, lecture halls, and research labs.[69]
Six years later a great icon of red sandstone emerged, rich with turrets and
battlements, known appropriately as The Castle.

A visual anomaly as much as the Capitol and White House, the
Smithsonian stood out as a lone Gothic sentry along the barren landscape
of the Mall. Citizens starved for scenic beauty even used the Institution's
grounds as an ad hoc resort.[70] But the building's magnificence made the
rest of the Mall look shabby and decrepit by comparison. This was especially apparent when anyone compared The Castle's lovely neo-medieval
form with the architectural attempt, just west, to honor George Washington with a great public monument. Indeed, no other building represented
so colossally the failure of federal politicians to aid a worthy cause than
the Washington Monument.

Monumental Struggles

Congress had been searching for a way to honor the nation's first president since the failure of the giant pyramid project at the end of the eighteenth century. The obvious solution to some was to preserve his house
at Mount Vernon, which certainly needed the help, as Harriet Martineau
observed in the mid-1830s:

> The land appears to be quite impoverished; the fences and gates are in
> bad order; much of the road was swampy, and the poor young lambs,
> shivering in the biting wind, seemed to look round for shelter and care.
> The conservatories were almost in ruins, scarcely a single pane of glass
> being unbroken; and the house looked as if it had not been painted on
> the outside for years.[71]

Members of the legislature, however, cared less about the fate of the general's estate than of his body, which was buried there.

Congress had wanted to entomb Washington in the Capitol almost as soon as he died, and they even built a crypt on the lower level to house the remains. On the centenary of Washington's birth, in 1832, Congress formed a Centennial Committee to devise a way to commandeer the body from Mount Vernon and spirit it to the Capitol. But certain Virginians would have none of it, vowing to "contend to the last for the body," and one Georgia congressman even warned of "the severance of this union" should Washington's cadaver be swiped from its vault at Mount Vernon.[72]

In the end, John A. Washington, the president's great-nephew, helped stop the congressional action. But just in case, Virginia passed legislation preventing the removal of the body, and leading politicians, North Carolina senator Willie Mangum among them, demanded the governor dispatch the state militia to stop the federal grave robbers at gunpoint.[73]

The attempt at "honoring" Washington didn't end there. Just after the jockeying for his body ended, Congress decided to commission a sculpture of the president, giving Horatio Greenough the task of creating a

Horatio Greenough's unloved statue of George Washington, depicting him as Zeus in a toga.

huge marble statue. The giant, twenty-ton carving arrived by boat in 1841 but shocked Washingtonians with its vulgarity. Greenough depicted the president as Zeus, enthroned and clad in a toga. Naked from the waist up, the great general looked angry, pointing at the sky for no particular reason. Congress didn't know what to do with the monstrosity, placing it first in the Rotunda and then exiling it to the east Capitol grounds, a wooden barn, the Capitol basement, and the Naval Academy.[74] (It now sits in the Smithsonian's American History Museum.)

Congress had racked up three failures in trying to honor a national hero. Still, the attempts continued—and in even more colossal form. In 1833 a group of civic-minded citizens created the Washington National Monument Society, Chief Justice John Marshall its president. The society held a design competition, which in 1836 Robert Mills won with a proposal for a five-hundred-foot neoclassical obelisk rising from a colonnaded base. The society didn't care for the base but accepted the obelisk and began raising funds for the monument,[75] to be located near the spot where L'Enfant once imagined a statue of Washington on horseback.

But raising funds for the monument proved slow going, and it took more than a decade for construction to begin. On July 4, 1848, the Masonic lodge of Washington City laid the cornerstone for the monument. But instead of sitting at the intersection of the axes aligned to the Capitol and the White House, the obelisk rose off-center, one hundred yards south, where the ground was higher, the soil not so marshy.[76] Construction continued apace for six years but then ground to a halt when the society ran out of money in 1854. The nativist Know-Nothing Party took over the society through violence and intimidation (about which more in the next chapter), and, though Congress rescinded its $200,000 donation, it did nothing to stop the interloping agitators from destroying the society's reputation. The result: a drab stump of granite that over the course of nearly three decades symbolized the repeated failures of Congress, and by implication the struggles of the capital itself.

Capitol Captives

In contrast to the bumbling of the national legislature, the philanthropy of wealthy Washingtonians helped keep the capital from collapsing or sliding into total poverty and structural decay. The rich dealt with such

The granite stump of the Washington Monument, which stood unfinished for nearly three decades.

problems because of the total lack of charity and good works from the town's other elite society—the politicians from around the country who congregated in Washington City but didn't consider it their home. These out-of-towners held power in the capital, but, despite being "public" figures, they lived lives even more removed from the average Washingtonian than did the planters and grande dames. It began with how they lived and with whom they chose to associate.

The seeds of the politicians' isolation germinated when the capital moved to Washington City in 1800. Few legislators wanted to live in the barren, undeveloped village year-round, so they looked for only temporary accommodation. Some entrepreneurs opened hotels, but most of these met with failure. Taverns made a poor choice because boarders had to share beds with random bunkmates—not an option for congressmen who needed privacy and workspace.[77] The answer came in the Washington boardinghouse.

This form of collective housing represented the only viable option for most legislators, almost all of them initially living in eight boardinghouses on Capitol Hill. Around these three-story brick structures

William Thornton described the early US Capitol, before it was remodeled, as a "large sugar dish between two tea canisters."

sprang up businesses and facilities that catered to every whim and need of their guests: barbers, bathhouses, bookstores, churches, clothiers, groceries, libraries, liquor stores, post offices, restaurants, schools, stables, and tailors.[78] Most of the time, though, the politicians just hung out in the House and Senate chambers where they aired their windy speeches.

A legislator might live in a boardinghouse with anywhere from two to seventeen or more boarders, often from his region or state. Proprietors advertised in newspapers their houses' spacious kitchens, fine gardens, and proximity to the Capitol. Lodging didn't come cheap, though, and they jacked up their prices whenever their customers came to town.[79] Their residents didn't have much choice but to accept the steep rates, so keeping a boardinghouse became one of the few profitable businesses in the District.[80] In his 1822 *Washington Directory*, Judah Delano fills the first eight pages of his guide with nothing but the names of Senate and House members, their states of origin, and the names of the boardinghouses where they lodged.[81]

Fortresses of Solitude

More than a few writers referred to the cloistered congressional life as monk-like, since the members lived, ate, socialized, killed time, and talked politics only among their kind.[82] Each house "had an invisible drawbridge and portcullis. One was a fortress for New Yorkers or the same party, another for Pennsylvanians, another for Ohioans."[83] They ignored non-politicians in the same house and often broke into smaller cliques based on state, party, or sectional interests, voting that way in Congress too. Their herd mentality held so strong that if a member defied his "fraternity" he was more or less excommunicated. Margaret Bayard Smith recalls one such apostate, who, after casting his vote against the wishes of his messmates, "looked wretchedly, tears running down his cheeks," and begged forgiveness; another who did the same was shunned by his fellows: "we let him continue with us, sit at the same table with us, but we do not speak to him. He is beneath anything but contempt, and he is an old man."[84]

This incestuous climate fed upon itself, until even the leisure and social life of congressmen became politicized with gossip and innuendo.

As James Sterling Young writes in his pioneering study of the life of politicians in the early District, "Who was and was not invited to a tea, a dinner, or a reception, who accepted and who declined, who was and was not calling upon whom, became matters pregnant with social significance."[85] But there was nothing genteel about the ways of those politicians in their private boys' club. On the floors of Congress they brought their hunting dogs (particularly John Randolph); they drank, whittled, yelled at friends in the gallery, took snuff, chewed tobacco, and spat anywhere they wanted.[86] Their boardinghouses sometimes looked even rougher around the edges. Anne Royall recalls a few houses known for their bullies and thugs: "It is out of the question even to have a card delivered to any member in the house without endangering life."[87]

These raw, aggressive attitudes came at a cost, though. The local elite weren't exactly rushing to welcome low-mannered congressmen to their balls and salons. As Constance McLaughlin Green writes, "cultivated Washingtonians felt no obligation to open their drawing rooms to congressmen of very modest political, and still less social, *savoir-faire*."[88]

Vortex of Ruin

Members of the executive branch, from cabinet secretaries to clerks, also clustered in houses and boardinghouses around the White House and the departments of State, War, Treasury, and Navy. They kept to themselves and had their own schools, churches, library, banks, and theater. With the president as the nucleus of their orbit, they had their own salons too, at which conversation, games, music, and poetry readings took place as well as celebrity visits by the likes of James Fenimore Cooper and Washington Irving.[89] Throughout the executive branch, in the so-called "Court end of the city," the need to be stylish and fashionable affected every rank and class." Even midlevel bureaucrats had to participate:

> *although their salaries are small and their means limited, they fancy it would be unpardonable not to ape those above them and be what is called fashionable, and thus they plunge into the vortex of ruin. They give evening parties, pay morning visits with cards in their own carriages, or any they can procure, give routs [nighttime parties], go to assemblies, and, in short, exhibit every folly their*

superiors think proper to practice because it is said to be haut ton,
*and they cannot think of being unfashionable, whatever may be the
result.*[90]

But they avoided social commerce with their counterparts on Capitol
Hill, from whom they kept a wary distance.[91] James Madison's secretary
of the Treasury, like those who worked for him, wasn't unusual in steer-
ing clear of congressmen: "Mr. Gallatin leaves no cards, makes no visits,
scarcely ever invites a member to dine, or even has a tea party."[92] The
high-minded pursuit of separating the branches of government wasn't the
only factor that encouraged such distance: Many members of the executive branch considered themselves superior to the rubes in Congress and
to people in general. As visiting critic William Faux saw it, "no men in
the world are more aristocratical than the heads of departments; they
spurn, and cannot even speak to, common men, unless it be to purchase
popularity cheaply."[93]

Thus Washington City's political elite comprised separate, warring
tribes, each with its own redoubts and its own enclaves, its own tightly
knit society and social codes, its own suspicions and hostility to outsiders. The same insularity applied to justices on the Supreme Court, who
worked in the basement courtroom in the Capitol and all lived and dined
at the same boardinghouse on Capitol Hill, an arrangement that lasted
until 1845.[94] Each political clan kept to itself, its members trusting only
those who slept, dined, worked, and relaxed in the same company. Some
commingled with the elite in town, but many didn't, and far fewer of them
socialized in any meaningful way with the slaves, free blacks, and white
mechanics who made up the bulk of the District's population. As for the
small middle class in town, it was more of a merchant class and consisted
of shopkeepers, clerks, artisans, and the like, but it never cohered as a
unified group. Its upper order sought out the company of the elite, while
its lower order were considered mechanics who had made a bit of money.
The old social divisions remained.[95]

Nobody's Constituents

Ultimately, national politicians considered themselves outsiders, not
responsible for correcting the problems that their policies obviously had

caused. The capital "was not 'our' community in the eyes of the governing politicians; it was 'theirs'—the townspeople's."[96] As a result, Congress regularly refused to upkeep the town's roads, streetlamps, sidewalks, sanitation, schools, and city canal, telling Washington City to tax itself—which it did heavily. But such efforts couldn't come to much when the prized real estate lay off-limits to taxation: the public buildings and the houses of the Congress and the president.

The capital remained a shambling mess throughout the first half of the nineteenth century, but the politicians, ironically, had the audacity to complain about it, calling the town "a hateful place . . . splendid misery . . . [producing] nothing but absolute loathing and disgust."[97] When local business leaders tried to jump-start the capital's anemic economy with a new railroad link in the middle of the century, Congress balked. Said one senator, "Washington was not intended to be a great business mart."[98] Instead, it was run by leaders indifferent to its plight and beholden to voters of other, increasingly distant states. As one irate letter-writer put it in the *National Intelligencer*: "Every member takes care of the needs of his constituents, but we are the constituents of no one."[99]

The situation reached such a crisis point that by 1835, with the legislature still withholding essential funds needed to modernize the town, Senator Samuel Southard admitted in a report to Congress that Washington City had exhausted its resources.[100] In response, he reasoned that the legislature should assume some of the city's debts and help pay for elementary services like road paving and lighting, sidewalks, poverty relief, and other functions. The stingy legislators needed to debate these urgent topics for a few more years, but at least they relieved the District's canal debt[101] and kept the American capital from going broke and being sold to the Dutch.

Walled off in its own fortress, Congress had crippled the growth and development of the capital, ensuring its abysmal physical condition and that it had few successful enterprises beyond slave trading and boardinghouses. Indeed, if it weren't for local elite society—with its elaborate social codes, gluttonous dining habits, fancy soirees, and extravagant outfits—Washington City couldn't have taken care of orphans, helped the poor, trained people for jobs, promoted art and science, or established museums and gardens. Thus the capital consisted of two distinct high societies: the elected one that completely dismissed the interests of the people it lorded over and the unelected one that didn't.

Twilight of an Englishman

Tom Law had a hard time of it in his final years, though you'd never know it from his cheerful demeanor and irrepressible charm. He and his young wife, Eliza, separated in 1804 and divorced seven years later, leaving great recriminations between the two and alimony payments for him for several decades afterward.[102] These, as we've seen, he couldn't afford, and he had to seek the assistance of friends and relatives to pay them. In the early 1820s, English critics Charles Janson and William Faux separately published salacious gossip that his wife had cuckolded him while she was "attached to the military, at the marine barracks in Washington . . . dressed *à la militiaire* in company with the officers."[103] Law skillfully fought the charge in print, but it only added to a reputation that he was as maladroit with women as he was with money.

But the worst was yet to come. In August 1822 his daughter, Eliza Rogers, died unexpectedly at the age of twenty-six, and less than two months later his son John, an attorney and city councilmember, followed her. Another son, Edmund, also a city councilmember, died at the end of the decade, and even his young ex-wife preceded him to the grave.[104] That shocking number of deaths in fewer than ten years, more than his financial failures or any other challenges, finally seemed to break his spirit. One Washingtonian saw him at a restaurant near the end of his life, recalling him "as a grave, sweet old man . . . who read a poem of his own composing, which served as a dessert after the oysters."

Look not in public places for a wife;
Be not deluded by the charms of sight.
Retirement only gives the friend for life
Who shares your grief and doubles your delight.[105]

Law died in 1834, at age seventy-seven, and was buried in an unmarked grave in Rock Creek Cemetery.[106] Like his gravesite, most of his endeavors have long since disappeared, including his spec developments, canal, theater, sugar refinery, scientific institute, country estate, and

Thomas Law House, one of the last remnants of Law's life in Washington City.

temporary capitol. Almost all that remains is the house that he and Eliza shared after their marriage. Located in the southwest quadrant of town, the Thomas Law House stands out among the sea of drab condos built in the frenzy of 1950s and 1960s urban renewal, which leveled so many other old estates but left this smart, elegant, unpretentious home as a fitting if lonely tribute to its long-forgotten owner.

SIX

COMING TO THE SCRATCH

The gentlemen of Washington City did more than just attend balls, feast with abandon, raise funds for charity, and live in their elite cocoons. They had other concerns too—such as trying to kill each other. The *code duello*, an elaborate honor code, enabled a gentleman whose pride or dignity was impugned to murder his adversary freely, as long as he did so with the proper etiquette and ceremony.

Dueling was only the tip of the sword of the varieties of violence in the Chesapeake, which spanned a broad range of socially tolerated mayhem in an era dominated by male bravado and almost cartoonish virility. Mobs rampaged, street gangs battled, and blood sport entertained, usually in combination with alcohol and social pressure, to create a heady climate of brutality that held sway from the colonial era all the way to the Civil War. Thomas Twining noticed how the region reveled in fighting, dueling, and "cruel sports," with eye-gouging and "other barbarities" among the special-ties.[1] Not just criminals out for blood took part. All creeds and classes participated in the bloodletting, using violence as a tool of dominance to keep pariahs in line and to enforce racial, social, and cultural codes. They often did so with a wink and a nod from the proper legal authorities, who had neither the inclination nor the means to fund an effective system of law and order. Disorder resulted and verged on anarchy during times of open conflict, when citizens could maim and mangle each other at will.

The Rules of Honor

Dueling represented the most acceptable form of social violence because this kind of attempted homicide "did not lower the would-be murderer in the respect and esteem of the elite of Washington society."[2] Treasury

Secretary Alexander Hamilton and Vice President Aaron Burr fought the country's most famous duel in 1804 in New Jersey, but countless other contests in the years after drew considerable attention as well, provided the adversaries had sufficient social standing to merit it. Indeed, some of the most esteemed gentlemen in the nation, and particularly in the South, became its most visible champions.[3]

By the early nineteenth century, refined dueling etiquette in the Chesapeake went something like this: One gentleman offended another by an insult real or imagined. The aggrieved party posted a note in a newspaper or other public place declaring his nemesis, say, "an unprincipaled villain and a coward."[4] The other party responded in kind, and the technical legwork began as the gentlemen and their allies, or "seconds," proposed a date and time, weapons (usually pistols), and choice of venue. All very formal and precise, it adhered to the *code duello* as the parties understood it. With the appropriate rules and ceremony, honor would be satisfied, regardless of whether it resulted in death or grievous injury.

The dueling ground at Bladensburg, Maryland, where gentlemen cordially met to kill each other.

The parties usually picked the dueling ground outside Bladensburg as their venue. Enclosed by hills with a little brook running through it,[5] the site made a stirring and romantic spot for mortal combat. More importantly, while Maryland had laws against its own citizens dueling, it said nothing about Washingtonians doing the same on the state's turf. In reality, the combatants were unlikely to be caught and arrested anyway: The District had no effective law against dueling,[6] and tradition kept them going back to the Maryland border to uphold the demands of honor, year after year.

The Power of Custom

Perhaps the most famous battle between American naval commodores took place not at sea but in a Bladensburg forest clearing. The challenger of the duel, James Barron, had commanded the USS *Chesapeake*, which in 1807 the British HMS *Leopard* had attacked and boarded in order to seize four deserters from the Royal Navy. The shameful encounter led to Barron's court-martial, after which the US Navy barred him from command for five years and resisted his appeals for reinstatement thereafter. Barron never forgot the humiliation and nursed a grudge against Stephen Decatur, the naval officer who had served on the court-martial and worked to keep him from commanding a ship afterward.[7]

Commodore Decatur, one of the most accomplished and legendary officers the US Navy ever produced, commanded a squadron against the Barbary states, fought in the War of 1812, and had a mansion near the president's. Decatur and his wife were planning a wedding reception in their elegant home for President Monroe's daughter even as Barron and Decatur were quietly exchanging notes in preparation for their duel. Barron felt Decatur had ruined his career and good name and demanded satisfaction; Decatur argued that his motives were strictly professional, not personal, but recognized the necessity of the contest. He had fought five duels before, killing an Englishman in one of them. Even though he philosophically opposed duels, he had no choice but to participate in them, due to the social demands of the dueling code, backed by "the omnipotence of public opinion."[8] The president had the power to stop the actions of such men in the military, but as William Faux saw it, "such is the power of custom, that he cannot and dare not do it."[9]

Separated by only eight yards, the commodores each shot the other in the hip, but Barron's bullet hit one of Decatur's major arteries. Decatur died on the evening of March 22, 1820, in excruciating pain. Barron lived for another thirty years. Thus, thanks to the near-random result of a socially sanctioned gunfight, a mediocre seaman who had embarrassed his country lived to a ripe old age, while "one of the first officers of our navy, the pride of his country, the noble-hearted gentleman"[10] expired early at age forty-one.

Blacklegs and Dressing Gowns

Not all duels took place at Bladensburg, nor did honor always have anything to do with dignity. One such counterexample occurred in April 1826 between Secretary of State Henry Clay and Virginia senator John Randolph. In one of Randolph's signature tirades in the Senate, he had quoted a foreign minister's denunciation of the John Quincy Adams administration, of which Clay was a key part, as a "puritanic, diplomatic, black-legged coalition" and dared anyone to take issue with that opinion.[11] According to the code, Clay had no choice but to challenge the senator to a gunfight. After some hemming and hawing on Randolph's part, the men met in a forest basin on the Virginia side of the Potomac, their loyal seconds acting as intermediaries and weapons loaders.

But instead of wearing a garment appropriate to the solemnity of the occasion, Randolph arrived in his flannel dressing gown, a billowy robe that fit him like a tent. The seconds were outraged by this flagrant disregard for the decorum of the contest, but Clay let it go. Then Randolph's hair-triggered gun fired into the ground by mistake, and one of Clay's allies threatened to call off the duel and leave. But again, Clay wasn't bothered. The contest finally began: Randolph took the first shot and fired gallantly into the air. But Clay, ironically known as "The Great Pacificator," took time to respond with his own, potentially fatal shot. He slowly counted down and took careful aim at the "vast circumference" of the senator in his "unseemly garment."[12] He pulled the trigger and shot a hole in it.

As Clay said later, "I might as well have tried to shoot at a pair of tongs as at Randolph." The senator had spread his legs under his gown to keep the bullet from striking him. He had played a sneaky trick, unbecoming of a gentleman, but it was technically okay since the dueling code said nothing about housecoats and wide stances. Dignity suffered, but honor was satisfied. With that unpleasant business out of the way, the men met cheerfully and later exchanged calling cards, and "social relations were thus formally and courteously restored."[13]

Hero of Anarchy

Events took a rather less genteel turn two years later when Andrew Jackson became president in 1828. "Old Hickory," an accomplished gunfighter and military man, carried lead in his chest from a prior shooting and served as a living symbol of the duelist triumphant. Under his reign, dueling drew in a wider class of people than just the elite, becoming "democratized" while also becoming cruder and bloodier as social climbers used one-on-one warfare to draw out and murder their rivals and make quick names for themselves.[14] Social critics such as Philip Hone took alarm at dueling's rapid rise and expansion. "Sanguinary semi-barbarous conflicts" appeared constantly in the news, as the combatants tried desperately to "write their title to fame in blood."[15] No longer were single-shot pistols the preferred weapons; instead, combatants used revolvers, shotguns, and even bowie

Andrew Jackson's 1829 inaugural party at the White House, at which drunken revelers incited a riot.

knives to enforce their own idea of the duel, which increasingly resembled the bloody brawl that it was instead of the dignified contest it pretended to be.[16]

Jackson perfectly embodied this increasingly democratic, increasingly malicious era. Exceeding any other figure of his time, his personality and actions—more than his politics—made him greatly popular, and he became a sort of "anarchic hero"[17] to a wide swath of Americans. Nowhere did this become more evident than at his inauguration celebration. It began as a friendly levee at the White House, its doors thrown open to the people. However, executive staff made the mistake of providing the crowd with buckets and tubs of punch and other liquor, potentially serving up to twenty thousand people. Soon, according to Margaret Bayard Smith, a "rabble mob" began smashing glass and china and almost killed their hero by accident. He was "*literally* nearly pressed to death and almost suffocated and torn to pieces by the people in their eagerness to shake hands."[18] The madness of the crowd reminded Smith of the worst aspects of the French Revolution. As Supreme Court Justice Joseph Story observed: "The reign of 'King Mob' seemed triumphant."[19]

Happy Animalism

The inauguration riot was hardly unusual. Civil disturbances around the nation in the Jacksonian age were common. Historian Paul Gilje, in his study *Rioting in America*, saw the violence growing out of the democratic, egalitarian impulses of the era.[20] The voting franchise expanded to wider classes of white men (though still not blacks and women) who used guns and fisticuffs to express their anger, fear, and resentment.

The chaos increased throughout Jackson's presidency until 1834, the "great riot year," with scores of battles involving anyone from gamblers and bankers to immigrants and anti-abolitionists.[21] These included Irish labor riots in New England, antibank riots in Baltimore and Portsmouth, anti-Mormon riots in Missouri, anti-Catholic and antiblack riots in the Northeast, and even an antiballoonist riot in Philadelphia.[22] The next year descended into even greater chaos with 147 riots fueled by similar grievances and loathing, including mobs lynching gamblers, abolitionists rioting in order to free slaves, Catholics attacking anti-Catholics (and vice versa), and, strangest of all, an anti–free love riot in New Hampshire.[23]

As electoral battles between Jackson's Democrats and rival Whigs turned nasty across the nation, strongmen at the polls told citizens for whom to vote, using verbal intimidation and outright attack to keep people from choosing the wrong side. In some cities, according to one historian, during Election Day's "genial mayhem [of] swearing, swilling and fighting, the black eyes and bloody noses and torn coats made this a time that tried men's bodies by smart raps and sound kicks" as the political process devolved into a "hell of happy animalism."[24] Jackson himself nearly fell victim to the chaos of the era when an attacker tried to kill him outside the White House in early 1835—the first assassination attempt in American history. After the would-be murderer failed twice to shoot him, Jackson subdued the man by beating him with his walking cane.

By 1837 the conflict so disturbed a young Abraham Lincoln that he saw an "ill omen" in the "increasing disregard for law which pervades the country" as "Accounts of outrages committed by mobs form the every-day news of the times."[25] Hezekiah Niles, the important but little-remembered journalist who published the *Niles Weekly Register* in Baltimore, took a more direct view:

> Society seems everywhere unhinged, *and the demon of "blood and slaughter" has been let loose upon us!* . . . *mobs growing out of* local matters—*and a great collection of acts of violence of a* private, *or* personal *nature, ending in death . . . We have executions, and murders, and riots to the utmost limits of the union. The character of our countrymen seems suddenly changed, and thousands interpret the law in their own way.*[26]

Riots Almighty

A black witness to the Chesapeake violence, Michael Shiner, kept a journal from his time as a slave and then as a free man, now preserved in the Library of Congress (and transcribed here from his colloquial shorthand). Born in Maryland in 1805, he spent the next thirty-five years as the property of the chief clerk of the Washington Navy Yard, Thomas Howard Sr.[27] Howard hired out Shiner to the Navy, where Shiner worked in the paint shop while also recording the details of what he saw around him, from ship construction and working conditions to mob attacks and racial hostility. In one 1828 instance of the latter, twenty young thugs surrounded and attacked him, during which "I had Christmas in me [as they] lit me up torch-like fashion with the firecrackers." A justice of the peace arrived in the middle of the mayhem, but instead of stopping the violence, he said "You scamp, what are you doing here?" and punched Shiner, who managed to escape into an alley. Later that year, Shiner had to flee from a vicious gang of sailors who took him for a runaway slave.[28]

Even when not being physically attacked, Shiner revealed just how threatening life could be for a common laborer in Washington City and for a slave in particular. Dangers that he faced or witnessed included falling overboard and nearly drowning in ice-cold river water, watching a fellow worker accidentally decapitated, and desperately trying and succeeding to free his wife and children from the confines of a Franklin & Armfield slave pen.[29]

In 1835 Shiner witnessed the Snow Riot. His fellow Navy Yard mechanics, on a break from their labor strike, attacked Beverly Snow's restaurant and destroyed it "Root and Branch." Later, they also nearly destroyed a jailhouse where a slave was being held under suspicion of trying to kill his master. Thanks to feeble law enforcement, the mob "raged with great vigor" until the secretary of the Navy detached a column of Marines to protect the jail. After the disturbance, instead of punishing the rioters, President Jackson inquired about their concerns and wondered if there was "anything he could do for them in an honorable way to promote their happiness." As a first step, he promised the thugs that "by the eternal God in this City" he would crack down on any "negroes [who] had violated any law whatever" and punish them severely for it.[30]

The eternal god of the city, however, had nothing on Andrew Jackson. The belligerent-in-chief cast himself as the stalwart tribune of democracy, someone who didn't need to follow the tired old rules of legal procedure when guided by his own sense of purpose, a man above the law who stood as the fulfillment of a righteous society rather than as a threat to it. Not surprisingly, a lot of his followers felt the same way. They rioted not against but *in favor of* the status quo in order to enforce their own sense of justice without worrying what the law had to say about it.[31]

Liquid Aggression

Shiner wasn't always a victim of his time. Sometimes he perpetrated the kind of violence he observed—before inevitably falling victim to it again. Alcohol often provided the fuel for conflict. After a heavy bout of drinking mysterious liquors called "Tom Cat" and "Run from the Gun," Shiner and another black worker got into a "tussle," during which Shiner threw him in a mud hole. Another time, he flung a man into a basement, "going crazy" with drink, before Marines wrestled him down and stuck a bayonet in his shoulder. Yet another drunken escapade resulted in Shiner getting mauled with stones and brickbats, arrested, and sent to navy lockup. Ultimately he escaped from lockup and went back at work as usual.[32]

None of Shiner's alcoholic tumults would have surprised Frederick Douglass, who saw liquor and slavery as inseparable. Slaveholders routinely used alcohol as a means to suppress rebellion and numb potential escapees into compliance. "In order to make a man a slave . . . it is necessary to silence or drown his mind," said Douglass. Other abolitionists and temperance supporters saw "Rum and Negro hate" as two sides of the same coin and worked to eradicate drinking altogether to dampen the spark that seemed to ignite so much racial violence.[33]

For their reward, the temperance advocates became a new target for the rioters, who saw any steps toward black self-improvement as a threat and made a special effort to destroy assembly halls that hosted temperance meetings, just as they did black businesses, schools, and churches—of course leaving brothels and dance halls alone.[34] A danger to the old order, black temperance found many supporters across the region, Michael Shiner among them. In 1836 he quit drinking, and "I never have had a drop of liquor in my mouth since that time."[35]

A Frenzy of Spirits

It wasn't so easy for others to stave off the power of liquor, however. Taverns offered a wide array of spirits, gambling, and other amusements, and they also featured dances, balls, and assemblies, with anything from a "wonderful mathematical dog [to] a collection of the works of some distinguished artist." They housed the Orphans Court and circuit courts in the early days, hosted political protests and rallies and nominating conventions for municipal politics, and offered an ideal place to celebrate George Washington's birthday in high style.[36] John Adams stepped into the City Tavern in 1800 to offer no fewer than seventeen toasts to the health of the country,[37] and later politicos stumped for votes over glasses of rum and whiskey. Drinking hard liquor and politicking went hand in hand, and election-day drunkenness was common.[38] William Henry Harrison won the presidency in 1840 with a campaign that boasted of his supposed log-cabin origins and taste for hard cider.

Non-political figures also drew crowds. Georgetown's Union Tavern hosted Talleyrand, Napoleon's brother Jerome Bonaparte, King Louis Philippe, inventor Robert Fulton, and Washington Irving.[39] Such figures lodged at taverns when few other accommodations were available in the District, and some continued to do so after proper hotels were built. The most prominent taverns provided little reason for visitors to go anywhere else. The Columbian Tavern, for example, advertised "good Beds and Boarding, with a variety of Liquors [and] Dinners dressed at the shortest notice," while others like Tunnicliff's and Rhodes acted as hubs for social activity and even a dancing assembly.[40]

But alcohol was still their prime draw. Americans drank more alcohol in the first third of the 1800s than at any other time in the history of the country. In 1830 the average American drank some five gallons of hard alcohol per year,[41] more than one shot of high-proof liquor a day. It's no accident, then, that the country's most brutal decade outside of war-time followed. "Violence often came in bottles," and countless conflicts occurred in and around taverns, occasionally punctuated by murder.[42] At the time, heavy drinking counted as a pursuit of proper manhood, and booze became the elixir of brotherhood and camaraderie, especially for the working class.[43] But this potent mix of drinking, violence, and social communion had grave consequences. It deformed everything from the way people interacted and communicated to how they solved problems and had fun.

Killing Games

"Fun" often meant watching animals tear one another apart. Blood sport was a prime source of antebellum entertainment. Taverns featured fights between men, dogs, and even rats[44] for the amusement and wagering of spectators. Providing such battles was technically illegal, but again the laws were rarely enforced and countless creatures became carcasses to satisfy drinkers' gambling lust. Baltimore even featured spectacles like bull and bear baiting,[45] in which a large beast in chains had to fight off a team of hunting dogs while bettors wagered on which creatures would survive. As early as the 1780s, English critic J. F. D. Smyth noticed how locals in the Chesapeake devoured all manner of "sport, gaming, and dissipation" as well as "that most barbarous of all diversions, that peculiar species of cruelty, cock-fighting."[46]

Indeed, if the capital was known for one blood sport, it was cockfighting. In this contest, owners of gamecocks would place their prized roosters into rings known as cockpits. The birds were fitted with little weapons around their legs, such as knives or gaffs—"sharp blades of finely tempered steel"—with which they could hack their rivals to death. Aficionados of the sport obsessed over the various breeds and types of birds, their proper fighting weights, and their various colors and plumages. Not surprisingly, arch duelist Andrew Jackson was a fan of cockfighting and even attended one public event in Bladensburg, which for once hosted a bloody contest between chickens instead of humans. The birds came from Jackson's own stock in Tennessee, and the president put great faith in them. But they never fought that day: The contest was canceled due to the sorry condition of their rival cocks, which were in no state to battle after a lengthy ride cooped up in a stagecoach.[47]

Many fowl fights occurred in taverns, though not all did. In Virginia, when local courts were in session, courthouse squares became popular sites for cockfighting, along with gambling, slave auctions, debt collection, and religious ceremonies.[48] Across the Potomac in Georgetown, cockfighting had been banned since 1796,[49] so its practitioners relocated to the Washington City circle at 23rd Street north of Funkstown. Christian Hines, in his recollections, reports that the site became the preferred place for blood sport of the human and animal varieties. During one match, a group of local cockfight fanatics tried to drive away interlopers from Georgetown using cudgels. Many suffered injuries, but one man made it all the way back home with a creative bit of self-protection: using a fence rail to deflect the blows of his attackers and beat them to the ground.[50]

The Rise of Fistiana

Although common, human fighting didn't become widely popular as a sport per se until the 1840s. One of its earliest guides, Patrick Timony's *American Fistiana*, lays out the rules for bare-knuckled combat and presents letters between famous boxers as a prelude to their battle. They read curiously like overtures to a duel. In one case, the challenger, James Sullivan, contends that reigning champ Tom Hyer "assailed [him] in a most cowardly manner" inside a saloon. Hyer disputes the charge by claiming Sullivan attacked him first, and he pledges to show no mercy to anyone who improperly assails him. The fight was on.[51]

Hyer's father, Jacob, was the first widely recognized American champion of the sport, but it didn't really take off until his son got into the ring with Sullivan. The match occurred in 1849 in a no-man's-land on the Eastern Shore of Maryland—a day trip from the capital—where federal and state jurisdiction was disputed, making it something like boxing's own Bladensburg. That didn't prevent authorities from trying to shut down the affair, but the boxers, along with a rowdy crowd of two hundred, escaped their clutches with an elaborate caper involving oyster boats.[52]

The match began with the two parties "coming to the scratch," that is, getting into the ring or field of combat. Soon they pummeled each other with rawboned vigor in a contest that a modern pugilist might consider unorthodox: Sullivan demonstrated "superior wrestling" moves in the first round. The men pounded each other mercilessly "with the rapidity of two cocks" in the second. Both were "clotted with gore" and barely able to stand in the ninth. Hyer tried to wrench Sullivan's arm from its socket in the fifteenth, and Hyer smashed his rival with both fists in the sixteenth, which finally did the trick. Hyer prevailed when Sullivan couldn't make it back to the scratch, which in the setting sun had become a gory crimson mess. The triumph was total: Hyer had won a stunning ten thousand dollars in a mere seventeen minutes, and the "hurricane fight" became greatly influential in making sportsmen in the Chesapeake and across the nation take notice of a new kind of blood sport, one that by comparison made cockfighting look almost humane.[53]

Serving Not to Protect

Boxing was one of several violent, technically illegal activities that occurred in the District due to the lack of an effective police force to stop them. In the early days of Washington City, the constables—a group of four, one per city ward—worked mainly during the day, keeping an eye out for disorderly persons; inspecting taverns, markets, and other public facilities; and rounding up wandering pigs and livestock.[54] As the town grew, however, this force became inadequate. By the mid-1830s, only a dozen officers patrolled an area that by the previous census had become home to nearly forty thousand people. After a group of hooligans caused a minor riot on the grounds of the White House—and with robberies, burglaries, and arson on the uptick—Congress established the Auxiliary Guard as a nighttime force in 1842.[55] Along with chasing thieves and firebugs, the guard was supposed to suppress riots and monitor the firehouse gangs that plagued the town. But with only fifteen men on duty, the guard never became an effective force of law and order, concentrating instead on harassing slaves and free blacks.

Unfortunately there was precedent for this brutal activity. Washington City originally paid its first constables fifty cents for each time they whipped a slave accused of violating the law.[56] Not surprisingly, one of the chief duties of the Auxiliary Guard was to hunt down any blacks out after curfew or presumably violating city ordinances.[57] The guard could arrest or fine them or flog them at the city jail, which had a whipping post for that very purpose.[58] The pattern was then set wherein the skeleton police force had a limited effect on controlling urban crime but a major effect on keeping blacks living in terror of being arrested, jailed, and put to the lash.

Officers of the Auxiliary Guard developed a lasting reputation, however, for sleeping at their posts, smoking cigars, and drinking heavily rather than walking their beats.[59] When they did feel like enforcing the law, most used noisy rattles instead of whistles and carried clubs with iron spearheads instead of guns.[60] By contrast, urban murderers were resorting to lethal force: From 1846 to 1860 their use of guns doubled throughout America to become the weapon of choice in a third of all killings.[61] Criminals shot and maimed a number of District officers and ran riot throughout town, committing what newspapers called "outrages of a most audacious and alarming character."[62] In response, members of Congress and the city council passed new laws, reorganized the police, and made fiery speeches decrying the free rein of miscreants, but nothing they did had much effect. The police were too few, their budgets too small, and they were fighting a mania of antebellum mayhem that afflicted both criminals and law abiders alike. In 1849 this was evident even during Christmas:

> Long before daylight began the fusillade by gun, pistol and cracker, the blowing of whistles and small horns, the beating of small drums and tin pans . . . At the same time there were bonfires blazing in different parts of the city . . . Primitive were the instruments used. The old-fashioned horse pistol, some with flint lock, the half-dollar brass pistol and Colt's revolver, then known as the pepper box, were for shooting purposes.[63]

One rotund fellow had the misfortune of resembling Santa Claus. After spotting him on a street corner, a crowd of a hundred hooligans surrounded him, mocked him with vulgar rhymes, and then chased him back to his house while pelting him with firecrackers.[64]

Ragged Parades

The local militia system wasn't much better than the guard. A law from 1803 provided for an armed citizenry to protect the town, but in later years this militia often operated without arms and equipment. Any effort to make the town folk perform their civic duty met with griping over "oppression and tyranny."[65] In one case, a group of local businessmen became so annoyed with militia drills that they organized a counterparade, with brooms for guns, a "general" who wielded a horse's shinbone as a sword, and old smokestacks dragged along like cannons.[66]

The real militia degenerated to the point where, in 1835, their attempt to present a proper parade resembled the ridiculous pantomime of those who had mocked them, prompting Michael Shiner's derision:

> They were the raggediest white people that ever I saw in my life, and their uniforms were of old rags . . . and they had drums and fifes and they had clarinets. Their drums were composed of old tin pans and old pots and all kinds of old sheet iron, and their flutes, clarinets and fifes and bugles were composed of ram's horn and oyster horns.[67]

A month later, the Snow rioters went on a rampage. The poorly trained and equipped militia could do nothing to stop them, which proved only how defenseless the capital was in the face of mob rule.* If not for the last-ditch efforts of the US military, the rioters would have completed the work started by the British in 1814 and incinerated the capital. The old militia system soon died, and the town had no effective means of civic order throughout 1836. A few companies were organized the next year, but they did little to provide for the basic security and safety of residents.[68] Even Georgetown and Alexandria had basic police services, as did countless other towns in the Chesapeake, but Washington City stood almost alone in its unguarded, helpless condition in the face of riot and disorder.

The Right to Riot

Members of Congress didn't help matters. The legislature hadn't even passed a law against rioting in the District and often watched feebly as violent events occurred on its watch. (By contrast, neighboring Maryland and other states not only had laws against riot and civil disorder but also an effective state militia with which to enforce them.) In 1848, when a simple law against DC rioting was suggested, some Southern congressmen argued residents had a "right to riot" in certain cases—against, say, abolitionists and other such threats.[69] The bill died. But at least the politicians deserved credit for a rare lack of hypocrisy, since they ranked among the most belligerent figures in town.

It was probably inevitable that the political boys' club—which encouraged chewing tobacco, whittling, yelling, and spitting—also embraced more violent behavior. Marked by aggressive bravado and occasional threats of bodily harm, the atmosphere was already threatening and no doubt worsened with members' drinking. In the 1830s, politicians attacked each other physically no fewer than eight times. These conflicts

---

* The federal response to mobs also depended on whom they were rioting against. The test case came in winter 1834, when rival groups of Irish mechanics digging the C&O Canal in Maryland violently went on strike. Unlike the gentle treatment he would show the Snow rioters, Andrew Jackson dealt with the workers by calling out federal troops. The US forces teamed with the state militia to arrest thirty rioters and throw them in jail, and a military presence remained on the canal the rest of the winter. The aggressive federal reaction was revealing—attacking the lives and property of citizens was one thing; attacking the property of the government was quite another. (Richard B. Morris, "Andrew Jackson, Strikebreaker," *American Historical Review* 55:1 (1949): 63–64)

ranged from a policy debate that turned into a fistfight—when one member called another "the tool of tools"—to actual murder threats on the House floor, which resulted in most congressmen carrying concealed daggers, bowie knives, and guns for protection.[70]

Even out-of-towners got into altercations with the local politicians. On visiting the District in 1832, former Tennessee (and future Texas) governor Sam Houston spotted his nemesis, Congressman William Stanbery, on Pennsylvania Avenue and severely beat him with a hickory cane. Stanbery pulled out a pistol and tried to shoot him, but the gun failed to fire, so Houston beat him some more until he was unable to speak. For this assault, a DC court fined the governor five hundred dollars.[71]

Others still resorted to the increasingly antiquated practice of dueling. In 1838 one of the last major contests pitted Maine's Jonathan Cilley against Kentucky's William Graves, the latter an exceptional shot. The event took place at Bladensburg as usual, but this time the duelists used rifles instead of pistols. After each man twice missed his mark, the parties took a third shot, and Graves hit Cilley in the groin and killed him.[72]

However, instead of the usual hosannas in praise of satisfied honor, the event sparked outrage. Northerners lionized Cilley, condemned Graves, and flooded Congress with petitions demanding an end to what they called "Murder Most Foul." Many Southerners resisted the change, but few in Congress wanted to go on record in favor of dueling,[73] especially as the practice was falling into disrepute thanks to the worsening climate of violence in general. After much debate, the legislators finally passed a measure in 1839 that not only made issuing or accepting a challenge to a duel illegal in the District but also wisely provided criminal penalties for doing so.[74] The law had plenty of holes in it, and it wasn't fully enforced, but it did provide a good legal justification for politicians to avoid mortal combat and gave an official stamp of disapproval to socially sanctioned murder. It did not, however, prevent politicians from fighting each other without guns.

Incendiarism

For some residents of Washington City, dueling and mob riots didn't happen often enough, and they required a more regular schedule of violent action. Firehouse gangs fit the bill by providing their members a chance

One of the early hook-and-ladder companies in DC.

to engage in fisticuffs and skirmishes with their enemies—as well as an opportunity to extinguish fires or even set them occasionally.

In the early days of the capital, fighting the town's fires was a responsible, respected, unpaid occupation. Households had leather buckets to help put out fires, and each ward had its own volunteer fire company.[75] Their members came from the working and middle classes and had stirring names like Union, Franklin, Alert, Star, Eagle, Vigilance, Perseverance, and Columbia.[76] Although the companies served ably for several decades, the older, more experienced men began dropping out in the 1830s because they had to do double duty with the town militia and found it a challenge to battle blazes across the vast distances of the capital. Into that void stepped rowdy gangs of teenage boys, who within a decade transformed the venerable companies into veritable gangs.[77]

Gang rivalries that had existed from the earliest days of the capital were initially petty, mostly limited to neighborhood fights and rock throwing in Frogtown, English Hill, or The Island.[78] Some of the more notable groups included the Gumballs, Round Tops, Never Sweats, Razors, Blood-tubs, Chunkers, and Rams.[79] (The last of these had its headquarters on Capitol Hill, though history doesn't reveal whether any of its members also served in Congress.) When the gangs took over the fire companies, though, they suddenly had access to fancy equipment and engines, and suddenly commanded a great deal more attention. The capital soon divided into warring fiefdoms, each based around a firehouse.

The gangs naturally proved better at fighting one another than fighting fires. If one engine house arrived on the scene of a blaze in their ward first, they might put it out. But just as often, buildings burned down if two or more companies arrived at a fire at the same time, as each group tried to prevent its rivals from extinguishing it—by hoisting a barrel over a over a street hydrant and sitting on it[80]—while the structure blazed. Sometimes the battles became violent, and a street fight that began with rocks and other small missiles grew into a full-fledged riot.[81] In 1844, exactly that happened right in front of the White House as various thugs battled one another with "stones, fence rails, and other dangerous weapons."[82] If authorities caught and tried the rioters, they usually received small fines (five dollars in one case) and often served no jail time.[83] Even worse, some gangsters even *started* fires in order to create chaos and enjoy a run with the fire engine—and then had the nerve to take credit for putting the blazes out.[84]

Newspapers carried all-too-frequent reports of "incendiarism," which told of the latest antics of the gangs in their efforts to start or extinguish local fires: "the fire-bells ring out, and the gangs of boys who have taken charge of the respective engines of the city are all on the *qui vive* [lookout] to run roaring and swearing through the streets . . . Who is to be burnt up next Saturday night no one knows, only some one must furnish the required food for excitement of undisciplined boys."[85]

Amid the turmoil, authorities had few means to stop the gangs. Although professional departments were rare in the antebellum South, Washington City lagged behind even Alexandria and other area cities in the organization and control of its firefighters.[86] Congress tried to attract more mature firemen by promising them exemption from militia duty, but the measure proved worthless when the militia system collapsed.[87] By the 1850s the fire company gangs had grown more powerful, extending their mayhem into local politics and using their pull to keep officials from regulating them. (But some still courted irony when even their own firehouses burned down.)[88] It took until 1856 for Washington City to establish basic safety and operational standards for volunteer firefighters, and a professional, salaried fire department didn't come into existence until the Civil War.[89]

Tourists from Mobtown

Some of the firehouse lads had ties to Washington's most notorious political party, the Know-Nothings, a virulently anti-Catholic and anti-immigrant group that meddled in District politics, usually for the worse. The most visible sign of their menace was the beleaguered Washington Monument, planned for decades but unfinished due to slow fund-raising and, later, their overt lawbreaking. In early 1854 they broke into the monument site at night, locked up the watchman, removed a memorial block of marble donated by Pope Pius IX, defaced and broke the stone, and threw the pieces into the Potomac. Soon after, they took control of the Washington National Monument Society by holding a sham "public meeting" in which they elected their own officers to its board and seized possession of its books and property.[90] This bold act of thuggery aroused such public ire that Congress withdrew its funding, and other donors followed suit. The Know-Nothings added several shoddy layers to the monument but gave up control of the society a few years later. The obelisk, however, remained an embarrassing granite stump for another quarter of a century.

Nearby Baltimore had an even worse problem with the Know-Nothings, who matched their anti-immigrant hysteria with armed intimidation at the polls and seized city government in several disputed elections. (In so doing, they offered cheeky campaign slogans that reminded voters of the tools they had used to menace voters, such as "Come up and vote: there is room for awl.")[91] The Know-Nothings found firm and brutal allies in the thugs that filled the ranks of the firehouse gangs,[92] who in turn spread so much turmoil that the violence spread beyond Baltimore and into the capital itself.

The gangsters' use of violence had deep roots in the Maryland city, going back to 1812 and before. Even Alexis de Tocqueville had heard of its fearsome riots on a trip to America.[93] The gangs caused unchecked havoc in subsequent years and gave Baltimore the well-deserved nickname of "Mobtown."[94] One visitor estimated that Baltimore had "a greater number of black-guards, for its population, than any other city in the Union."[95]

Baltimore's gangsters had many colorful names: the Rip Raps, Rough Skins, Ranters, Rattlers, Black Snakes, Thunderbolts, Little Fellows, Blood Tubs, and Decaturs.[96] But it was the Plug Uglies who took a break from their Maryland violence in 1857 and paid a visit to Washington City. Their local allies in the Know-Nothing Party joined them in an effort to intimidate the District's voters and prevent those deemed "foreigners" from voting.[97] The joint force attacked a naturalized citizen trying to vote in one ward, wounding the ward commissioner in the fracas, and then fired a volley of pistol shots at other voters.[98] As Michael Shiner saw it, the out-of-town rioters "raised such an excitement that the mayor and the whole police force could not stop them."[99] Desperate for help and unable to control the mayhem, Mayor William Magruder wrote to President Buchanan that hooligans armed with "firearms, clubs, knives, and stones" had managed to drive the voters from the polls, chased off the election commissioners, and were threatening further violence.[100]

At the president's behest, the secretary of the Navy had to call out the Marines again, as in 1835, but this time the rioters didn't disperse so easily. Some in the crowd seized control of a "six pounder swivel gun"—a cannon—and hurled stones and fired revolvers at the Marines who tried to capture it.[101] According to Shiner, "one of the Marines was shot in the face and severely wounded, and it was supposed that the Marines fired through a mistake of order, and there was several people killed and wounded."[102] When the carnage ended, eight people lay dead, twenty-one injured, almost all of them citizens of Washington City. The Plug Uglies escaped back to Baltimore that night.[103]

The election riot of 1857 offered yet another example of how the town had no real defense against disorder. A visiting goon squad easily overwhelmed the capital's police force to indulge in a bit of mob tourism. To quell the protests of residents over the threat of such violence, six months after the riot the city council authorized expanding the daytime police force by the grand number of just ten men, for a total of fifty-seven officers—twenty-seven policemen during the day and thirty Auxiliary Guardsmen at night—to patrol a city of sixty thousand people.[104] A Senate committee summed up the terrible state of affairs in an 1858 report:

The police force is both feeble and inefficient. Riot and bloodshed are of daily occurrence. Innocent and unoffending persons are shot, stabbed, and otherwise shamefully mistreated, and not unfrequently the offender is not even arrested. It is hardly necessary to add, that such acts are a disgrace to a civilized society, and, if not put down, must result in disastrous consequences to society, and bring a lasting reproach on this Federal city.[105]

But Congress had little interest in turning the DC police into an effective crime-fighting force. This impasse derived from its usual lack of action in passing legislation that could help the District in any way and from legislators' inability to approve almost anything because of the growing enmity among them. Indeed, by the middle of the 1850s, the "riot and bloodshed" on the capital's streets had once again moved into the halls of Congress itself.

House of Combat

The most infamous bloodletting was the assault by South Carolina congressman Preston Brooks on Massachusetts senator Charles Sumner in 1856. The attack developed from the ongoing battle over the admission of Kansas as a free or slave state, which produced great invective between abolitionists of the North and slavery apologists in the South. Infuriated by Sumner's speeches against human bondage, Brooks found him at his desk in the Senate and, in his own words, took action:

I struck him with my cane and give him about 30 first-rate stripes with a gutta percha cane which had been given me a few months before . . . Every lick went where I intended it. For about the first five or six licks he offered to make a fight, but I plied him so rapidly that he did not touch me. Towards the last he bellowed like a calf. I wore my cane out completely but saved the Head which is gold. The fragments of the cane are begged for as sacred relics.[106]

Brooks did in fact become a hero to the South, just as Sumner became a martyr to the North, drenched in his own blood and nearly dying in the assault. Northerners saw Brooks as a demonic figure and called for quick justice, but he received no jail time for his attack and was reelected to the House after he made the voluntary gesture of resigning from it. (Before Brooks could retake his seat, however, he died of a respiratory disease. By contrast, Sumner recovered, lived long enough to see the South lose the Civil War, and helped oversee Reconstruction.)

Another brawl occurred two years later, again over slavery, as Brooks's ally Laurence Keitt called Galusha Grow a "black Republican puppy." Grow responded by calling his accuser a "negro-driver." Keitt tried to choke Grow, and the House exploded into a melee of bodies and fists flying. The speaker wielded the ceremonial House mace as a weapon, and one congressman even tried to brain people with a heavy stone spittoon. The fracas finally ended when one member tried to grab another by the hair to punch him in the face but pulled off his toupee instead. The chamber erupted in laughter, and the internecine battle ended—for

The infamous 1858 battle in Congress that included punching, choking, and even toupee pulling.

the moment.[107] But no amount of mirth could make people forget that, throughout six decades, the violence between "gentlemen" had degenerated in Congress just as it had around the country. What had begun with mortal contests to preserve honor had devolved into a grotesque spectacle of cane beatings and open brawling.

Final Pages of a Diarist

As the 1850s ended, Michael Shiner surprisingly managed to steer clear of much of the era's violence. He saw plenty of mayhem on the streets, but he personally experienced less of it as the years passed—or at least he grew less fond of writing about it in his journal. Quitting drinking helped him avoid conflict more easily, as did his manumission in 1840. Like some other urban bondsmen, he paid for his freedom through years of labor in the slave-hiring system, but afterward he continued to work at the Navy Yard until he was age sixty-five, living another ten years after that. During that time, he rose to prominence as a successful businessman, a leader in Republican Party politics, and a well-known figure in the black community.[108] His journal provides but a glimpse of the Civil War and the years that followed. What remains, then, are his vivid anecdotes of an earlier era of socially sanctioned violence—a time when duelists, mobs, and gangs ruled by gun, club, and knife, and community bonds frayed and civil order nearly collapsed.

SEVEN

ILLICIT CONGRESS

Washington City had another socially sanctioned activity that, like street violence, is almost always illegal today but was practiced openly then. It had a devoted class of customers from all stations of society, prominent locations near the Capitol and the White House, de facto impunity from any kind of effective prosecution, and intelligent, driven promoters who became some of the best-known figures in the underworld. Its employees went by a variety of colorful euphemisms, from "painted Jezebels" and "fallen angels" to "daughters of Eve" and "gay young ducks" in their pursuit of the "illicit congress" of profiting from human desire.[1]

Prostitution wasn't technically illegal, but it did operate in a gray zone that enabled police to make busts when needed (usually due to political pressure) under the charge of "keeping a bawdy house" or a "disorderly house." The houses weren't dangerous themselves necessarily, but they did attract rougher types of crime since they operated in neighborhoods rife with thievery and street violence. Despite the danger of visiting a brothel in a bad neighborhood, countless men did so in Washington City, helping to make the capital one of the prime centers of the sex trade on the East Coast during the nineteenth century. Opportunities for sin lay within easy reach of any wayward politician, businessman, or merchant, and this vice became one of the capital's most pervasive.

Boardinghouses to Brothels

Although records are scarce, prostitution likely dated to the earliest days of the District, when brothels emerged from some of the lower-end boardinghouses in town. Of course these weren't the same houses that hosted legislators and executive staff members in individual state and party delegations—as far as we know. Instead, they were another sort of rooming house. Tenants included young, single women employed in shops and factories and often impoverished, earning about half the salary of their male counterparts. Many struggled through economic crises, the disappearance or death of a breadwinning spouse or parent, and other financial problems. To make ends meet, some turned to friends and family for support; others became "charity girls" who accepted material gifts in return for sexual favors.[2] In time, the boardinghouses where they lived housed both working girls and "working girls." The latter had some of the highest incomes in the house and quietly conducted their business from their rooms.

An older woman typically operated the house, and, if sufficiently impressed by her tenants' underworld revenue, she might boot out the aboveboard residents and become a madam. In so doing, her boardinghouse became a brothel. Soon, enough boardinghouses had turned into whorehouses that critics saw prostitution as one of the capital's most prominent and regrettable industries. John Ellis, in his salacious guide to town, *Sights and Secrets of the Nation's Capital*, remarked:

> *Boarding-house life is not pleasant anywhere. In Washington it is simply abominable. . . . The "young ladies" are devoted to you, and expect you to take them around, and spend your spare cash on them in the most liberal manner . . . your peace of mind, if you are at all sensitive, is destroyed by the scandal which is soon set afloat about you. You meet with sundry women, who have no visible means of support, and sometimes in the effort to be civil to them, you compromise yourself in a manner you little dream of at the outset.[3]*

Tax and census records euphemistically called prostitutes "boarders," "substitutes," or "inmates," and the line between boardinghouse owner and brothel keeper was often so thin as to be imperceptible.

The Rise of a Madam

Among the several women who owned or managed property in town, Mary Ann Hall ranked among the most notable—or notorious—as a pioneer in the sex trade. She began her career in the 1840s, then in her

twenties, and built a three-story brick edifice on The Island when most
of the surrounding structures were little more than tumbledown wooden
shacks. Government records don't reveal the source of the initial capital for
her investment, but there's little doubt it came from sex. While most single
women in the neighborhood worked as seamstresses or laundresses, Hall's
official title was "substitute," an occupation shared by her housemates, who
included her sister and several other women.[4] It didn't take her long to create the biggest and possibly the most profitable operation in town. Early
records list some eighteen "inmates" working at her establishment,[5] with
potentially more sex workers showing up for part-time duty.

Located at what was then 349 Maryland Avenue, Hall's brothel was
erected at some distance from the central red-light district north of the
Mall. This isolation proved profitable for Hall and her employees because
here she could construct a sexual fantasyland for her elite clientele of
bankers, merchants, and congressmen, who easily could afford the expensive rates and tastes on offer.

Capital Inmates

Upon entering, a visitor would find a house exquisitely furnished with oil
paintings, silver-plated candlesticks, mahogany and rosewood furniture,
marble tables, porcelain and ironstone dishes, plush lounges, and Brus-
sels carpets.[6] Escorted to one of the bedrooms, he'd find the decor no less
eye-catching: French mirrors, brass candelabra, Chinese vases, assorted
decanters and wineglasses, finely carved wooden beds—and of course the
women.

It's hard to know exactly how Ms. Hall's prostitutes appeared or how
they entertained visitors, but a few artifacts and baubles recovered from
the brothel site by Donna Seifert and other archaeologists in the last few
decades provide a clue. One might expect the mirror fragments, hairpins,
combs, and jewelry, but the array of black-glass buttons that the ladies
wore stand out as totems of high-priced dresses that few working-class
women could afford.[7]

The clothing of the "inmates" wasn't the only expensive aspect of the
place. The food and drink that they and their clients enjoyed were con-
sistently among the best in town: expensive steaks and roasts, fish, turtle,
wild game and mutton, not to mention berries, peaches, grapes, figs, and

even coconuts. Tea and coffee filled porcelain cups, pipes and later ciga-rettes held the finest local tobacco, and copious amounts of champagne flowed.[8] All of these details suggest that Hall's clients weren't just pop-ping in for a quickie. Clearly they expected to spend substantial time at her house, enjoying a fine meal, drinking tea, smoking, perhaps even con-versing after a long day at the office. Her brothel thereby functioned more like an upscale, European-style salon with benefits rather than a stereo-typical whorehouse with drunken johns chasing trollops in bloomers.

Although we know precise details of the fashion, food, and flair of Hall's elite (or "upper-ten") brothel, the identities of her johns remain mysterious. Doubtless she drew visitors from the Washington business district and the plantations of Virginia and Maryland, but uncovering the names of her Capitol Hill customers requires more speculation since no "little black book," if ever one existed, has survived. Suffice it to say, though, that the proximity of Capitol Hill gave Hall a ready and eager clientele,[9] which contemporary sources indicate wouldn't have been unusual.

Tales from the Cattery

J. W. Buel, in his sensationalistic *Mysteries and Miseries of America's Great Cities*, describes how "the assignation houses of Washington are sustained almost wholly by members of the two houses of Congress." Buel even claims that within the House of Representatives there was "a reception room, which has been denominated by newspaper correspondents as the 'Cattery'. . . . In many respects it is an assignation place, maintained at public expense for the benefit of salacious congressmen." Of the Senate side, he reveals even more:

> *It is well known that upon special occasions, through the influence of senators, women of easy virtue are admitted, and that they give recep-tions therein to those who write notes on official [desks] underneath. Queens of the lobby have entre there, and from this lofty and flattering perch they become objects of unctuous admiration, displaying to excel-lent advantage their gorgeous apparel, with half revealing monu-ments of maternity peeping over brilliant bodies, and arms dressed in a rouge that helps nature amazingly.*[10]

Official Capitol records don't report the presence of prostitutes in the galleries, but other published accounts hint at their presence, including that certain enterprising women manipulated politicians to effect policy changes. One Lucy Cobb, for example, could "get a pardon [for her customers] where anybody else would fail. She probably picked up a few hundred dollars in this precarious way. . . . Policemen, folders, pages, and Congressmen all knew her, and she would walk through the Capitol unannoyed by the stare of people, and was able to make her way into almost any of the committee rooms."[11] The author of this passage, George A. Townsend, reports similar tales, as do comparable salacious books of the time that covered any scrap of Washington scandal and intrigue that their writers could find.

A Division of Hookers

During the tumult of the Civil War, the sex trade expanded, and Washington City became well known for its illicit congress. The town attracted not only johns from the East Coast but prostitutes from as far away as the Midwest looking for a new place to set up shop, drawn by the capital's lax enforcement of vice laws, overwhelmed police force, willing clientele, and plentiful brothels. At their peak, more than 450 such houses of ill repute operated in the metropolitan area, with "ladies of easy virtue" plying their trade in bordellos, hotel rooms, gambling dens, music halls, saloons, private apartments, even parks and alleys.[12] Much of the activity took place around Pennsylvania Avenue between Capitol Hill and the White House. One government inventory listed some eighty-five known brothels along with their locations and proprietors. Some of the more memorable establishments included the Haystack, the Ironclad, the Wolf's Den, the Devil's Own, the Blue Goose, Madame Russell's Bake Oven, and Madam Wilton's Private Residence for Ladies.[13]

Modern estimates of the number of DC prostitutes range from 3,900 to 15,000,[14] and with so many sex workers in town the city council briefly considered licensing them to exert some control over their industry. However, General Joseph Hooker, head of the Army of the Potomac, had a simpler plan: He herded them into an area below Pennsylvania Avenue, near the Treasury building, where he could keep an eye on any troops who might pay a visit. This consolidation of downtown brothels was known as "Joe Hooker's Division," then "Hooker's Division" or just "The Division,"[15] which gradually became the name of the neighborhood over the years, along with the old moniker of Murder Bay.

Red Light, Green Light

Though the general's name didn't give rise to the synonym for prostitute—a dubious honor that goes to New York several decades earlier—Hooker made official what was already developing in practice. Most boardinghouses left in the area already had switched to housing mainly prostitutes, or else they acted as safe houses for petty thieves, fugitives, thugs, and other miscreants. Guides to Washington, if they mentioned The Division at all, predictably thundered against it, as do modern histories of the era. When mentioned, it's described as a place where "shrieks and revelry rent the midnight air," and, outside one brothel, "the hacks of the sporting men were thickly ranked, and saucy women flounced in and out in full view of the horrified churchgoers on Sunday,"[16] which raises the question of why anyone was going to church there in the first place.

Some of the many brothels of the downtown red-light district known as The Division.

There's little doubt that the red-light district was a bleak, downtrodden area where criminals outnumbered police and poverty ran rampant. But the grim conditions of the zone did little to deter business, and a trip to The Division became something of a rite of passage. Its bordellos, music halls, and markets always had plenty of customers from beyond the neighborhood, and even its gambling halls saw their fair share of military officers and government officials.[17] Slumming was as popular in the nineteenth century as it is today, and otherwise upstanding middle-class men weren't above getting a few cheap thrills from venturing into the rough part of town.[18] Since the district lay conveniently between the White House and Capitol Hill, an enterprising john could easily take in the town's major sights in an afternoon. Pennsylvania Avenue, "America's Main Street," connected them all.

Of course, the brothels in The Division didn't quite reach the level of Mary Ann Hall's establishment. They came much closer to our modern conception of an old-fashioned cathouse than anything resembling an intimate salon. One visitor's testimony describes a brothel so clichéd that it could have come from Central Casting: In an elegant parlor featuring a sleek velvet couch and gas lights, an overdressed madam appeared in jewels and other finery while half a dozen prostitutes stood by in scanty garments and thick makeup.[19] Only the fringy red lampshades and a player piano were missing.

War, Debauchery, and Reaction

The consolidation of downtown prostitution into Hooker's Division didn't bring the trade under control. Instead, as Washington City exploded during the war with troops, camp followers, and support staff, the underworld followed suit and tailored its gambling, thievery, and sex-trading operations to the new martial class.

Brothels expanded into the better parts of town, into elegant mansions with gardens and smart brick houses in the more upscale neighborhoods around Lafayette Square, the White House, and churches.[20] Among the more elite sex-trading sites were Sal Austin's brothel near City Hall and Julie Dean's bordello in Marble Alley, a prostitution enclave three blocks west of the Capitol.[21] Both establishments provided close and convenient access for the rich and powerful clients they entertained.

Many neighbors of these bordellos, however, took issue with all the activity taking place there. The press seized on stories of prostitutes consorting with army officers and exploited the tales to lurid effect, as described by Margaret Leech:

Painted equestriennes, in riding dresses and gaily feathered hats galloped beside their spurred and booted cavaliers. In satin and pinchbeck, the women of the town staggered boisterously into the restaurants; and the attendance of respectable citizens at the theatre was disturbed by scenes of bawdry in the audience. One officer attended the Campbell Minstrel Show at the Odd Fellows' Hall with a harlot on each arm.[22]

As the spectacle of drinking and whoring grew louder and more chaotic, the upper crust of Washington City rose up to demand a crackdown on prostitution in general and Hooker's Division in particular. In due course, the army's Provost Guard, led by former clergyman Lieutenant W. G. Raymond, made a public show of raiding the brothels, arresting johns and prostitutes, and hauling them before a judge, night after night.[23]

March of the Rogues

As the Civil War developed, Washington City had become a home base not only for prostitutes but for criminals drawn there because of the money to be had from the luckless soldiers in town, who proved to be willing dupes for various kinds of fraud and chicanery. There were the expected counterfeiters and con men, as well as all manner of pickpockets, from gentleman thieves to the lowliest handkerchief snatchers.[24] In this lively carnival of vice centered around the brothel districts, the streets and houses of amusement thronged with "dancers and singers and comedians, prize fighters and gamblers, vendors of obscene literature and proprietors of 'rum-jug shops,'" who fueled the spectacle with free-flowing illegal liquor, all combining to create what one observer called the "wildest and wickedest city in the history of the world.'"[25]

To control all the vice, the Provost Guard wasn't above a few publicity stunts. An early effort involved a roundup that paraded suspects through the streets with red signs identifying each troublemaker's crime while a band followed along playing "The Rogue's March." A more famous event saw six hundred secessionist-minded criminals receive an offer of safe passage across the border into the South, regardless of whether the Confederacy wanted them. (Some seventy prostitutes happily accepted.) Then came the dozens of sensational, well-publicized arrests. The infamous Light family, for example, featured a mother and three daughters all engaged in the sex trade. To entertain their clients, they hired an organ grinder and his excitable monkey and "danced their clothes off to the rhythm of mechanical melodies, until the racket brought the police, and they were carried, monkey and all, before the magistrate."[26]

Madam in Trouble

One madam who had no need for such primate antics was Mary Ann Hall, who during the war maintained her Island brothel's status as the largest and most well-funded operation in DC. For years prior, the police had considered Hall and other upscale madams off-limits, likely on account of the embarrassment that might ensue if they found a wealthy banker or senator among the rest of the johns. But one indignant madam by the name of Maria Kauffman argued in court that the police were focusing obsessively on brothels like hers, in poorer neighborhoods, while pointedly ignoring the "upper-ten" houses of Austin and Hall.[27] Spurred by the press, the authorities finally took action.

Hall was arrested and brought before a judge in a two-day trial. Nothing exceptional was stated for the record: Women were seen lounging on her property without any visible means of support. Carriages brought strange men at all hours of the night. The house was decorated with suspicious luxury. No legitimate work seemed to be going on there. Many of the witnesses were police officers and detectives who curiously betrayed a rather intimate knowledge of the place.[28] Hall was summarily convicted, yet no record of her punishment survives. Given the typical penalties of the time, she likely paid a fine of just a few dollars.

Ultimately, despite brash headlines and dramatic activity, the Provost Guard and other police agencies failed to stamp out prostitution. By the end of the war, more bordellos were operating than at the beginning, and countless madams and prostitutes prospered even if they had to pay a small fine or spend a night in jail now and then. They even learned a trick or two from their well-paid lawyers and could navigate the legal system much better the next time around—or could offer a well-placed bribe to keep from being hauled in at all.

The authorities, however, were far from the only issue that denizens of Hooker's Division or The Island had to contend with. A much bigger threat was the ubiquitous pollution of such neighborhoods, which had only gotten worse during the war and now threatened to overwhelm the capital with disease and decay.

Filth in the City

No matter how many fine cuts of steak or magnums of champagne a madam bought or how exclusive her guest list, she still had to deal with the surrounding neighborhood, and in most cases that neighborhood was dreadful. Upper-shelf bagnios could front such major streets as Pennsylvania Avenue and Ohio Avenue, but the nastiest dives lay in the alleys behind. In the slum geography of nineteenth-century Washington City, hundreds of these cramped little roads interlaced the interiors of

Filthy and decrepit alleys lined many interior blocks of the city, persisting well into the twentieth century.

the wider blocks,[29] giving access to the capital's most wretched gambling halls, saloons, shacks, and rubbish piles.

The Island, for example, contained the forbidding Louse Alley, regularly mentioned as the worst street in town, which lacked running water and featured dozens of unkempt privies and piles of garbage.[30] Predictably, it hosted all types of crime and of course vermin. But this wretched urban lane didn't lie just down the street from Mary Ann Hall's elite brothel—it ran right outside her back door. Indeed, Hall's fantasyland for the upper crust stood in an area that was home to half the crimes committed in the entire District.[31] One particular concentration of alley housing lay south along F Street, where many migrants with little money or job prospects settled. An 1854 report by the town's Board of Health found a high death rate for children living in such squalid conditions, and "The higher proportion of these deaths are among the children of negro, of foreign, and of destitute native parents."[32]

Overall, though, Hooker's Division was the bleakest of all. It too had plenty of alleys, making it an underworld warren where criminals could practice their crafts with impunity, but its biggest problem was the city canal, that fearsome "miasmatic swamp."[33] When last we encountered it, in the 1830s, the underfunded and poorly designed waterway was silting up at both ends as garbage collected in the center section near downtown. By midcentury, the canal had worsened considerably. Poor funding meant a lack of even basic maintenance. Sedimentation virtually prevented end-to-end navigation. Garbage and sewage turned the shallow channel into an ongoing health menace.[34] Some critics called it a "death-ditch," responsible for the town's regular outbreaks of disease, its "green, stinking water" making the capital noxious to the nose and eyes during the summer months.[35] During spring rains, the canal often flooded, sending the whole vile stew into The Division's streets and basements as far north as 7th Street.

Economics of the Oldest Profession

Despite the toxic, crime-riddled zones where most of the brothels stood, no amount of pollution or violence seemed to limit their appeal, as they grew and expanded during and after the war and remained among Washington City's top attractions, licit or illicit. They also provided one the few reliable sources of employment for thousands of women.

Sordid, lower-class houses in The Division barely paid their sex workers enough to survive, but midrange brothels offered adequate salaries to their employees, plus regular meals and serviceable lodging. They in turn bought goods from vendors who specialized in selling overpriced wares to prostitutes—everything from cosmetics and perfume to laundry services and medicine.[36] The patent medicines that they bought also encompassed narcotics, such as cocaine and morphine.[37] (The more unusual cure-alls included Putnam's White Satin Bouquet, Mrs. Winslow's Soothing Syrup, and something called Valentine's Meat Juice, meant to relieve venereal disease as well as influenza and tuberculosis.)[38] Houses of prostitution functioned as what economists call a "multiplier," creating new jobs for traders doing business with a house and establishing an economic incentive for the expansion of the sex-trading market.

The market continued to draw new employees because, for many young women who didn't come from middle-class or elite families, selling sex provided a decent wage. Ruth Rosen's groundbreaking study *The Lost Sisterhood* makes it plain: For women doing aboveboard work in shops and factories, salaries averaged about six dollars a week by the end of the nineteenth century; for prostitutes, the pay was forty to fifty dollars a week.[39] The downsides were the moral qualms one might have about undertaking such work, the risks of venereal disease and vice arrests, and the physical discomfort and potential danger of fornicating with strange, possibly violent men.

Intelligent critics, then as now, were not ignorant of the links between economic desperation and prostitution for the capital's underprivileged women. William Sanger, in 1876, saw a widespread bias against women as contributing to their financial troubles that led to the sex trade.[40] That same decade the Women's Christian Association undertook a groundbreaking series of interviews with sex workers and public hearings on the trade. The group successfully convinced the police vice squad to delay its brothel raids to allow time to create a health dispensary and charity that catered to the needs of these working women. Establishing the dispensary was a forward-thinking idea and proved to be controversial in its time. However, it was only in operation for a few years before it had to close due to the death of its landlord, Mary Ann Hall.[41]

Hall's End

Hall met her end in 1886, and by all accounts her life had been a success: Aside from a brief tussle with the law, she avoided jail and the pitfalls of disease, addiction, and bankruptcy. She owned property throughout DC

Angelic statue in Congressional Cemetery memorializing Mary Ann Hall.

and a farm in Virginia, and her assets at the time of her death were valued at $67,000,[42] about $2 million today. Her estate was large enough for her heirs to fight over it—and luckily so, because court records preserved a description of what her house of ill repute featured and a hint of how it operated.

As a final touch, Hall honored herself with a prominent funerary monument in Congressional Cemetery. On its capital kneels the plaintive figure of a woman lost in thought, which could be mistaken for an emblem of grief or some virtue or another. In reality she represents a lady of the night who ran one of the most lucrative enterprises in town. Thus, through death and with time, Mary Ann Hall finally became legitimate. In a touch of irony that she might have enjoyed, she lies in peaceful repose under her column, in a well-tended plot of land, close to the grave of J. Edgar Hoover.

Twilight of a Fantasy

The rise and triumph of prostitution in the District of Columbia offers a telling case study of how far the original plan of the capital had fallen. The carefully laid blueprints of its designers, both physical and moral, had turned to mud. Pierre L'Enfant and the Founding Fathers had envisioned the city as a political lodestar and glistening centerpiece of the new republic. Instead, Washington City inverted that dream.

Between the Capitol and the White House, where L'Enfant imagined elegant mansions for statesmen and diplomats, there were filthy tenements and hovels. Where he saw useful canals and beautiful fountains, there were sewers and stagnant water. Where he saw grand avenues for strolling, there were dirty lanes and broken pavements. Where he saw smart theaters, churches, banks, and salons, there were squalid alleys, gambling halls, and bordellos catering to criminals and johns. The city had become a grotesque parody of everything that he and his contemporaries had envisioned, the inevitable legacy of seven decades of congressional indifference and incompetence, and the dangers posed by unelected, unaccountable leaders. And at the dawn of war, the capital was about to enter its darkest and most tumultuous period of all.

EIGHT

SEEING THE ELEPHANT

By 1862 the antebellum landscape of Washington City had vanished. The old town—long derided as a failed blueprint, a stillborn utopia, a national disgrace—suddenly became the key to victory for the Army of the Potomac and the Union itself. Holding and fortifying the capital became critical, as did making it a base for the federal government's prosecution of the war against the rebel states. The transformation wasn't hard to see: Barracks peppered the hillsides, hospitals occupied public spaces, nearby cemeteries began filling up, and camps for runaway slaves sprang up in ever larger numbers.

The textbook history of the capital's role in the Civil War usually focuses on the life and actions of Abraham Lincoln. It makes for epic, stirring biography, but it barely describes what Washington City resembled during these dark years or what its residents saw and experienced inside the battle lines. As the war moved the center of power from the halls of Congress to the White House and the War Department, the entire District of Columbia experienced more dramatic change from 1861 to 1865 than perhaps any other urban center in the North. Accordingly, the federal government unleashed its full, formidable might to fight secessionists and subversives—even if that meant ignoring more than a few constitutional liberties—and forced Washingtonians to confront the legacy of slavery by engineering its abrupt conclusion.

Volunteer Work
Trouble began almost as soon as South Carolina seceded on Christmas Eve, 1860. It readily became apparent that other slaveholding states would follow quickly in its wake, forming a daunting bloc ready to defend

its actions by force. The national government knew it would have a hard time stopping it. Worse, many residents of the new Confederate states had their eye on the District of Columbia as a great prize in the coming battle; the rebel secretary of war even planned to fly the Stars and Bars over the Capitol once they had captured it.[1] Southern armies would have plenty of sympathizers too if they invaded the capital. Members of aristocratic, slaveholding families held many positions in the Buchanan administration, from high-ranking politicians and diplomats to military officers and an array of midlevel clerks.[2] Nearly half the residents of the District had family ties of one kind or another to the South.[3]

More depressing for Unionists in the capital, the new Lincoln administration wouldn't be taking the reins until March 1861—and as was customary for the timing of the transfer of power then—leaving the town's defense in the hands of the doddering lame-duck president Buchanan and "Old Fuss and Feathers" general Winfield Scott, whose service to the country began in the War of 1812. Scott, however, astutely recommended that Buchanan promote US Army topographical engineer Charles Stone to the rank of colonel and to the role of inspector general of the District so he could provide an overview of what defenses the capital possessed.[4] What Stone found wasn't pretty.

While there were three hundred to four hundred Marines at their barracks and fifty-six officers and ordnance men at the Arsenal, the local militia looked suspect.[5] Units such as the National Rifles swarmed with secessionists, and outgoing Secretary of War John Floyd had supplied them plentifully with arms and ammunition, including a few howitzers.[6] Moreover, instead of obeying General Scott's order to reinforce federal garrisons in the Southern states, Floyd shipped 115,000 muskets and rifles to rebel arsenals and planned to send 120 cannons from Pittsburgh to the Deep South as well.[7] Luckily, Floyd's latter order was overturned before it went into effect—after which he resigned and took up arms for the Confederacy. (Floyd later became known for helping lose the Battle of Fort Donelson, which handed an obscure Union commander named Ulysses S. Grant his first major victory.)

Despite the efforts of turncoats like Floyd, Charles Stone did his job well, and by February he had organized twenty-five militia companies and purged the National Rifles and other companies of their subversives.[8] He

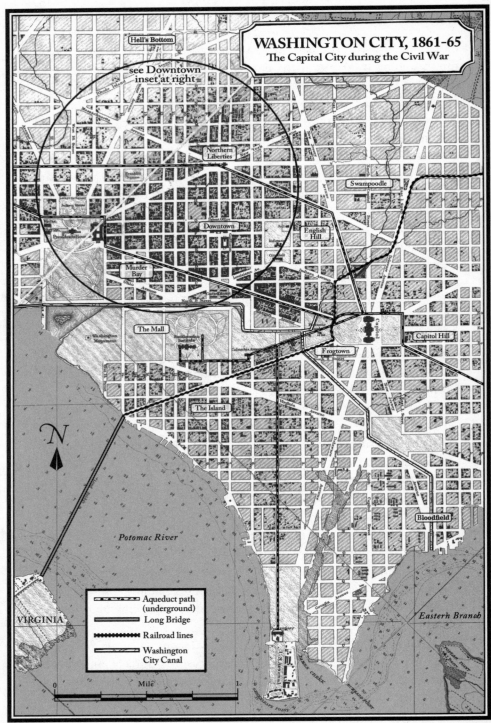

WASHINGTON CITY, 1861-65
The Capital City during the Civil War

Hell's Bottom

see Downtown
inset at right

Northern
Liberties

Swampoodle

Downtown

English
Hill

President's House

Murder
Bay

Capitol

Capitol Hill

The Mall

Washington
Monument

Frogtown

The Island

Bloodfield

N

Potomac River

VIRGINIA

Eastern Branch

Aqueduct path
(underground)
Long Bridge
Railroad lines
Washington
City Canal

0   Mile   1

Source: Albert Boschke, topographical map of the District of Columbia, 1861.

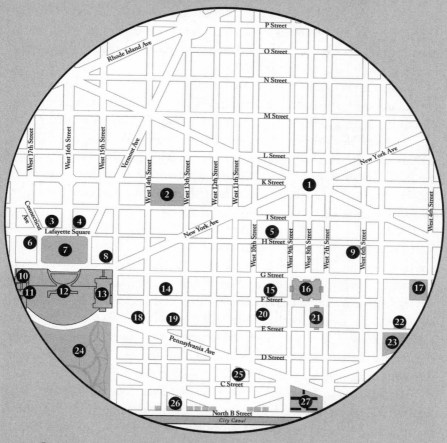

DOWNTOWN WASHINGTON CITY, 1861–65
The Capital City during the Civil War

① Northern Liberties Market	⑮ St. Patrick's Church
② Franklin Square	⑯ Patent Office
③ Corcoran Mansion	⑰ DC Jail
④ St. John's Church	⑱ Willard's Hotel
⑤ Orphan Asylum	⑲ National Theatre
⑥ Decatur House	⑳ Ford's Theatre
⑦ Jackson Statue	㉑ General Post Office
⑧ Riggs Bank	㉒ Judiciary Square Hospital
⑨ Surratt Boarding House	㉓ City Hall
⑩ War Department	㉔ White Lot (Army Camp and Corral)
⑪ Navy Department	㉕ Harvey's
⑫ Executive Mansion	㉖ Contraband Shacks
⑬ US Treasury	㉗ Centre Market
⑭ Sanitary Commission	

brought together two thousand infantrymen, two hundred cavalrymen, two batteries of artillery, and a company of engineers for militia training and service.[9] This complement of citizen-soldiers formed a critical defense for the capital when it lay almost completely exposed to hostile forces. It wouldn't be strong enough to fight off a Southern army, but at least it provided a better defense against the pro-slavery mobs and other hooligans who had run riot in earlier years.

More drama came in short order, including a twelve-day threat to the capital in April, when Maryland secessionists isolated the town from the North by cutting telegraph wires and burning bridges near Baltimore. The Seventh New York and other regiments saved Washington City by arriving just in time to populate the capital with its first major complement of Union troops.[10] Many more arrived in the coming months as the US military transformed the District of Columbia from a sleepy, dysfunctional village into a smart and efficient martial colony.

Oaths of Iron

Even before the Northern troops arrived in the capital, the more overt secessionists made a quick exit, including hundreds of families of Southern slaveholders, government clerks, and army officers.[11] Despite the disappearance of the more vocal rebels, a climate of fear and paranoia took hold of the capital as rumors abounded over conspiracies involving saboteurs trying to deliver the District into the hands of the Confederacy. The federal reaction was swift, imposing, and effective—some even called it dictatorship.

Lincoln began to suspend the writ of habeas corpus during 1861, and the following year he denied it to all persons detained under military order. Confederate sympathizers were labeled "Copperheads" and found their houses searched, their property confiscated, and themselves carted off to prison with no expectation of trial, legal counsel, or often any explanation of the charges against them. Secretary of State William Seward led the charge in hunting down potential rebels with a team of crack detectives to do his dirty work. (Secretary of War Edwin Stanton later took over responsibility for this branch of state security and released a number of the wrongly imprisoned.)[12]

By August, Congress provided an additional tool for rooting out subversives by imposing an oath to the Constitution and the Union on all government employees. Among them was the mayor himself, James Berret, a Southern Democrat. Initially declining to take the oath, Berret sat in prison for three weeks until he changed his mind . . . and relinquished his office.[13] More than a hundred other officeholders refused the oath and were driven from their positions, along with more than three hundred army officers in 1861 alone.[14] The following May, an even more "iron-clad oath" applied to all residents of Georgetown and Washington City trying to vote in municipal elections.[15]

The Fallen Capitol

Wartime paranoia reached ridiculous extremes—some even imagined Secretary of the Smithsonian Joseph Henry sending covert signals to secessionists in his castle turrets[16]—but Southern spies did operate in Washington City and did anything they could to mine information on troop movements, battle plans, public morale, and anything else of value to the Confederate leadership. The most famous spy in town, Rose O'Neal Greenhow, a holdover from the old Southern gentry, hadn't left town like so many of her peers. Instead, she relayed secrets from her sources in the federal government to Confederate general P. G. T. Beauregard, which helped the South rout the North in the First Battle of Bull Run.[17] She was summarily arrested and imprisoned, but even from her cell she was said to be adept at passing information to her associates outside the prison walls.

Taking the lead in the arrest and detention of potential and actual spies was the army's provost marshal,[18] who—for enemies of the state, including Rose Greenhow—favored the ominous and much-feared Old Capitol Prison, a building with a long and unexpected history.

Thomas Law and others had conceived it as the Brick Capitol, the temporary home for Congress after the British burned the town in 1814. The sturdy three-story brick structure played a valuable role in the late 1810s, temporarily housing the legislature when countless schemers tried to displace Washington City as the national capital. In the years following it became a private school and a boardinghouse for congressmen, as well as the publishing site of Anne Royall's newspaper *The Huntress*, until the federal government purchased it and converted it to a prison in spring 1861.[19] A block south stood a line of tumbledown wooden buildings known before the war as Carroll Row, the site of one of the capital's first hotels

Postwar view of the former Carroll Prison and Southeast DC.

and boardinghouses. Rechristened Carroll Prison, the structures took their name from civic leader and property speculator Daniel Carroll. The jail also employed runaway slaves from Virginia as an ad hoc labor force.[20]

Virginia Lomax, wrongly imprisoned at Old Capitol Prison for inquiring about her friends held there, later wrote a famous account of her ordeal and described her "accommodations" as follows:

> *The room was one mass of dirt; spiderwebs hung in festoons from the ceiling, and vermin of all kinds ran over the floor. The walls had been papered, but dampness had caused most of it to fall off, while all over that which was left were great spots of grease . . . The furniture consisted of an iron bedstead, pillows, and mattress of straw, a pair of sheets, and a brown blanket. Between the windows stood a small table, on which was a stone jug containing water, and a tin cup. A tin basin was on the floor. One wooden chair completed the inventory.[21]*

The prison held a surprising number of women prisoners, not only Lomax and actual spies Greenhow and Belle Boyd but all manner of upper-crust matrons—"ladies of education and refinement," according to the prison superintendent—whose sympathies lay on the wrong side of the conflict. The warden, William Wood, found it useful to detain such Southern sympathizers, since they could serve as useful sources of information about rebel spies and other activity. Wood employed a complex system of intercepting and reading prisoners' mail, used his own spies within the prison to figure out what the inmates were doing, and allowed Colonel Lafayette Baker, like "a tiger on the loose," to interrogate suspects in the fearsome Room 19.[22]

Baker took over the job of Union spymaster and intelligence director from the famous Allan Pinkerton in 1862. Using a force of two thousand men, Baker essentially ran his own secret police, investigating anyone alleged to be committing treason, fraud, counterfeiting, profiteering, or bounty jumping, along with gamblers, prostitutes, their johns, and dealers in black-market medicine and illicit liquor. For his efforts, Baker's enemies branded him a tyrant, but few doubted the efficacy of his organization. He had a knack for offending those in power, usually by spying on them, and then getting fired; federal officials then decided they once again needed his special brand of skills and rehired him. (He most famously tracked down the conspirators in the Lincoln assassination.)[23]

As a result of all of this activity, the capital veered closer to a police state than perhaps any major city in American history. Democracy still flickered here and there in the sharp protests from well-protected members of the upper class and in the vigorous dissent in Congress over the conduct of the war. But the executive branch exercised almost unchecked rule in most areas of civic life.[24] Not surprisingly, newspapers in the early years of the war represented only a narrow slice of acceptable politics, from the *National Intelligencer* and *National Republican* (moderate to conservative Republican views) to the *Daily Chronicle* (radical Republican views).[25] Even the strongly Democratic-leaning and widely read *Evening Star* quickly came around to supporting the Lincoln administration, though it maintained its criticisms of the dismal state of urban infrastructure.

Rise of a New Force

Paradoxically, even as the federal government was expanding its power over spies, secessionists, and saboteurs, the local government was proving thoroughly inept in dealing with garden-variety criminals. The District of Columbia had fallen far behind other US cities in law enforcement. New York created a formal police department in 1844, as had Boston, Philadelphia, Chicago, Baltimore, and New Orleans in the 1850s.[26] When the Metropolitan Police finally came into being in August 1861, covering Washington City and Georgetown, it bore some of the hallmarks of those other forces: The District had ten precincts, each under the control of a police sergeant; station houses administered each precinct; and a superintendent oversaw the entire department, the first being William Webb.[27]

It looked good on paper, and almost anything would have been an improvement on the city's dysfunctional constables and Auxiliary Guard. But the DC force faced significant challenges, thanks to the unwillingness of Congress—once again—to fully fund or staff an organization it had created. For a start, the department had far fewer patrolmen than it needed: only 161 officers to cover 75,000 people in 1860 and 140,000 people at the wartime height of 1864.[28] An early report from the police commission in 1862 didn't gloss over the daunting challenge of having one officer for every 625 citizens, most spread out across 307 miles of roads and alleys.[29] Allowing for sickness, absences, and double beats, the average officer beat stretched four miles, and covering it proved next to impossible.[30] The town, the report claimed, needed a minimum of 545 officers to patrol such a huge, crime-ridden place, which also contained "the very worst and most disorderly class of residents from other cities."[31]

The duties of these beleaguered officers didn't extend just to preserving the peace and tracking down lawbreakers. Instead, Congress made sure to pile on the work, directing them to fix just about everything that made the District of Columbia unpleasant. Some of these labors included cracking down on pawnbrokers, auctioneers, gamblers, drunks, vagrants, and disorderly citizens; guarding firefighters and property around burning buildings; maintaining blue laws on the Sabbath; looking after visitors new to town at docks and rail depots; protecting the public from illness and disease; and dealing with all manner of public nuisances, from "dead horses, bone factories, and garbage," to filthy stables and hog pens, leaking privies, broken sewers, and manure and ash heaps.[32]

Malicious Mischief

The appearance of the police didn't exactly inspire fear in the hearts of criminals. At first the officers didn't even have weapons, badges, or uniforms. They were given a small oil band reading METROPOLITAN POLICE to drape around their hats, and for protection they had to create their own clubs or mallets from whatever woodpile they could find.[33] They were better outfitted as the months went on, but the difficulty and brutality of the work didn't change.

More than half a century later, veteran patrolman Lingan Anderson gave an interview to the *Washington Post* in which he detailed the raw, barbaric nature of early police work. One of the biggest challenges was trying to corral enraged or drunk suspects and take them back to the station house. Sometimes they used horses for the task, but other times they had to force a suspect to walk a great distance, even as he tried "to straddle your chest so he can beat your head off." In one case, Anderson recalled having to strong-arm one brute, nearly a foot taller, a mile and a half to the station, trying to keep the man from escaping or punching him along the way. Finally, armed with a club, Anderson "belted him so hard that he had to lay down for a little while before he could get up and go on." Anderson ended up hauling him in a wheelbarrow for the rest of the journey, during which the suspect's mood brightened considerably: "All the way to the station the prisoner kept singing 'Nelly Gray' at the top of his voice, and when we finally landed him [at the station] he told us he'd had a fine evening."[34]

Anderson was shot in the leg during one of the worst episodes of violence he witnessed, a ferocious barroom brawl and gunfight between pro-Southern sympathizers and abolitionists. He tangled again with the Copperheads when a group of them paraded down 4th Street, "up to devilment." Their infernal strategy included outnumbering the cops, one hundred to one, and trying to pull them from their horses to beat them. The police responded with guns and clubs and finally rode down the rioters on horseback.[35]

The levels of street crime could be staggering. During Election Day skirmishes in June 1862, the force separated crowds from their knives, clubs, and guns in one part of town, halted scattered fighting between partisan zealots in another, and joined the army in stopping a fusillade of bricks and stones near City Hall in yet another.[36]

Despite their meager numbers, the Metropolitan Police force arrested a huge number of people: 22,000 in the first year and 24,000 in 1863, amounting to a rate three and a half times that of Brooklyn.[37] Most of the offenses, however, didn't concern violent crimes but drunk and/or disorderly conduct. Assaults, burglaries, and various kinds of fraud and thievery made up most of the rest of the offenses, along with a handful of arrests for adultery, bigamy, fast driving, vagrancy, and the catchall "malicious mischief."[38]

Cops versus Cops

With so many people up to devilment, the task of keeping public order strayed well beyond the ability of the Metropolitan Police. But they weren't the only cops in town. As soon as the war began, the army's Provost Guard began patrolling the town at night to keep soldiers from committing crimes—including a law passed by Congress to keep liquor out of their hands—then arresting them when they did break the law.[39] A few months later the Provost Guard expanded its mission to include daytime patrols and arrested citizens of the District along with army personnel.

The Metropolitan Police force arrested its own share of soldiers, nabbing 5,750 of them during its first year of operation, more than a quarter of its total arrests.[40] As Lingan Anderson recalled, the soldiers "filled up on forty-rod liquor . . . and if we interfered we were their meat."[41] Not all the offenses related to possessing illegal liquor, though. Sometimes rogue soldiers raced their carriages down Pennsylvania Avenue at breakneck speed and the police tried to stop them—despite the risk of being dragged by their horses or sustaining broken ribs.[42] Other times garrulous troops fought with citizens. The police interceded, only to be beaten themselves by the soldiers, who often escaped arrest or court-martial.[43] The War Department increased the potential conflict by ordering the police to hunt down army deserters and anyone resisting the wartime draft. While some officers did their duty, others exploited their power and became "substitute brokers," pocketing a handsome fee for finding someone willing to enlist in lieu of the draftee. One particular cop managed to pocket $125 for each substitute he found.[44]

The hostility between the Metropolitan Police and rogue soldiers peaked in September 1862, when a full-scale riot broke out downtown after some drunken troops got into a dispute with a merchant and beat him. Soon the furious soldiers vented their rage on passersby and then on area blacks. A trio of police officers tried to intervene, but a volley of bricks and stones greeted them, and the mob chased them for several blocks. The Provost Guard made a belated appearance and arrested more than twenty-five malefactors.[45] It was one of the most violent riots in wartime DC, made even worse because members of a military force who had sworn oaths to protect the Union had instead disgraced it.

Muddy Footprints

The lawless character of the town matched its physical appearance. Margaret Leech, in her magisterial history of wartime Washington City, described the place as "sour as a medieval plague spot," thanks to its rank odors and lack of ventilated buildings.[46] The increased presence of military wagons and foot traffic buried some streets in almost a foot of mud, and great dust clouds arose in the dry months to envelop the town in a hot, choking atmosphere.[47]

The lack of proper sanitation for soldiers garrisoned in the capital posed a particular challenge. The local Board of Health declared many of the barracks to be filthy and a public health hazard. (It didn't help that some soldiers new to town bathed in the fetid waters of the city canal.) Such poor living conditions, combined with a meager diet in the early war years, kept the men "half-starved, living on crackers and cold water." Soon enough, illnesses such as measles, whooping cough, and diarrhea claimed the good health of a number of the soldiers regardless of whether they had experienced combat.[48] Adding insult to injury, the military located Camp Fry, one of its largest encampments, in the capital's own disease central, Foggy Bottom,[49] best known for its equally large encampments of infectious mosquitoes. Here they put thousands of troops in barracks, supplies in warehouses, and horses and mules in stables.

The Union Army used the forlorn grounds of the Washington Monument as a
livestock corral, with slaughterhouses nearby.

A great necessity for military transport and provision, livestock also
created major sanitation problems, including the excrement of thousands
of draft animals matched with a lack of effective measures to deal with
it. The army built slaughterhouses for its droves of cattle, butchered them
freely within city limits, and pastured its herds on the grounds of the
Washington Monument.[50] Soon enough, the stench of feces from the
live animals and of the carcasses of the dead ones left in the street overwhelmed the town.[51]

To the army, these concerns paled in comparison to the more critical mission of keeping the country together and subduing the rebellion.

Accordingly, the war forced the city to grow and expand as a vital supply base and staging point for battle. The most visible examples of this change included not only the countless soldiers billeted here on their way to campaigns in the South, but also the hospital workers who attended to them when they came back.

Under the Blade

The waves of casualties came by land, rail, and sea. They arrived over rutted roads from Virginia in two- and four-wheeled horse-drawn ambulances. They came via the railroad depot on The Island, in boxcars and flatcars on mattresses or bare boards. They arrived at the wharves at 6th and 7th Streets on riverboats, where they lay in cabins and on decks, in saloons and on stairs.[52] But few general hospitals existed to care for all the wounded, so the army had to improvise. It requisitioned schools, hotels, barns, homes, and even boats to the task of keeping soldiers alive.[53]

Hospital wards and operating rooms sprang up inside the old Braddock House, where George Washington once held councils of war.[54] Wounded men found themselves in the Insane Asylum, the halls of Congress, and the Patent Office—where they shared space with miniature models of inventions.[55] Even churches saw their pulpits, cushions, and hymnals stashed away, their pews covered with boards for operating tables, and their doors greeting ambulances of the dying instead of the carriages of the pious.[56] The amenities for the wounded were as spartan as the facilities themselves. Sacks of straw or corn shucks doubled as mattresses, and, where there were no mattresses, old boxes, benches, and woodpiles had to suffice.[57]

Nor were there enough surgeons for all the casualties—at most, one doctor per every seventy-five[58]—so an injured soldier might have to wait three to five *days* before seeing a physician. When he did receive care, he might expect a mixture of chloroform and whiskey to disinfect his wounds, if anything at all, and the same kinds of fluids to be consumed as painkillers. In the days before germ theory, elementary hygiene suffered: Soiled bandages were reused, wax and lard were applied to suppurating wounds, and sponges were dipped in dirty water and applied to multiple patients.[59] Predictably, gangrene ran rampant, and when necrosis developed a surgeon could saw off a damaged limb in as few as forty seconds.

Such speed barely lessened the terror of the blade, though. Some hospitals had piles of severed arms and legs outside, and after particularly bloody battles, such as Fredericksburg, a given hospital could become "a house full of amputated limbs."[60]

Infectious diseases also afflicted the Army of the Potomac, both when its soldiers occupied the field and when they had gone to the District for treatment. In the early years, typhoid fever, malaria, and measles posed the major threats, and as the carnage continued diarrhea, chronic dysentery, tuberculosis, and an unsettling typhoid-malaria combination also ravaged the troops and those who tended to them.[61] (Typhoid in its various forms was one of the top killers of the war, felling an estimated 81,360 in the Union army alone.[62]) Shockingly, soldiers had a greater chance of survival on the battlefield than in the hospital. More soldiers died from infections than bullets.[63]

At various times, up to fifty-six hospitals operated in the capital and held some fifty thousand soldiers[64]—more than the town's entire population just a dozen years earlier. Of varying sizes, the facilities usually employed a team of doctors, stewards, chaplains, clerks, cooks, launderers, gardeners, grave diggers, and guards. But for many of the wounded, the most visible and benevolent presence belonged to the nurses.

Dix's Legions

Our modern conception of nurses doesn't quite fit who they were and what they did in the Civil War. The majority of nurses were men,[65] but for women the term usually applied to white ladies of the middle and upper class. "Matron" was a more generic term for a woman who assisted in medical care and also cooked and did laundry. If such women were black or working-class white, they were called "cooks" or "laundresses," even though many performed nursing duties. Some of the latter found the designation financially crippling after the war. Maria Bear Toliver, who had worked in camps for runaway slaves and risked her life in a smallpox hospital, tried for more than three decades to get a pension from the federal government—to no avail.[66]

Nurses handled a great number of tasks. They changed wound dressings, assisted in surgical operations, and provided medicine to patients.[67] They acted as personal secretaries for injured men, writing their letters home or reading to them. They provided what we now call physical therapy or psychiatric care to soldiers suffering physical or mental trauma. They listened to the confessions of dying men, and they sang and played music to lighten the otherwise grim proceedings. They worked sixteen-hour days, sleeping in designated quarters if they were lucky or, if they weren't, making do with luggage or supply rooms as bedchambers. Most were aging widows with sons in the military or were longtime activists for abolition or women's rights.[68]

At the head of Union nursing efforts was Dorothea Dix, already nationally well known and admired for her reform efforts in jails, alms-houses, and asylums.[69] The supervisor for the hiring and assignment of all nurses for the army, she had a reputation for being conscientious and driven as well as rigid, brusque, and capricious. She insisted that any nurse brought into service have strong morals, dress plainly, know how to cook, and look unattractive (the last to ensure that bedridden men would avoid sexual temptation—even as they struggled to breathe).[70] Other prospective nurses went through Protestant organizations like the Christian Commission, Catholic groups like the Sisters of Charity (which provided a steady supply of nuns), and most importantly the US Sanitary Commission.[71]

The commission united the work of charitable groups and individuals to provide food, medicine, and care to the sick, anything from "sugar, shirts, crackers, farina, drawers, and some chicken and oysters" to woolen underclothing and head rests.[72] The commission also operated soldiers' homes for rehabilitation and recovery, home lodges that offered convalescent care for soldiers just out of the hospital, sanitary fairs throughout the country to raise funds for veterans, and a nurses' home in Washington City that provided rest and relief to medical workers overwhelmed by all the bloodshed and suffering.[73] It also published regular bulletins that detailed its work and issued meticulous, pedantic recommendations for nurses: using a "noiseless step" when walking, ensuring "no door or window in the patient's room shall rattle or creak," being "as motionless as possible" when speaking to patients, and never speaking to an invalid from behind.[74]

Tales of the Armory

Armory Square Hospital, the capital's highest-profile facility, sat on the eastern side of the Mall between the Smithsonian Castle and the city canal alongside a militia armory. It featured fifty white wooden buildings grouped into ten wards, each of which acted as its own mini-hospital.[75] Unlike other local facilities, the Armory Square was well lit and ventilated, which made it one of the most modern hospitals around. The facility certainly needed to provide the best care in town, because it saw the worst casualties of the war. It lay a short distance from the railroad depot at Maryland Avenue and the wharves to the south. As such, it served as the hospital of first resort for grievously injured and dying men who needed immediate attention as soon as they returned from the battlefield. Not surprisingly, it also had the greatest number of wartime deaths of any facility in the region.[76]

Contemporaries realized the significance of Armory Square, and it attracted some of wartime Washington City's most able chroniclers. One was Amanda Akin, the "Lady Nurse of Ward E," whose diary details the mortal struggles faced by the men and her challenges in providing care to them. While she considered her hospital "the most complete and best conducted institution of its kind during the Civil War," she had no

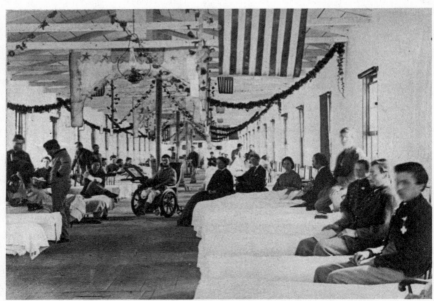

A ward at Armory Square Hospital, the most renowned of Washington City's many wartime hospitals.

illusions about the suffering of the soldiers, which ranged from hemor-rhages and violent headaches to "neuralgic pain" and limb amputations.[77]

But Akin doesn't dwell on the misery of her patients. Instead she details what she did to provide mirth and distraction. She played back-gammon with them, staged impromptu classical concerts, delivered new and interesting foods such as "guava jelly," read literature and poems aloud, and even composed goofy rhymes for her coworkers. Her purpose in entertaining the wounded was clear: "anything that will keep them from despondency, and will not add to anyone's sufferings is welcomed with pleasure."[78]

Armory Square's most famous chronicler was Walt Whitman, who composed some of the war's most poignant and memorable descriptions of death and suffering. Working as a nurse in several of the capital's wards, he spent much time at Armory Square, which attracted him "because it contains by far the worst cases, most repulsive wounds, has the most suf-fering & most need of consolation—I go every day without fail, & often at night—sometimes stay very late—no one interferes with me, guards, doctors, nurses, nor any one—I am let to take my own course."[79]

The hospital tolerated Whitman, but it didn't exactly welcome him. The controversial poet's then-scandalous work *Leaves of Grass* challenged conventional notions of moral propriety and poetic form. It made him a celebrated figure in some literary quarters, but the more devout ladies at the Armory Square had their doubts, Akin among them. She called him an "odd-looking genius" who "has written some very queer books about 'Free Love,' etc. . . . When he stalks down the ward I feel the 'prickings of my thumbs,' and never speak to him. . . . With all his peculiar interest in our soldier boys he does not appeal to me."[80]

But propriety had its limits, and throughout her book Akin exhibits a strange fascination with America's bold new poet and itinerant nurse, however much she disapproves of his ways. She tellingly gives an entire chapter in her diary to an excerpt from Whitman's work, in which he praises a hospital concert featuring convalescent soldiers and nurses: "I am not sure but I received as much pleasure under the circumstances sitting there as I have had from the best Italian compositions. . . . The sounds and scene altogether have made an indelible impression on my memory."[81]

Camp Misery and Beyond

The conditions at other Washington-area hospitals were much worse: no
concerts, games, guava jelly, or famous poets. Julia Wheelock, another
author of a fine memoir, *The Boys in White* (named for the shrouded bodies of the dead), found herself at Camp Convalescent, aka "Camp Misery,"
near Alexandria. She unsparingly recorded her contempt for it:

> *Pen would fail to describe one-half its wretchedness. Here were ten
> to fifteen thousand soldiers—not simply the convalescent, but the sick
> and dying—many of them destitute, with not even a blanket or an
> overcoat . . . sick with fever, pneumonia, or chronic diarrhea, eating
> raw pork and lying upon the cold, damp ground . . . the wonder will
> be, not that they died, but that any recovered.*[82]

Only after several soldiers froze to death in winter 1862 did the camp
finally close and relocate.

Camp Convalescent represented the nadir of hospitals in the capital
area, but many run-of-the-mill facilities were almost as bleak. One of

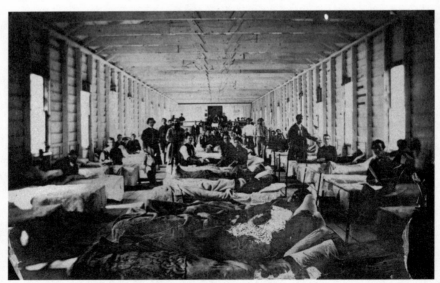

The grim confines of Camp Convalescent, also known as "Camp Misery,"
represented the worst of DC's hospitals.

the most well chronicled was Georgetown's Union Hospital, a converted hotel. Its darkened hallways and cold floors provided a sense of "universal depression" to the enlisted men confined there and to the nurses who dealt with living conditions almost as bad as those of the patients.[83] A Sanitary Commission report in 1861 described "narrow, tortuous and abrupt" hallways, a lack of functional sinks and bathrooms, decaying woodwork, undrained cellars, and worst of all no morgue.[84] Louisa May Alcott, who worked there briefly as a nurse before *Little Women* made her famous, called it the "Hurly Burly Hotel," a place where "disorder, discomfort, bad management . . . reduced things to a condition I despair of describing." Her patients stood "ragged, gaunt and pale, mud to the knees, with bloody bandages untouched since put on days before; many bundled up in blankets, coats being lost or useless; and all wearing that disheartened look which proclaimed defeat."[85] Hospital typhoid afflicted Alcott herself, forcing her to leave the hospital. She survived, but at the physical expense of a long and painful recovery.

Soldier of God

Another trenchant wartime diarist at Union Hospital, Alcott's boss Hannah Ropes, a Christian activist, had a background in abolitionist politics that gave her a radical stance on injustice where she found it. Ropes hailed from Massachusetts, wife of one William Ropes, who abandoned his family and left her and their son and daughter to fend for themselves. Her son, Edward, became a homesteader in the worst possible place: Kansas during its "Bleeding Kansas" phase of internecine guerrilla warfare over slavery.[86] She and her daughter followed him there, and, as she described in her book *Six Months in Kansas*, they soon found themselves under the threat of pro-slavery Missourians, for whom "To kill a man is not much more than to shoot a buck." In response, she had no qualms about the reality of self-preservation: "How strange it will seem to you to hear that I have loaded pistols and a bowie-knife upon my table at night, three of Sharp's rifles, loaded, standing in the room," and "Now the hour for action has come . . . and may Heaven speed the RIGHT!"[87]

Six years later, after Edward enlisted in the Union army, Ropes entered the fray again, this time a bit farther from the front lines. She came to the capital—"the ugliest and dirtiest city I ever saw"[88]—with no proper experience in nursing, armed only with her knowledge of Florence Night-ingale's influential *Notes on Nursing*. Despite her inexperience and lack of training—typical for most nurses in the war, before the development of professional organizations and proper licensing—Dorothea Dix accepted her as a ward matron for Union Hospital. Ropes started in July 1862.[89]

Frightful Grandeur

Ropes had great sympathy for the soldiers in her care and great impa-tience for the cogs of bureaucracy that hampered that care. She gath-ered supplies from donations, the Sanitary Commission, and anyone with influence and recorded her observations of the men in their bleakest hour. The workers around her generally provided good care, but the head sur-geon's treatment of the soldiers disgusted her. She claimed that he cared "no more for a private than for a dog" and that he released soldiers not fully healed or recovered: "the poor men in all the hospitals barely escape with life or clothes or money."[90] She had already encountered the dark-est side of human nature in Kansas, had "seen the elephant"—a popular nineteenth-century term for an intense emotional experience, often in combat—and didn't shrink from it. Thus, she resolved to act even if doing so meant upsetting the hierarchy of the medical system.

At Union Hospital, as with others in the capital, the top surgeon, A. M. Clark, reported to US Surgeon General William Hammond and, above him, Secretary of War Edwin Stanton. Below the chief was an array of assistants, contract physicians, medical students, and wardmasters who assisted both doctors and nurses.[91] Hannah Ropes's main nemesis, though, was the hospital steward, a devious (unnamed) character who withheld food from the injured men, stole their clothes, and sold their rations.[92] After he suggested to Ropes that they form a ring to purloin hospital food and supplies, she reported him to Clark, but the high-handed surgeon dismissed her complaints. She went over his head to Surgeon General Hammond, who referred her complaint back to Clark, who again dismissed it out of hand. Finally, when the steward attacked a patient with a chisel and created his own little prison for disfavored patients in the damp, rat-infested cellar, Ropes took dramatic action. She ignored the chain of command entirely and set up a meeting with the secretary of war.[93]

At Stanton's office, as Ropes mentally prepared herself to be locked away for insubordination among "the rats and cockroaches," the secretary entered: "a large man with dark beard, bald head, and legal brow" whose eyes "gleamed with the fire of a purpose." Ropes stated the case about the problems at her hospital as succinctly as she could.

Stanton's response: "Call the Provost Marshal."[94]

The marshal charged into Union Hospital with his investigators in "a frightfully grand scene." He released one of the steward's victims from the cellar and arrested the steward and sent him to the Old Capitol Prison—to the "pale terror of the head surgeon" and the fearful reaction of his subordinate officers. Soon after, head surgeon Clark himself went to prison, and a medical inspector came to the hospital. He looked around and questioned Ropes about the relationship of the steward and chief surgeon. She compared the former to a whispering devil and the latter to a tyrant, "harsh and unsympathizing." Her words kept them imprisoned a while longer.[95]

Ropes had engineered a shocking, unexpected outcome. Not only had she upended the protocols between surgeons and their supposed subordinates, she had struck a powerful blow against the culture of greed and corruption that had held sway for decades in Washington City. What replaced it, at least for a few years, was a new military efficiency, intolerance for bureaucratic incompetence, and frightening use of absolute power.

Within the Fray

Countless other nurses and support staff took on miscreants in the medical system where they found them, from administrators unfairly withholding food and supplies from needy patients to rogue surgeons threatening and harassing their staff.[96] Even though many surgeons acted heroically and diligently to save the lives of soldiers, they had fraught relationships with the female nurses below them. Nurse diarist Georgeanna Woolsey wrote, "Hardly a surgeon of whom I can think received or treated them with even common courtesy . . . [they] determined to make their lives so unbearable that they should be forced in self-defense to leave."[97]

Joining the nurses in the wartime workforce were great numbers of women who filled jobs throughout the capital. These included clerks at

the US Treasury and other departments—unheard of before the war—
workers at the Government Printing Office, and weapons makers at the
Navy Yard and Arsenal. Their pay predictably was low, and in some pro-
fessions they earned about half what their male colleagues did.[98] Still, the
war helped challenge antebellum notions of the role of women, and it did
so in combination with social reform movements and Christian charitable work.[99] Hannah Ropes had ably chronicled and actively participated
in both. Perhaps a bit too actively.

Because of her regular proximity with sick and infected patients, she
regularly took ill with one disorder or another, complaining to her daughter, "We get *lousy!* and dirty. We run the gauntlet of disease from the disgusting *itch* to smallpox!"[100] In her last journal entry, dated December 29,
1862, in her description of a dying soldier, she had a sense of something
darker on the horizon:

> *two eyes like live coals roll, gleam, recede in terror behind their own*
> *pupils, or soften to tears before mine; two cheeks, purple with fever,*
> *a sweet mouth and beardless chin, teeth a girl might envy, and a*
> *wide fair brow, from which light brown hair, dank and curlless,*
> *falls away . . . .[The doctor] pronounces him* very sick *and orders an*
> *anodyne—still, no closing, hardly to wink, of these bright, restless,*
> *beautiful blue eyes.[101]*

Typhoid finally did what the medical bureaucracy couldn't do and
conquered Hannah Ropes in January 1863.[102]

Rise of the Contrabands

Ropes wouldn't have said her death was in vain. She had a keen sense of
what the war was really about, and why soldiers like her son were fighting. As she wrote the month before her death, "If in the beginning our
President had declared freedom for all, and armed all, the rebellion would
not have lasted three months . . . the only way out of this trouble remains
just where it did before, only to be gained by *immediate, unreserved eman-*
cipation."[103] Instead, freedom for slaves proceeded piecemeal, by moderate
gestures and accidents. One of the biggest such accidents, however, fun-
damentally reshaped the racial and social landscape of the District.

Slaves had been coming to the capital even before the war started. Their masters and other Southern whites fled and either abandoned their "property" or made keeping track of it difficult in the growing chaos.[104] Farther south, in May 1861, three slaves escaped to the Union lines at Virginia's Fort Monroe, one of the few federal installations still held by the national government. General Benjamin Butler decided not to send them back to their masters as required by the Fugitive Slave Act of 1850. Instead, improvising his own military law, he held them as "contraband of war," or commandeered enemy property. After Lincoln reluctantly confirmed Butler's decision, thousands of "contrabands" escaped their plantations in the South to take shelter behind Union lines, a number that grew to half a million by the end of the war.[105]

The District of Columbia, not far from the fighting in Virginia, became a major draw for escaped slaves, who arrived via the Long Bridge and within two years formed a community of ten thousand people in Washington City and three thousand more in Alexandria. They took exceptional risks in the first year of the contraband policy, when Maryland slaveholders could have them held as fugitive slaves if they had come from that state and when they could be arrested for the slimmest of reasons and confined to the municipal jail (and the whims of its racist warden).[106]

This situation changed on April 16, 1862, when President Lincoln signed the Compensated Emancipation Act, which freed slaves held within the District of Columbia and provided up to three hundred dollars for their owners,[107] the only time such an act occurred during the war in any US city or state. This act predated Lincoln's much more famous Emancipation Proclamation—which freed slaves only behind enemy lines and didn't apply to slave states that remained within the Union—by nine months, and 996 slaveholders came forward to get their recompense. All they had to do was prove their ownership and take a loyalty oath, so the federal government essentially rewarded them for owning human chattel and staying in town. The total cost ran to more than two million dollars—owners typically claiming their slaves were young, sprightly, and in excellent health, while bondsmen argued the opposite—but the act was much less sweeping than it sounded. Slaveholding whites composed only 2 percent of the District's population in 1862.[108] In the end, while it did free 3,100 slaves in the District,[109] compensated emancipation also provided an undeserved treat for slaveholders. Abolitionists knew as much at the time and endeavored to make sure the policy was never repeated anywhere else in the future.

Camps and Villages

The Emancipation Proclamation went into effect at the beginning of 1863 and only increased the flow of slaves across Union lines. In response, the army used them as workers in trenches, kitchens, hospitals, and even plantations.[110] In Washington City, the federal government employed thousands more, hiring them as "carpenters and masons, teamsters and blacksmiths, nurses and orderlies, and laborers of every description to move supplies, chop wood, haul coal, tend animals, build roads, and dig fortifications." For such work, the government paid them up to thirty dollars a month, the same as whites, but with an unpopular monthly tax of five dollars deducted to defray the costs of operating the sites where many of them lived.[111]

The Department of War tried to provide at least a minimum amount of assistance, which included clothing, food, shelter, medicine, and education for the former bondsmen, consigning them to on-site settlements known as contraband camps.[112] Conditions there were often grim, though. The camps faced a lack of sanitation and supplies, a surfeit of poverty and disease, and an inability to handle the seemingly endless flood of new arrivals. In due course, the healthier men and women with contacts elsewhere in the region departed the camps, leaving behind the poorest and sickest individuals.[113] One of the most prominent outposts was Camp Barker, near Washington City's northern boundary. Built over a former brickyard and cemetery, its swampy conditions made it notorious as a plague center. In one of the camp's deadliest outbreaks, the six hundred residents suffered through a smallpox epidemic in 1863 that killed three to five people a day, worsened by the lack of access to water and vaccines.[114]

Encampments closer to town didn't fare much better. Just a few blocks from the heart of Pennsylvania Avenue, freedmen found dreadful accommodation in the disease-ridden shacks and hovels that lined the poisonous city canal, making for a shantytown between the White House and Capitol known as Murder Bay.[115]

The shanties of Murder Bay, where escaped slaves, or "contrabands," took refuge amid deplorable conditions.

Such dismal living conditions shocked the residents of the capital but persisted for years afterward. As late as 1866 the superintendent of the Metropolitan Police reported to Congress that whole families packed into shanties "without light or ventilation," barely protected from rain or snow, exposed to the "most disgustingly filthy and stagnant water." Even if sanitary standards were ever fully enforced, "these places can be considered as nothing better than propagating grounds of crime, disease, and death; and in the case of a prevailing epidemic, the condition of these localities would be horrible to contemplate."[116] (The Bureau of Refugees, Freedmen, and Abandoned Lands—the "Freedmen's Bureau"—had the postwar task of improving this and other substandard conditions for blacks, and we'll see in chapter ten.)

By the summer of 1863, the military had to address the crisis. As a partial solution, it created Freedmen's Village, a mini-town with fifty houses and two families per residence, just across the river in Virginia. It also had schools, churches, a home for the elderly and disabled, streets and parks, and a tailor and other artisan shops. It provided job training for men in such fields as blacksmithing and for women in sewing, which paid the meager wage of ten dollars per month, minus five dollars for the contraband tax.[117] Freedmen were charged rents of one to three dollars per month, which didn't leave much money to spare, so many African Americans there found other sources of income, including working as military laborers, defending the siege works of the District, and working in local fields and gardens.[118] Eventually the army constructed barracks to hold 250 families at much lower rental costs, and the village ultimately grew to 1,500 people.[119]

Life in the quasi town was marginal, but at least it improved on the awful conditions of the contraband camps. It also held great symbolic value. The village sat on the Custis-Lee estate, where Robert E. Lee lived before the war in Arlington House.[120] On this former slave manor, African Americans now lived willingly and earned pay for their labors, where once they would have lived as prisoners at the behest of the Confederates' top general.

New Authorities

The Union army also opened Freedmen's Hospital on the site, a groundbreaking facility where African Americans could receive treatment for diseases and other ailments in the camps.[121] Its most famous employee was the legendary Sojourner Truth, who before the war had been an activist for abolition and women's rights, an agent on the Underground Railroad, a preacher, and a lecturer. Already in her mid-sixties, she helped bring about the integration of the horse-drawn street railway by riding in whites-only cars, had a private audience with President Lincoln, and lobbied Congress for establishing proper training for doctors and nurses. During her time in Washington City, she also organized the cleaning of Freedmen's Hospital to help prevent disease at a time when few recognized, and most ignored, the need for medical sanitation at other hospitals in the District.[122]

Other employees of Freedmen's Hospital may not have shared her fame, but they proved just as critical to the health of black soldiers and former slaves who needed care there. One of them, Dr. Alexander Augusta, had fought widespread racism directed at black professionals to become an army major and the surgeon in chief at Camp Barker. In 1863 his authority was transferred to the new three-hundred-bed Freedmen's

Hospital, where he and eight other doctors became part of a select fraternity: African-American physicians who worked in a District medical facility. Augusta's second in command was Dr. Anderson Abbott, a prominent Canadian who attended levees held at the White House, became an acquaintance of the president, and fit well into local middle-class black society, despite his foreign origins. He was even present at Lincoln's deathbed, and the first lady later gave him the president's plaid shawl, "a most precious heirloom," as a reminder of his time in the capital and friendship with the chief executive.[123]

Unlike the more reserved Abbott, hospital director Augusta cut a controversial figure in some circles because of his activism for racial equality. Like Sojourner Truth, he protested segregation on the capital's street railway and helped force the integration of the "c'yar boxes," as the streetcars were known, by lobbying Congress for action.[124] Augusta's actions raised his public profile just as they raised the jealousy of his white peers. In 1864, these doctors forced his removal as chief surgeon, and Abbott assumed control of Freedmen's Hospital, continuing Augusta's policies.

Fighting Old Demons

Charles Sumner aided Augusta's antisegregation cause by bringing it up in the US Senate and by threatening to revoke the streetcar company's charter if it didn't remedy the problem.[125] Other abolitionist politicians joined him in such attempts to lessen racial bias in public accommodations and helped pass laws that gave black-oriented schools a proportion of the municipal school fund and expunged some parts of the Black Code, including the hated ten o'clock curfew.[126] However, racism remained alive and well: White District residents protested any assistance shown to African Americans, and laws like the one funding black schools existed more on paper than in reality thanks to the recalcitrance of the City Council.[127]

The crazed mobs that had enforced the racial status quo before the war returned with a vengeance too. After such events as the Emancipation Proclamation or the enlistment of African-American troops, crowds of reprobates hurled stones and shattered glass at black churches, convalescing soldiers attacked minorities at random on the street, and interracial hostility increased throughout the capital.[128] The law often gave sanction to such violence. Not only could blacks not testify against whites in many courts or even take the stand as witnesses, but they could be held as lawbreakers just for defending themselves from mob attack.[129]

Similar prejudice existed in the military, as black troops became more visible defenders of the Union in 1863 and after. Many in the city and the nation resisted the idea of sending African Americans to fight in the war, and even Lincoln had his doubts.[130] The army didn't enlist black troops out of magnanimity; it just needed more men, 150,000 more. Surprisingly, despite being offered less money than white soldiers and severely limited in rank and command, more than the requested number of African Americans enlisted, including many ex-slaves.[131] It made for dangerous service, even when the bullets weren't flying. Local thugs occasionally attacked camps where these soldiers were billeted, and, if Southerners captured any of them, they stood a good chance of being massacred on the spot—infamously so at Fort Pillow in 1864. Nonetheless, black troops proved themselves to be able, vigorous combatants in the field, and their courageous service in such battles as Port Hudson and Milliken's Bend in the Deep South made their detractors less vocal if not necessarily more tolerant.

Village No More

By the end of the war, the racial landscape in Washington City had changed dramatically. No longer was the capital a backward village of plantation owners and white gentry with a minority of free blacks and slaves bound by law and custom. Instead, according to a special census in 1867, the capital boasted 106,000 people, a third of them black and none of them slaves.[132]

At least one general in Washington City knew the value of African Americans as soldiers, laborers, and citizens of the Union. He happily employed contraband labor against the Southern enemy.[133] He ordered that black soldiers buried at the humble Freedmen's Cemetery be reinterred in a more prominent facility.[134] He developed a plan to give slaveholders' property to freed slaves, and he understood how "the loyal inhabitants of the country, white or black, must be compelled to assist" in the war since they were "animated by the strong desire not merely for political but for personal liberty."[135] He was the city's greatest master builder, Montgomery Meigs.

An Engineer's Apotheosis

An officer in the US Army Corps of Engineers, Meigs cultivated an interest in just about everything: architecture, engineering, fine art, history, languages, literature, photography, and science.[136] No ordinary engineer, he held thirteen patents on innovations from fire hydrants to file cases.[137] Most importantly, Meigs devised and constructed the huge Washington Aqueduct that utilized only gravity (not steam pumps or other devices) to bring freshwater from Great Falls, Maryland, through 18.6 miles of reservoirs, bridges, conduits, tunnels, and pipes at a cost of more than two million dollars.[138] His aqueduct had a capacity of sixty-seven-million gallons, twice what New York City needed and four times what Paris required.[139] In the history of Washington City, only the Capitol itself had a higher price tag[140]—which Meigs himself, as chief engineer, had helped reconstruct in the 1850s, the great white iron dome the most visible example of his exceptional ability.

Before the war, the turncoat Secretary of War John Floyd had shipped Meigs to the distant Dry Tortugas island chain. Instead of moping about his fate, Meigs instituted an immediate campaign to strengthen

The ingenious arches of the Washington Aqueduct, which doubled as pipes carrying water into the city.

the defenses of the federal post there, Fort Jefferson. By February 1, 1861, he had bolstered the fort against potential attack, and three weeks later his political allies aided his return to Washington City.[141]

In June, Lincoln promoted him to brigadier general and gave him the title of quartermaster general of the US Army, overseeing the administration, procurement, and supply of military troops. When he arrived, the shambling, debt-ridden condition of the quartermaster's office didn't help the massive organizational task, nor did the insidious fraud and corruption of federal contractors. Yet Meigs succeeded beyond expectation and helped the Union army dramatically improve its logistical planning and deployment of troops, equipment, and supplies—everything from shipping food, clothing, tents, and blankets to delivering gunboats and expediting railroad construction.[142] Meigs also succeeded in the monumental feat of delivering huge numbers of horses, mules, wagons, and ambulances to the capital to aid the Union cause (while, more regrettably, tramping the town's roads into muck). But that wasn't the only way he altered the local landscape.

In fall 1862, Stanton named him to a commission to fortify the District of Columbia against Confederate assault.[143] By the end of the war, it had become the most fortified city in the world, with sixty-eight forts and ninety-three batteries manned by twenty thousand troops along a thirty-seven-mile defensive line. Countless battles took place in the Chesapeake region, but only Jubal Early's July 1864 raid breached this line when the rebel cavalry general attacked Fort Stevens in Washington County.[144] Meigs participated in the battle, commanding a force of some fifteen hundred men in rifle pits between Fort Stevens and Fort Totten, the latter appropriately named for the general who first brought Meigs to Washington City in 1852 to fix the town's water supply.[145] Union troops repulsed Early's raid, and the capital remained secure.

Ghosts of War

For all he did to provide clean water, engineer the Capitol, and help win the war, Meigs's most lasting contribution lay not within Washington City but across the river in Arlington, Virginia. Here the great engineer made a mark on the landscape of the capital that remained long after the war ended, the hospitals and military camps closed, and the

During fifteen years, Montgomery Meigs built an aqueduct, engineered a new US Capitol, and helped the Union Army win the Civil War.

decrepit antebellum village of Washington City disappeared from view and memory.

On the huge Custis-Lee estate, in a neoclassical manor rising above the Potomac, Robert E. Lee had once held court. His wife, Mary, had luxuriated under blooms of honeysuckle and jasmine here, and old George Custis had danced and cavorted with his wealthy guests. But Meigs had very different plans for the estate.

The federal government confiscated the property shortly after the outbreak of the war and claimed outright ownership of it in 1864 after Mary Lee failed to pay her property tax in person (though she had tried to do so via courier). With battles in Virginia causing eighty thousand casualties a month, local hospitals bursting with wounded and dying men, and the dozen Union cemeteries in the capital filling up rapidly, Meigs recommended the estate become the grounds for a new national cemetery to hold the bodies of deceased soldiers.[146] Edwin Stanton concurred, and by the summer of 1864 plots for the Union dead began to populate the grounds.

Meigs's resolve only strengthened when he learned that his son had died in the Shenandoah Valley on an army scouting mission. He vowed that Lee's estate would never again serve as a leisurely retreat or pleasure garden. Instead, with its sarcophagi, memorials, and tombstones, it would stand as a testament to sacrifice and death.[147] He located one of the biggest pits near the manor house, ordering Mary Lee's garden excavated and filled with the remains of two thousand unknown soldiers.[148] Mary Lee fought for decades afterward in Congress and court for the return of her estate,* but Meigs served just as long as quartermaster general, continuing to expand and develop the property as the nation's foremost burial ground, adding temples, arches, and an amphitheater to the landscape. As he did on the aqueduct he created, Meigs took care to have his name engraved prominently and proudly on a column near the entrance, so all the world could see who had built this grand tribute to the fallen.[149]

---

* Mary Lee achieved her aim in an 1882 Supreme Court case, after which she sold her estate back to the federal government for $150,000. The official buyer was the Secretary of War—Robert Todd Lincoln. (Robert M. Poole, "How Arlington Cemetery Came to Be," *Smithsonian* (November 2009): 4, accessed at www.smithsonianmag.com/history-archaeology/The-Battle-of-Arlington.html)

Conceived as revenge, Arlington National Cemetery in many ways became the ideal gesture. This estate, which sat on some of the area's most scenic property, never saw the Confederate general and his wife live out their twilight years in splendor. Instead, the hillsides embraced thousands of American heroes and warriors, officers and enlisted men, Supreme Court justices and presidents, explorers and reformers, black and white, North and South. And as Arlington grew, so too did the town on the flat-lands below. Through terrible carnage and tumult, the capital city stood bloody but unbroken, straining to live and grow, watched over by armies of the dead.

NINE

SUSPICIOUS CHARACTERS

As the Civil War ended in 1865, many of the bodies filling up cemetery plots in the capital weren't only casualties of battle. A good number of the newly deceased were victims of cruel and often random attacks that epitomized the postwar explosion of violent crime and brutality. Murders, stabbings, and shootings became a daily occurrence,[1] and rampant fighting and assaults gave the capital a well-earned reputation for mindless bloodshed and thuggery. Thieves robbed their victims in their hotels or on the streets, con artists and counterfeiters enjoyed a profitable trade, and houses of gambling and prostitution experienced a surge in popularity.[2] The District turned from being the cornerstone of the Union to "a perfect Gomorrah of sin, violence, and corruption."[3]

The wartime growth and military importance of the capital attracted a range of newcomers: discharged soldiers without jobs, former slaves without homes, army camp followers, vagrants, and troubled youth without any prospects at all. More than a few of these arrivals turned to crime in the absence of work or opportunity, while others came to town for the express purpose of preying on the local citizenry, whether by making a killing off them in thievery or just killing them outright. In later years, some compared the conditions in the capital to the worst corners of the Wild West, with levels of lawlessness as bad as Cripple Creek, Colorado, or Tombstone, Arizona.[4]

Long, Hard Beats

During the fifteen years that followed the war, Congress expanded the Metropolitan Police force to 238 men, but time and again it refused to provide adequate funding and then salted the wound by cutting officers' salaries and their already meager benefits. In 1876 policemen went without half their full pay (six hundred dollars per year) for two months, and some of their station houses slid into such a deplorable condition that they actually collapsed.[5] In later years, with the District's growing population, only one cop patrolled the streets for every nine hundred residents, and a beat could stretch for as long as ten to fifteen miles. An 1880 police report, summing up the era, decried "the total inadequacy of the force" to cover a city that had little to no police protection on most of its streets and alleys.[6] One police officer walking seven blocks to the Capitol witnessed fourteen fights along the way. Another became exhausted from the endless conflict:

> *Like the others, I used to spend the entire day in making arrests. As fast as I would return from taking one prisoner to the station-house I would make another arrest, and sometimes I used to leave two or three people calling "Help!" and "Police!" simply because I had my hands full and could not tend to any more. . . . I remember that one night the old Central Guard House contained seventy-one prisoners arrested within a space of six hours for disorderly conduct, fighting, shooting, &c.*[7]

Deep in the Hole

The Metropolitan Police made countless arrests, but just because they took criminals off the street didn't mean they ended up in jail. Many faced lenient judges or juries at trial, but just as many faced unfair or inconsistent sentences. As an example, David Barnett stole a few hundred dollars and received a year in prison, while Samuel Uber received a five-dollar fine for assault and battery.[8] Anyone unlucky enough to go to jail experienced conditions nearly on par with the the Old Capitol Prison. The Washington County jail held twice the capacity for which it was designed in 1830 and stuffed up to ten men into each of its eight-by-ten-foot cells. It had a filthy jail yard and an unsanitary lack of toilets and windows. Each corridor of cells had only a single daily tub of water for washing up. The secretary of the interior himself compared it to the Black Hole of Calcutta and with good reason. Delinquent teens convicted of minor offenses went into the same cells as the worst criminals, which provided them with little rehabilitation but extensive training in other, more savage kinds of crime. They emerged in a state of "precocious villainy."[9]

Elsewhere, so-called "workhouses" combined the functions of jails and poorhouses, giving those in poverty the added humiliation of having to share their living quarters with actual criminals.[10] Near the Arsenal, the federal penitentiary closed during the war for conversion into a storehouse for military ordnance and ammunition.[11] Although some convicts headed north to a state prison in Albany, New York,[12] the closure ultimately resulted in an even greater lack of space to house local criminals, inevitably allowing them once more to take to the streets. One police board report charged that no other city in America was so "inadequately supplied with prison accommodations," yet a congressional bill in 1864 to fund a new penitentiary failed, and many years passed before the legislature even attempted to build a new one.[13]

Far-Flung Duties

Congress and police superintendents made the work of already overwhelmed police officers even more arduous by piling on extraneous duties. One of the most tedious was upholding strict enforcement of liquor laws even after the war had ended and most of the soldiers—the original targets of the Provost Guard for their drinking habits—had left. Temperance advocates demanded that officials strictly control or else reject liquor licenses. The police brass responded by detailing officers to crack down on illicit saloons and tippling shops, forcing patrolmen to chase down rogue bartenders instead of thugs and murderers.[14]

The Metropolitan Police continued to take charge of one far-flung duty after another, no matter how far each stood from the primary goal of law enforcement. In a government town with ironically few government agencies, the police often served as the only recourse for fixing problems. The department's annual report from 1880 provides a detailed list of some of the many tasks—or "incidentals"—performed by officers, who in many cases acted as much as repairmen, utility workers, and social service agents as enforcers of the law:

- abandoned infants found (26)
- broken lamps reported (174)

- dead infants found (47)
- dangerous holes in carriageways and sidewalks (106)
- filthy alleys reported (67)
- hydrants out of repair (123)
- loads of coal weighed (1,171)
- lodgers accommodated (7,461)
- lost children restored to parents (195)
- owners of insecure buildings notified (13)
- sewers in bad condition (46)
- trees and tree boxes broken (1,121)
- water notices served by police (7,017)[15]

Age of the Swindle

With the police distracted by their ever more varied assignments, under-paid and exhausted from their labors, and outnumbered by lawbreak-ers, crime increased in frequency and complexity. In just the category of fraud and thievery, thousands of shady characters concocted schemes to steal goods and money from the public. While pickpockets and shoplift-ers were a strictly local menace, forgers, con artists, and fencers of stolen goods conducted elaborate operations across state boundaries, sometimes using aliases and disguises. *Professional Criminals of America* by Thomas Byrnes provides a key look at the assorted thieves in the Gilded Age with whom the urban police in America dealt:

bank burglar: *the "intelligent and thoughtful rogue" who invades a bank and attacks its safe with "patience, intelligence, mechanical knowledge, industry, determination, fertility of resources, and courage—all in high degree."*

bank sneak: *part of a group of bank burglars, "who stealthily steals behind the counter and robs the cash box or a bundle of bonds."*

confidence and bunco men: *those who practice "the safest, pleasantest, and most amusing way for a shrewd thief to make his liv-ing," employing all types of subterfuge, fraud, and gamesmanship "in helping themselves to other people's money."*

forgers: *falsifiers or counterfeiters "of a writing, bill, bond, will, or other document" who "prostitute their talents by imitating the handwriting and workmanship of others."*

receivers of stolen goods: *middlemen thieves "extremely careful in their negotiations with professional rogues" in buying purloined "bonds, securities, diamonds or silks," among other commodities.*

sawdust men: *operators of get–rich–quick schemes who solicit rubes to purchase bags of stolen or counterfeit money at a discount before switching bags and leaving them with a sack of worthless blank paper sometimes weighed down by sawdust.*

sneak thieves or house thieves: *"Daring and desperate rascals" known to invade homes by breaking through doors and windows, some of them housebreaking at night "in search of plunder and with masks on their faces and murder in their heart."*[16]

One of the most notorious operations was the "circular swindle" or illicit lottery. In this scheme, thieves mailed handbills proclaiming the easy money to be had from buying tickets to a random drawing. There was no such drawing, however, and the criminal pocketed the money, changed his or her address, and moved on to the next group of marks.[17] More traditional underworld gambling also proved popular and used various methods of cheating either through stacked odds or confidence games. Gambling houses became so pervasive that an 1876 congressional investigation revealed widespread police corruption in protecting such illegal establishments, the detectives either on the payroll or receiving money under the table.[18]

Murder Bay to Hell's Bottom

In an era of unprecedented corruption, the White House perhaps appropriately lay near the heart of District crime. Most police arrests, about one-quarter, came in the First Precinct,[19] roughly a ten-block arc east and southeast of the White House, which included one of the District's bleakest neighborhoods: Murder Bay. Here in 1869, a lunatic wielding a club with a glass insulator strapped to it attacked President Grant and tried to smash his head in. After police apprehended the assailant they found a loaded revolver on him.[20] (Other unconventional weapons of the era included an umbrella to gouge out a man's eye, a gas-pipe bomb meant for a judge, a "cheeser" to scourge someone's flesh, a walking cane used by a rapist, and a "bogus infernal machine" used for God knows what.[21] The police sometimes responded in kind with medieval-style weaponry, in one case with a nightstick that deployed steel barbs with a turn of its handle.[22])

A contraband camp had arisen in Murder Bay during and just after the war, but the area's material conditions hadn't improved much since then. Thick with thieves, cardsharps, and pickpockets, it stood within close, uncomfortable view of the White House, roughly bounded by 11th and 15th Streets NW, Pennsylvania Avenue, and the city canal. Murder Bay had its own main street, Ohio Avenue, which paralleled Pennsylvania Avenue to the north—though with a decidedly more dismal aspect: thick with low-rent industries like foundries and industrial works, numerous gambling halls and saloons, and the ubiquitous brothels.[23] Looking back on the neighborhood's worst years, the *Washington Post* described the area as a place "where life itself was frequently sacrificed on the turning of a card [and] Thieves and unprincipled men and women, as ready to cut a throat as pick a pocket, flourished and walked the streets in certain sections in open daylight."[24]

The old "Island" slums stood southwest of the Capitol.

Murder Bay wasn't even the worst of the District's neighborhoods, though. Some of them were so fearsome that the public didn't dare venture into them by day nor the police at night. The canal and railroad tracks cut off stretches of The Island from the rest of town and made it an expansive slum, with shanties and crowded tenements home to some of the town's most pervasive crime.[25] Bloodfield near the Navy Yard and Swampoodle north of the Capitol were equally grim, packed with gambling houses and assorted thieves and thugs.[26] But the most shameful was Hell's Bottom.

Located above the major boulevards, at the northern tip of Washington City, this down-at-heel neighborhood sat on low-lying marshy ground that bred malaria and other waterborne diseases and fostered dense criminal activity. It had evolved from a contraband camp at the close of the war to a forbidding enclave ignored by the police and left to the control of criminals preying on the predominantly black residents. In this forlorn place, "Money was scarce and whiskey was cheap." Fights routinely turned into riots, but no police court existed to try suspects.[27] It had little in the way of elementary housing or sanitation, and the local and national governments provided almost nothing in funding or services to alleviate the misery. If highly visible areas like Murder Bay suffered from dreadful crime and poverty, then of course more distant neighborhoods like Hell's Bottom would be much worse.

Revolving Door

Not confined to just a few dangerous neighborhoods, crime existed everywhere, in areas rich and poor and practiced by criminals of a variety of looks, methods, and backgrounds. The National Archives holds several volumes of arrest books for the Metropolitan Police during the postwar era. Better than any dry statistics, they explain who these suspects were and what they were accused of doing. A few scattered violations concerned rarely enforced laws against abortion and profanity, but most of the offenses related to some form or other of stealing, drinking, and fighting—often in combination. A few of the listings are quite telling for what they reveal about the capital's standard of law and order, including the following cases from a sample page of the arrest books, during the late summer of 1874:

August 14: Mary Adams (servant), intoxicated and disorderly
Like many of those arrested, Ms. Adams was brought in for being drunk and, we can assume, causing a spectacle or threatening someone. Her case was dismissed, possibly after she spent a night in jail to sober up.

August 14: John S. Mosby (lawyer), suspicion of dueling
Times had changed dramatically in half a century for would-be duelers as the crime drew closer to a capital offense than an "affair between gentlemen." Mr. Mosby was held on a five thousand dollar bond to await requisition.

August 31: Tom White (thief), grand larceny
The arrest ledger lists Mr. White's occupation as a thief, so he may have been well known to authorities. Despite being accused of a major crime, he was given only ninety days in the workhouse.

September 6: George Nickens, John Talbert, Richard Queen, Frank Bell (laborers), affray
These four were hauled into the station just before noon for fighting and received the light but not uncommon fine of five dollars each.

September 7: John T. Matthews (merchant), receiving stolen goods; Charles Kennar (servant), petit larceny; William Henry (liquor dealer), obtaining goods under false pretenses
These three suspects were booked consecutively for unrelated crimes of thievery (though the order of their arrest does suggest an air of complicity). As with so many nonviolent criminals at a time when fraud ran rampant, they were not prosecuted, marked as *"nolle prosequi"* in the books.

September 12: William J. Dees (schoolmaster), insanity
The ledger doesn't reveal what led police to charge this teacher with madness, but they nonetheless arrested him and sent him to the Insane Asylum, the inevitable repository of the mentally ill.

September 14: Susan Simpkins (prostitute), assault and battery with intent to kill

Unlike the madams and prostitutes occasionally arrested in the sex trade, Ms. Simpkins was accused of a more serious crime and remanded to authorities in Virginia, most likely where the act was committed.[28]

Of the forty-nine suspects on this page of the ledger—arrested from August 14 to September 16, 1874—only ten faced serious charges of a stint in jail or a later court date. The thirty-nine others either had their cases dismissed or not prosecuted, spent a night in jail, or paid a small fine, usually five dollars.[29] It wasn't that almost 80 percent of these suspects were innocent or deserved only a light slap on the wrist. The beleaguered justice system simply couldn't prosecute so many accused criminals and had to focus on the worst violators by letting lesser offenders go.

Criminal Trading Cards

The National Archives contain many vivid images of area suspects as well, from steely-eyed murderers to winsome pickpockets, in a series of cabinet cards that police once used to identify persistent wrongdoers. Mostly dating from the 1880s, these pocket-size mug shots resemble criminal trading cards, with the suspect's image on the front and biographical details, including alleged crimes, on the back.

Here we see long-forgotten figures like the portly and goofy "swindler" George Gardiner and his walrus mustache; Harry Smith, an ancient horse thief who looks barely able to steal a pencil, let alone a draft animal; the cane-bearing, top-hat-wearing Isaac Vail, a dapper confidence man; the sullen figure of pickpocket William Johnson; the surly Italian immigrant Agostino Caliagno, who "can't speak English" but is notorious for "false pretense"; and little Ida Prather, a petty thief only five-foot, four-inches tall but who "carries herself erect." Numerous figures are listed as "suspicious character," a catchall term for criminals clearly up to something or otherwise familiar and notorious to law enforcement. Some of them do indeed look suspicious, especially Charles Leonard with his "long thin fingers" and freakish eyeglasses and Jack Wilson, aka "Boston Charley," with a face like an Old Testament prophet.[30]

Police "cabinet cards" identifying alleged criminals. To the right, Agostino Caliagno, known for his "false pretense."

Charles Leonard, a "suspicious character."

Pint-size pickpocket Ida Prather.

William Johnson, "false pretenses."

The swindler George Gardiner.

Horse thief Harry Smith.

Jack Wilson, aka "Boston Charley," a suspicious character.

Isaac Vail, the very image of a confidence man.

Especially telling is the line for "Color" on the back of the cards. For most African Americans, it records a highly specific shade. Some of the descriptors are quite inventive and include anything from "bright yellow," "copper," and "dark copper mulatto" to "dark ginger" and "gingerbread."[31] Such adjectives, for all their vagueness today, could be useful to nineteenth-century police in recognizing a suspect, but of course no comparable descriptions exist for Caucasian suspects, such as "milky," "eggshell," or "ivory." Instead, the line simply remains blank.

Racial Conflict Redux

The majority of suspects during the war were either Irish immigrants or African Americans, but, as the years went on and the number of black residents increased in the capital, so too did their arrests, up to half of all District arrests in 1888.[32] Statistically black crime was no greater than white crime, but African Americans received most of the blame, especially when Reconstruction was winding down and segregation and Jim Crow laws were increasing. The *Washington Post* even blamed blacks for a "reign of terror" involving murder, rape, thievery, and arson, seeing them as the primary culprits for all crime in the capital.[33]

In fact, blacks more often fell victim to crime than perpetrated it. Violent criminals attacked them in their own neighborhoods knowing that police would turn a blind eye. Angry mobs still targeted them even years after the abolition of slavery and the Black Code. In one example, in the summer of 1865—after the war had ended—the soldiers of the army's 20th corps descended upon blacks on The Island. After guzzling "bad whiskey," smashing doors and windows, and assaulting citizens, the soldiers had free rein to destroy as much of the slum as they wanted until a different group of soldiers interceded and arrested them.[34] Four years later, almost to the day, another mob attacked black voters on Election Day. The police almost quelled the disturbance, but soon the crowd swelled and erupted in an antipolice riot, hurling rocks and wielding sticks at officers until the cops fired on them. The only person killed in the melee was black.[35]

A New Class of Officers

Despite police inability to protect African Americans from the fury of racist mobs or from opportunistic criminals in their neighborhoods,[36] one point had changed. Blacks had joined the force itself. A month after the 1869 Election Day riot, the Metropolitan Police swore in its first black officers, Charles Tillman and Calvin Caruthers.[37] However noble the move may have seemed, it had less to do with the open-mindedness of local officials than with the difficulty that white officers had in patrolling minority neighborhoods and the need to find any policemen who could.

The new class of officers faced great hostility at times. Many residents in minority districts—who of course had reason to distrust all police—didn't accept them. The amount of crime in their precincts was overwhelming, and newspapers and public officials chastised them for being too lenient when they arrested black suspects and for being too firm when they arrested white ones. Within the department, they faced discrimination from their peers, rarely received promotions, and sometimes were forced to quit the force altogether.[38]

Nonetheless, despite these drawbacks and challenges, it was a significant step that African Americans entered the force. Beginning in 1869, their presence as enforcers of the law dramatically reversed the

An early group photo of Metropolitan Police, including several black officers.

grim situation of just a decade earlier, when the Auxiliary Guard rounded up blacks after dark and whipped them when they broke the rules or were thought to be disobedient. African Americans had become agents of executive authority, not just objects of it, and were expanding their roles beyond the servants, cooks, drivers, and laborers of the prewar years. That they met strong, often violent opposition on the streets and hostility within the department was perhaps inevitable, but their status as members of the police force—an arm of the national government—ensured that they had achieved a small but critical foothold on power in the capital.

Indeed, the hiring of blacks for the police force and the federal government's control of that force gave a clear sign that the old Washington City was changing. The war had introduced the most dramatic transformations—the expulsion of the pro-slavery elite, the rise of Republican power, the martial efficiency—but the threat of backsliding remained. At any time, the city could slip back into the shadows of a poor, benighted village underfunded by Congress and ignored by national politicians. The creation of the Metropolitan Police attempted to push the changes forward as these officers of the law, with all their thankless duties, tried to remake the capital into a modern, functional city, even as they patrolled a landscape almost feudal in its violence and poverty.

TEN

THE FALL OF WASHINGTON CITY

On February 20 and 21, 1871, the capital threw a big party. It didn't celebrate the end of a bloody uprising or the abolition of slavery but something much more prosaic: the laying of new wooden pavement across Pennsylvania Avenue to replace the old stone pavers.

The stretch between the White House and the Capitol stood packed with ten thousand spectators who reveled under flags, streamers, and Chinese lanterns as fireworks erupted overhead. The entertainment included spirited races between citizens on foot and in sacks, horses in teams of four and six, and even contests between goats and wheelbarrows. Lively floats paraded down the avenue, including one depicting the inauguration of a female president. Along with a bevy of games and tournaments, a carnival delighted the spectators during the day, and masked balls enchanted the elite at night.[1] As one newspaper remarked of the spectacle, taking place amid unexpected winter sunshine, "The very heavens lent the charm of their approval," marking "a complete transformation of the city into a thing of happy life, the beginning of a new era."[2] However, this celebration wasn't honoring just the new era of a wood-paved Pennsylvania Avenue. It also marked the repeal of the charters of Washington City and Georgetown, the dissolution of their mayors and city councils, and the institution of a new form of territorial government.[3]

The festival marked the end of a failed era of local government and its replacement with a fresh regime that many hoped would illuminate the benighted capital with major new projects and improvements. Indeed, the changes of the 1870s did begin the reinvention of the capital from embarrassing Chesapeake backwater to locus of national power and prestige. Yet the sacrifice proved harsh. In exchange for a bold modern

The 1871 public gala that celebrated the long-awaited paving of Pennsylvania
Avenue . . . as well as the official end of Washington City.

city, Washingtonians lost the right to choose their local leaders, mired
themselves in webs of debt and corruption, and relinquished the power
to shape their city's image and infrastructure. Through dramatic twists
and turns, the new capital emerged from the tragicomedy of its history
as a markedly different place that scarcely resembled the old Washington
City. It wouldn't even be called Washington City anymore.

Postwar Capital

In the years after the Civil War, the capital lay in tatters. Inadequate sewage and an unreliable water supply crippled the city, darkness cloaked the streets, roads and bridges were falling into disrepair, and Congress wouldn't pay for any significant upkeep or improvement. Henry Latham, a visiting Englishman, described a patchwork landscape still reminiscent of the 1820s, with its scattered marble public buildings surrounded by brick and wooden houses, while beyond stood blighted sheds and fields. Unlike the rest of the country, "It is the only place we have seen which is not full of growth and vitality."[4]

Barnyard animals still roamed at will despite laws that forbade the practice, and it wasn't uncommon to see cows grazing on the commons or unregulated slaughterhouses plying their trade throughout the capital.[5] Hogs still had free rein and delighted in destroying people's gardens, creating wallowing holes in the streets, and scattering mud and feces everywhere. Municipal attempts to control waste of the human variety also failed. Citizens dumped "night soil" in unclean pits and privies and helped give the town's streets and alleys a ghastly odor.[6] Some city lots still lacked privy boxes and even plumbing, and decaying offal and organic matter in the streets only helped spread infectious disease.[7] The situation was worst in the poor and working-class parts of the capital, which held low-rent houses and tenements with deplorable sanitation and barely livable conditions.

GOP on the Rise

Once again, the dismal state of local affairs fired the enthusiasm of critics to move the capital elsewhere. Such detractors had never really disappeared in the half a century since the British had burned Washington City in 1814, and with the town in such a ragged condition after the chaos of war, many felt the time had come to relocate the capital farther west. *New York Tribune* publisher Horace Greeley thought St. Louis an excellent location for a world-class capital, and he wasn't alone.[8] Former Union general John Logan also felt the Mississippi Valley would make for a fruitful site, imagining that the nation's archives, art, and even federal buildings could be carted off wholesale to the Midwest, leaving the District home only to the "maiden ladies and widows who kept boarding houses."[9]

But the critics had a formidable enemy in the White House: Ulysses S. Grant, former head of the Union armies and, as of March 1869, president of the United States of America. He opposed any congressional scheme to relocate the capital from Washington City and threatened to veto any such measure that proposed it. He realized, however, that it would require an intensive campaign of public investment to make the town a worthy site for the seat of government. His Republican Party had reconstructed the capital as the political and constitutional heart of the reunified country, and there was no way that he'd lose such a potent symbol of federal supremacy over the states to the Midwest or to the clutches of his political enemies.[10]

The GOP dominated the legislative branch with two major wings: Radical Republicans, who came from safe districts and favored civil rights for blacks and harsh Reconstruction measures for the white South, and more moderate Republicans from swing districts regularly contested by Democrats. After Grant replaced Andrew Johnson, the GOP ruled the executive branch as well. That meant that the party could dole out choice Washington jobs to such Northerners as bureaucrats seeking opportunities in the federal government and entrepreneurs seeking contracts for business with that government. Those Yankee Republican newcomers, derisively called "carpetbaggers," secured political and economic control over the District and further marginalized the old Southern ruling class[11]—many of whom had absconded to Richmond and other points south, and returned now in the hopes that their unfortunate sympathies could be forgotten or, for the right price, overlooked.

But there was no getting around the fact that, for the first time in the capital's history, Southerners were in the minority.[12] During the 1860s, the capital grew from 56,000 to 131,700 people, both the fastest numerical and percentage rise of the nineteenth century.[13] Among these arrivals came a fresh new class of well-connected politicians, merchants, bankers, and robber barons who refashioned high society in the District in their own image.

Antiques and Parvenus

With the emergence of this new ruling class, the town's upper crust soon divided into mutually suspicious camps. On one side stood the "Antiques," the old-line, Southern-oriented, secessionist-friendly Democratic stalwarts who privileged rank, status, and lineage above all else. On the other stood the "Parvenus," the neophyte, Northern, pro-Union Republicans who valued money and property above the quality of a name or family line. The Parvenus threw notoriously lavish balls "overflowing with roses, heliotropes, and camellias" while "On the buffet sparkling with gold, silver and crystal sat the bottles of red Bordeaux and Burgundy and the buffet tables were loaded with terrapin and truffle, spiced meat and salads, pastries, elaborate confections and choice fruits."[14] The only items missing from the old days were the canvasback ducks, minuets, and enslaved servants.

Madeleine Dahlgren's *Etiquette of Social Life in Washington*, an essential guide at the time, codified the social rules of the great men and women to prevent any unusual or untoward behavior among the unknowing. Among many other topics, Dahlgren detailed the proper manner by which to enter a ballroom, the ideal way to leave a calling card, the preferred gastronomy for a feast, and the most tasteful forms of attire and presentation—which did not include a gentleman wearing white gloves with his black dress suit instead of the more sensible choice of "lavender or any delicate tint."[15]

On the plus side, few of these gentlemen were slapping each other in the face with their lavender gloves as a prelude to a duel, and the elevation of money over honor did much to diminish the importance of rank and status. However, the reign of the Parvenus appalled the Antiques, who avoided contact with such philistines—especially if they were "upstarts and grafters" in Congress.[16]

Nonetheless it took a great deal of money for the average congressman to keep up with high society. After all, a politician had to make a good show among his peers. Luckily, he had ample opportunity through bribery. In their novel *The Gilded Age*, Mark Twain and Charles Dudley Warner helpfully tallied the costs of buying public servants for business magnates who wished to secure favors—such as a handy change of law or a lucrative appropriation—from the legislature:

majority of Senate committee members: $40,000
committee chairman: $10,000
male lobbyist: $3,000
female lobbyist: $10,000

"high moral" congressman or senator: $3,000
backbenchers: $500[17]

In possibly the most avaricious era in American history, providing under-the-table payments represented part of the cost of doing business. This laissez-faire style of corruption helped fund the indulgent lifestyles of the region's richest citizens, fueled many of the major projects of the time, and created a strong, if perverse, incentive for the reconstruction of the District of Columbia. Its greatest practitioner was Alexander Shepherd.

The Making of a Boss

Like many of his upstart Republican peers, Shepherd came from humble circumstances, born in Washington City to an unexceptional middle-class family in 1835. After his father died, the teenaged Shepherd had to find work to support his mother and six younger siblings.[18] He did drudge work for a time until a plumbing and gas-fitting company employed him in the 1850s and 1860s, giving him a hands-on understanding of public infrastructure that shaped his perspective in years to come. (During this time he also served a brief stint as a soldier in the Union army, for which he was eminently unsuited.)

Life in the plumbing business was good, and he eventually became the owner of the company. Like any good bootstrapper, he parlayed his business success into other areas, securing a seat on the boards of directors of banks and paving, construction, and railway companies and entering the political field with a seat on Washington County's governing Levy Court.[19]

Shepherd also took partial ownership of the *Evening Star* newspaper, had a knack for speculative real estate, and belonged to several prestigious gentlemen's clubs. A champion glad-hander, he had a keen understanding of human politics, though partisan ideology engaged him less. He shifted from a pro-Southern stance in his early years, to a more pro-Union—though still conservative—perspective in his middle years, to an ardent Republican posture in his peak years.[20] Self-made magnates such as Shepherd particularly attracted the attention of President Grant, who took him into his confidence as a member of his secretive "Kitchen Cabinet,"[21] even though Shepherd had worked to defeat his nomination for president in 1868.

The most powerful figure in the history of DC politics, Alexander "Boss" Shepherd laid the groundwork for the future city.

A transient political partisan, Shepherd did have one ongoing commitment as a businessman: the development of the material conditions of the District. As many citizens were beginning to understand, if urban progress were to take place, it had to happen in a functional and well-built capital that could stave off threats of relocation to the Midwest. While Shepherd stood out as the most prominent figure to advocate for major capital improvements, he certainly wasn't the first. The Army Corps of Engineers had been doing so for decades.

Capital Designers

Montgomery Meigs—engineer of the US Capitol, builder of the Washington Aqueduct, wartime quartermaster general—helped prompt Congress in 1867 to transfer control of the Office of Public Buildings and Grounds from the Interior Department to the War Department.[22] This was no small feat. Henceforth the corps oversaw all public buildings in town and designed the blueprints for the modernization of the capital—for which later politicians like Shepherd were only too happy to take credit.

Meigs spent a crucial year in Europe, from 1867 to 1868, investigating the cities of Germany, Austria, Italy, and the UK, with a stop in Paris for the World's Fair.[23] He made extensive sketches and notes on infrastructure with an eye toward using some of the best ideas to improve Washington City. He wrote of the proper layout of pavements, laid "at right angles to the line of travel." He detailed the color and composition of stone walkways and the effect of weather on them. He described boulevards featuring trees, paths, promenades, and parking as a means of reducing the scale of roadways. All while keeping an eye to the possibility of exporting the functional aesthetics of the Old World to the New.[24] He sent his observations to Nathaniel Michler, the superintendent of public grounds and buildings of the army corps, who took Meigs's notes and recommended them to Congress as a starting point for capital improvements.[25]

Michler, an engineer and brigadier general, had distinguished himself in running the Topographical Department of the Army of the Potomac. He created defensive works for Grant's bloodiest battles in the last phase of the war and even witnessed Lee's surrender in 1865.[26] After the war he had the responsibility of finding a new home for the White House, which sat on a swampy site prone to malaria, with the filthy city canal running nearby.[27] (An 1864 engineering report called the site "a dangerous miasmatic swamp . . . the noxious exhalations from which during the summer and early autumn months [have] made the Presidential mansion so notoriously unhealthy as a place of residence."[28]) Michler issued a report proposing to locate the president's new residence to a pastoral setting such as Harewood, far from the grit and grime of downtown Washington City.[29] Despite Michler's considerable efforts, though, Congress ultimately disregarded them because, as one historian wrote, "The men who were in the process of trying to impeach the President [Andrew Johnson] would hardly be enthusiastic about building or buying him a new home."[30]

Michler's other proposals met with more success. He detailed a way to modernize Pennsylvania Avenue and other thoroughfares, based partially on Meigs's recommendations, with streetside parks, abundant trees, and graceful promenades.[31] He recommended the creation of a network of public parks, centered around a great "National Park," perhaps at Rock Creek, which would give residents the opportunity to "seek its shades for the purpose of breathing the free air of Heaven and admiring nature."[32] He developed a plan for the town's public parks, squares, and reservations—most in notorious disrepair—proposing to enclose and cover them with foliage while removing the decrepit structures that littered them.[33] He also advocated for the replacement of the "dilapidated and unsightly" Centre Market with a new structure. The building burned down in 1870, and two years later Adolph Cluss designed a new structure acclaimed as "the largest and most modern food market in the country."[34] (Further out on a limb, he envisioned ornamenting the bedraggled Mall with walkways, equestrian paths and gateways, and graceful water features such as "jets d'eau, fountains, miniature lakes" amid artistic statuary.[35])

With more immediate and practical application, he argued for a bevy of ambitious goals that came to pass in the coming decades: converting the city canal into a sewer, dredging the Potomac to improve navigation, repairing and remodeling DC bridges, and reclaiming the disease-ridden Potomac Flats as dry and healthful public lands.[36] The Flats—the shallow sections of the Potomac River where low tide exposed higher ground as mudflats—notoriously hosted legions of disease-breeding mosquitoes and, in the popular imagination, "gazeous miasms, which, absorbed by the body, produce weakness, sickness, and death."[37]

Few of Michler's ideas came to fruition during his tenure, aside from fixing up some small public parks and public reservations. Nonetheless, Washington City had found in him, like Meigs before, an urban planner who combined romantic visions with a knack for practical application. He also provided the Army Corps of Engineers even more credence as the capital's preeminent designers. In 1871 Michler stepped down as superintendent to make way for the more industrious and controversial Orville Babcock. Before he left, however, Michler served as one of the commissioners overseeing the successful paving of Pennsylvania Avenue and the high-spirited carnival that followed—as good a sendoff as any.[38]

Struggle for a New Era

Along with the continued efforts of the Army Corps of Engineers and the new Republican elite, the dramatic changes of the 1870s couldn't have taken place without the increased presence of African Americans. The black population of the capital was expanding rapidly: from 14,316 before the war to 38,663 in 1867, a growth rate driven by former slaves and free black migrants looking for work.[39] During this and subsequent decades in the nineteenth century, blacks composed around a third of the population, and lived in all wards of the capital, with particular concentrations in northwest and southwest DC, sometimes in racially mixed neighborhoods.[40] Most worked as laborers, launderers, seamstresses, masons, and plasterers as well as the old antebellum jobs of waiters, drivers, servants, and midwives.[41] A small but growing number of wealthy African Americans was emerging too, including hotel and drugstore owner James Wormley, lawyers John Cook and Charles Thomas, and hoteliers John Gray and Alfred Cook. Business magnate and early trade unionist George Downing even opened a restaurant at the Capitol, pushing for both races to be served there, and lobbied for African-American access to public galleries in the building as well.[42]

The most famous black citizen of the District was Frederick Douglass—escaped slave, renowned autodidact, abolitionist, activist for equal rights for women as well as blacks, correspondent of Abraham Lincoln, newspaper publisher, lecturer, and author of several famed memoirs. He retired to his home in Rochester, New York, after the war and the abolition of slavery, but Washington City drew him back as the publisher of the reformist *New National Era*.[43] Despite the newspaper's failure—a "misadventure" as he called it, which cost him nearly ten thousand dollars[44]—Douglass stayed in town and came as close to an icon as a Washingtonian could get without serving as president. Douglass also involved himself in local politics, a turn of events that could humble any legend, as we'll see.

Although Douglass had educated himself, many other notable black professionals had studied at Howard University, chartered by Congress in 1867 to provide higher education and opportunity to students regardless of race. Endowed with funding from the Freedmen's Bureau and helmed by militant Christian general Oliver Howard, the university attracted pupils from around the world, including a wide range of black students as well as poor whites.[45]

Howard became a valuable ally of Radical Republicans in Congress, who helped create the Freedmen's Bureau to assist blacks in the post-war era. During its existence, from 1865 to 1872, it had a huge array of tasks assigned to it: protecting the civil rights of African Americans, reuniting families separated by war and slavery, maintaining hospitals and settlements in the District (such as Freedmen's Village on the former Lee estate), overseeing and operating black schools, and supporting industrial and vocational schools that provided job training. It also had the monumental job of trying to improve the sanitation and livability of tenements in such neighborhoods as The Division and, failing that, razing the buildings and moving their residents to new facilities, including some remodeled from old hospital wards. It later provided food, fuel, blankets, and clothing to the destitute and coordinated with private aid societies for ongoing relief—sorely needed in view of the high death rate and infant mortality for local African Americans.[46]

The bureau was controversial at the time. The idea of a government agency overseeing social welfare and services was almost unheard of in the mid-nineteenth century, much less one directed toward the betterment of blacks, whom so many of the town's white citizenry still viewed with suspicion and contempt. Nonetheless, the Freedmen's Bureau, like the Army Corps of Engineers, operated with military efficiency[47] and stood as yet another example of the War Department forcing change on the capital while most other public institutions stood idle.

Rise of the Black Vote

Oddly enough, the other institution improving the capital was Congress. The Republican Party swept the national elections of 1866, and the GOP found itself with two-thirds majorities in both the Senate and House and therefore the ability to pass anything it liked. Near the top of the list for the Radical Republicans, the most active and dominant force in the party, was black suffrage in the District. In short order they passed the measure and easily overrode President Johnson's veto.[48] Some, such as Charles Sumner, saw the measure as a test vote for extending suffrage to blacks nationwide, despite its broad unpopularity with local whites.[49]

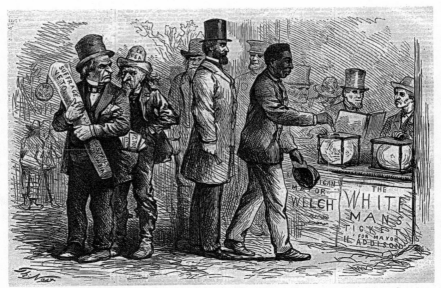

Thomas Nast cartoon of "the Negro at the Ballot Box," watched over by
President Johnson holding a suffrage veto like a club.

The GOP didn't flinch at this disapproval, since it continued to see
most native white Washingtonians as potential secessionists and saboteurs. The suffrage bill even included a plank denying the vote to anyone
"convicted of any infamous crime or persons who may have given aid and
comfort to the rebels in the late rebellion."[50] In this way, the politics of the
"Old Democracy" had turned on their head: Congress had come under
the control of New Englanders instead of Southerners. Former abolitionists ruled instead of slaveholders, nationalists instead of regionalists,
moguls and generals in place of planters and gentry.

Black enthusiasm for suffrage was immediate. Political clubs for African Americans met in assembly halls and churches, and the new voters
organized into groups such as the Radical Republican Association with
the goal of entrenching and extending the power of Lincoln's party. The
franchise expanded considerably, and by the close of registration for the
next election, nearly as many blacks as whites had registered.[51]

Reaction from the other side was predictably livid. The *National Intelligencer*, guardian of the hidebound customs of the old DC, claimed a

modest number of whites had registered because they feared having to sit alongside blacks in jury boxes drawn from voter rolls.[52] Mayor Richard Wallach asserted that no "pauper race" should ever rule the capital. Other entrenched politicians charged black voters with fraud and other crimes.[53] Later, the *Daily Patriot*, a local paper with funding from pro-secessionist banker and art collector W. W. Corcoran, bemoaned that the District ever became a beachhead for black suffrage and "an experimental garden for Radical plants."[54]

Frederick Douglass had a markedly different view, that "to guard, protect, and maintain his liberty, the freedman should have the ballot; that the liberties of the American people were dependent upon the Ballot-box, the Jury-box, and the Cartridge-box; that without these no class of people could flourish in this country."[55]

The Brief Reign of a Reformer

As it had in the 1830s, violence broke out at the polls in the city elections of 1868. Each party exaggerated the extent of the chaos and blamed the other side's voters for it. One conservative newspaper imagined a "Carnival of Blood" taking place as African Americans went out to vote, and Democrats accused Republicans of importing nonvoting blacks by the boatload from Maryland and Virginia to swing the elections. The *Georgetown Courier*, a Democratic mouthpiece, even envisioned a sort of Gilded Age horror movie arising from the interracial vote: "The races are now pitted against each other in deadly animosity and but very little added excitement is required to drench the streets of the capital with human blood."[56]

After the bloody carnival had ended, former abolitionist and city postmaster Sayles Bowen became mayor by a margin of just eighty-three votes, a narrow victory for the Republican Party. The closeness of the count prompted the usual charges of fraud from Democrats, and lame-duck mayor Richard Wallach even refused to hand over the keys to his office. Bowen had to use a locksmith to claim his rightful title.[57]

A prime figure in the Freedmen's Aid Society, which sent assistance to former slaves in the South, Bowen controversially used the Republican spoils system to reward his allies with key positions in local government, which prompted Democratic newspapers to dub him "Six Teat Bowen." He employed African Americans as laborers on urban improvement projects, and he continued his previously private support of black schools with mayoral efforts to fund and promote them citywide, even proposing to integrate public schools, which alarmed moderates as much as it heartened radicals.[58] He also helped pass laws that forbade discrimination in public accommodations such as theaters and hotels and levied fines of fifty dollars on businesses refusing to serve blacks as customers.[59]

Despite his noble efforts and good intentions, though, Bowen was a disappointment as mayor. He found it difficult to fund his many projects. He depleted the city treasury after increasing pay for local officials. He met with unrelenting hostility from white residents and many newspapers. He even oversaw a city election in 1869 as violent as the one the year before, featuring the familiar stone-throwing mobs that attacked passersby and ransacked people's houses.[60] He lost support from his allies, both black and Republican, and in 1870 the more moderate Matthew Emery deposed him in a landslide.[61]

The Territory Emerges

Voicing the attitude of the capital's upper crust in her memoir *Ten Years in Washington*, journalist Mary Clemmer Ames decried the "extravagance and venality" of Bowen's administration, which stood uncorrected by his successor, Emery. The elite didn't have the numbers to sway an election, so their only recourse was "the absolute necessity of a vigorous and radical reform."[62] In other words, they wanted to scrap the old system of government altogether. In this instance, the Antiques and the Parvenus united in their contempt for politicians like Bowen and Emery, but they needed a champion to push forward a solution to the messy complications of local democracy. Alexander Shepherd was more than ready to meet their needs.

There had been efforts in Congress to eliminate the franchise for Washington City citizens completely, even for city elections, as early as 1865. Two years later, Shepherd, in his position on the local Board of Trade, proposed stripping the cities of the District of their charters and replacing elected representatives with appointed commissioners.[63] In 1868, in laying down his position on democracy and progress in the District, he affected an air of a disgruntled king more than that of a former plumber: "The taxpayers of this city did not want elections of any kind, and had not wanted them for more than 20 years. If the people trifled with these petty little elections, the city never would come to anything. . . . A board of Commissioners of men of the right stamp could do better than any elected officials . . . in ten years the oldest inhabitants would scarcely recognize the city."[64]

The incompetence of the Bowen regime immeasurably aided his cause. Bowen had led the city into such desperate fiscal straits that an 1870 legal judgment resulted in the seizure of the furniture in the mayor's own offices. In an atmosphere of yawning social need and an expectation for comprehensive public improvements, Bowen squandered his opportunity: City debt mushroomed while the streets lay unpaved.[65] Shepherd attacked Bowen's failures through the newspapers over which he had influence and proposed once again scrapping the current system of government. The city charter had expired in 1868—to be renewed one meager year at a time—and critics again were pressing their demands to move the capital farther west. More than anything, though, what aided Shepherd's cause was the desire of white Washingtonians to relinquish their own suffrage completely to skirt the electoral power of newly enfranchised blacks.[66]

Even before the wheels of local democracy had run over Sayles Bowen and replaced him with Matthew Emery, Alexander Shepherd was busy lobbying Congress to revoke the charters of the District cities and institute a new form of government. Both Shepherd, a Republican, and W. W. Corcoran, a Democrat, lobbied congressmen with treats and favors, including a ride on a Potomac yacht complete with champagne, food, and music.[67] In a telling sign, outside Democratic politicians like New York ward heeler Fernando Wood—known for his vehemently racist rhetoric—praised a bill restricting the franchise in the District,[68] as did a good number of the town's Republican newspapers, power brokers, and upper-crusters. Some, like the soon-to-be jobless Matthew Emery, derided the lack of democracy in such proposals, but to no avail.[69] Emery was doomed to be the capital's last mayor for more than a century.

On February 21, Congress created the Territory of the District of Columbia in the Organic Act of 1871, which stripped Georgetown and Washington City of their charters, removed the jurisdiction of the Levy Court over Washington County, created a unified District of Columbia ruled by an appointed governor, and consigned the name of Washington

City to history's dustbin.[70] On the very same day, the parades and grand masques of the great carnival of Pennsylvania Avenue were taking place over clean wooden pavements. The festivities celebrated a brave new capital progressing inevitably toward urban glory, and its citizens had little power to stop it even if they wanted to. The carnival was the last great gasp of Washington City, which on June 1, 1871, would conclude its seven dark decades and cease to exist.

ELEVEN

A GILDED CAGE

Local democracy in the District didn't die overnight. The new territory had twenty-two wards, each allowing voters to send a representative to a lower chamber of the legislature, the House of Delegates. But the president appointed the upper chamber, the Legislative Council, and all executive offices including the governor.[1] This arrangement gave the chief executive a great deal of power over local matters, which Ulysses S. Grant was only too happy to use.

A month after the creation of the territory, Grant installed financier Henry Cooke, brother of Republican banker and power broker Jay Cooke, as territorial governor and appointed other Republican stalwarts to major offices. Democrats fumed, and in April they raged even more when Norris Chipman, Grant's handpicked and nonvoting delegate to Congress, was elected to the House of Delegates along with fifteen Republicans, among them two African Americans. The reactionary newspaper *The Patriot*—the instrument of W. W. Corcoran, who turned against the Republicans who had helped him lobby for the Organic Act—cried fraud, the first in a long string of verbal brickbats that it leveled against its enemies.[2]

But battles over DC voting habits had become passé. Everyone knew the real power lay not with the territorial legislature, the congressional delegate, or even the governor. Instead, the Board of Public Works flexed the muscle behind the capital government, and its new vice president was Alexander Shepherd.

The Ruling Ring
Henry Cooke frequently left town to attend to financial matters in the Northeast, and his stand-in, Edwin Stanton—eponymous son of the

former secretary of war—happily acted as rubber-stamp governor. (Technically the territorial governor acted as president of the Board of Public Works, and Stanton, like Cooke, acted as chief executive in name only.)[3] When the Board of Public Works took control of the executive machinery of the District, *The Patriot* and other old-line interests took alarm, warning of "Ring Rule" if Shepherd and his cronies were allowed to dictate policy from their perch on the board. In response, Shepherd assumed the rhetoric of an Old Testament patriarch, warning that if his extensive program for the improvement of the District weren't enacted:

> *You shall continue the same old patchwork system which has rendered the nation's metropolis a disgrace and an eye-sore at home and a by-word and reproach abroad. You shall continue to drive over unpaved streets and exposed ravines and be as successfully lost in the blinding dust as was Elijah of old in the clouds which enveloped him as he ascended into the sky.[4]*

To tamp down any such dust, Shepherd advocated a series of proposals for the capital that cost six million dollars, a third of it coming from increased taxation on properties adjoining the improvements and the rest through a loan. Opponents had a US district judge issue an injunction against the plan, but Cooke and Shepherd appealed the decision and went for broke by calling a snap election in November, gambling that voters might approve four million dollars themselves in a plebiscite.[5] As part of their high-risk strategy, they put all of the seats in the House of Delegates up for a revote—just seven months after the last election. The gambit paid off: The Republicans enjoyed a landslide victory and won all but two seats in the House. At nearly the same time, the US Supreme Court overturned the injunction. The Board of Public Works was in business.[6]

Fractured Franchise

Shepherd still faced the suspicions of African Americans in the District, though, who had won the vote only four years earlier and now saw their franchise dramatically crimped, having to settle for five seats in the neutered House of Delegates. It didn't help his cause that Shepherd's own father had owned slaves or that many black leaders had protested Shepherd's rise to executive power as a politician hostile to their interests.[7] Still-bitter Sayles Bowen even charged that Shepherd opposed equal education for blacks in the District as well as mainstream Republicanism. In response, early in 1871, Shepherd engaged in a Gilded Age version of spin control, exchanging a series of public letters with O. O. Howard in which he called himself a friend to African Americans, a supporter of "unified" education for both white and black students, and an opponent of racial discrimination in any form—while conspicuously avoiding the topic of black suffrage.[8]

In reality, Shepherd was no more or less prejudiced than any white mainstream Republican of the era, and he didn't count race his primary concern anyway. He wanted to limit the franchise of any voter without property—white or black—on the dubious premise that anyone whose votes could be bought with "whiskey and money" inevitably would abuse the local elites.[9] In this way his views mirrored those of other Parvenus in the GOP, who had little patience with old-fashioned ideas of democracy. Seven decades of District voting had resulted only in stagnation and decay, and these merchants and magnates didn't want to wait any longer to force change upon the decrepit capital.

Still, Shepherd knew that he had to appeal to core supporters of the Republican Party in the city, most of them African American. He accordingly made a vocal effort to support striking black railway workers in summer 1871[10] and later steered a good number of construction jobs to blacks and other party loyalists. He also had the good fortune to have a firm, notable ally in the black community.

The Ship and the Sea

Frederick Douglass had been appointed to one of the seats on the Legislative Council. The position was one of five appointed jobs in District government that Douglass filled in the postwar era, but probably the least important of them. (He served only two months before turning the job over to his son Lewis.) Nonetheless, despite his minor role in the chamber, Douglass remained an important figure, both for his prominence and for his allegiance to the GOP, of which he said, "The Republican Party is the ship and all else the sea."[11]

Initially the newspaper that Douglass had purchased, the *New National Era*, vented hostility at Shepherd and his Board of Public

Works, but it soon came around to argue that they "deserve the earnest, active support of the city, and the earnest, active, practical support of Congress."[12] "Practical" was the key word here, for if blacks and other citizens of the District lost their voting rights, Congress had to provide something in return, such as sufficient funding for urban improvements and full political support for civil rights. In due course, Lewis Douglass introduced a bill into the Legislative Council that outlawed segregation and discrimination in restaurants, saloons, and soda fountains. A year later the bill passed, and the governor approved it. In 1873 the law was strengthened, and that same year a theater antisegregation bill passed the council too.[13] Realistically, the Republican Party represented the only real alternative. Local Democrats remained wedded to antebellum notions of racial relations and the white supremacy that went along with them, and the GOP had demonstrated more than once at least a passing interest in the black voters who regularly helped it win elections in the District— even as those elections counted for less and less. With the firm support of Frederick Douglass and other African Americans, along with the already fervent backing of the nouveau riche Parvenus and the president, Alexander Shepherd had a clear road to change the capital, starting with the roads themselves.

Capitalizing the District

Emboldened by his success in court and at the ballot box, Shepherd threw his Board of Public Works into hasty action. Major property owners wanted him and his board to pay for public improvements as they went, but the man increasingly known as "Boss" Shepherd was having none of it. In autumn 1871, he ordered work to start in all wards of the city at once and enlarged the board's staff to more than two hundred employees. They took on the huge challenge of leveling the roads—a dream project if ever there was one. The District's streets had long been a hodgepodge of different slopes and angles, and clear perspectives down the thoroughfares had proved elusive because only Pennsylvania Avenue had ever been leveled.[14] Shepherd demanded that asphalt or wood be used for the paving instead of a cheaper macadam surface, and he ordered uniform grades on the major boulevards and avenues, including those directly around the US Capitol, without authorization from Congress.[15]

The board's work on the roads went beyond just making them functional. Employing three arborists, the board planted sixty thousand trees during two years, which helped narrow the giant, inhumanly scaled boulevards with green strips and foliage. It also provided new street parking for horses and carriages.[16] Shepherd further ensured that major roads had illumination by ornamenting them with thousands of gas lamps, the largest street-lighting program in the city's history to date. Never one to miss an opportunity, Shepherd allowed for his own plumbing and gas-fitting company to submit bids for the work, including placing fifty-eight lamp-posts around the Capitol itself.[17]

In earlier decades, fixing and lighting the roads would have presented an enormous enough task, requiring years to get started. But the board wasn't working only on the streets. It was adding even more duties to its agenda, including a redesign of the water system.

Water Work

The grand aqueduct of Montgomery Meigs had been a good start, but large parts of the capital on higher ground still didn't have access to water. The board addressed this problem by laying 180 miles of new water mains, largely in 1872, and giving residents of the District more water per capita than any other city in the world.[18] New sewer lines followed as the old inadequate system of drainage gave way to a more streamlined network that included freshly laid conduits like those along Slash Run. Doing so turned one of the capital's last major creeks, with all of its bogs and marshes, into a channel for the filth and runoff of the city.[19]

To scrape up more funds for his water projects, Shepherd created new sewer districts and assessed each a tax, then levied additional taxes on those areas improved by the conduits.[20] As a further sanitary measure, the territory passed new laws in 1871 to control barnyard animals. Two years later it outlawed scavenging and began cleaning privies with the aid of the Odorless Evacuating Apparatus Company.[21] It was one business Shepherd thankfully didn't have a hand in.

However, one dirty bit of business he couldn't help but be involved in was the town's longest-standing problem: the pestiferous ditch known as the Washington City Canal. In 1864 former mayor Richard Wallach had commissioned a comprehensive survey illustrating just how noxious the open sewer running through the center of town was. Even for a dry civil engineering report, the conclusions were damning. Not only was the canal dysfunctional and stagnant, it posed an active and ongoing health hazard. Rich with "putrescent and decomposing organic matters" that were "tough and viscous," it was enriched by runoff from "the offal of kitchens, and the soil and filth from water closets which are brought in by the sewers discharging in the canal." It was strewn with "carcasses of all kinds, from the bloated horse to the skeleton kidden which have found their way into the canal by divers modes."[22] The canal's rank pollution extended beyond the water: "The accumulated filth and excrement of the city is constantly held in a state of semi-solution in this hot-bed of putrefaction, by means of the ebb and flow of the tides, over a surface of more than a million square feet . . . the miasma from which contaminates every breath of air which passes, from that direction, through or over the city."[23]

With powerful members of Congress threatening to withhold funding for urban improvement unless the canal was removed, Shepherd and his board took quick action. By the end of 1871, Shepherd's men had filled in a large stretch of the ditch from 3rd to 14th Streets. They followed that with halving the width of the canal flowing south of the Capitol and making an actual sewer out of it.[24] Within two years, the old canal vanished beneath pavement. Taking its place was an enlarged B Street, which was later named Constitution Avenue.

Orville's Industry

Shepherd wasn't alone in cleaning up the capital. Orville Babcock, head of the Office of Public Buildings and Grounds for the Army Corps of Engineers, nearly matched Shepherd in his undertakings. A former aide-de-camp to Ulysses S. Grant when he was a Union general and his executive secretary as president,[25] Babcock rose in power above his predecessor, Nathaniel Michler, thanks to Grant's influence, becoming more heavily involved in the Republican machine than almost any engineer up to that time. A buddy of Shepherd, Babcock helped establish an almost incestuous relationship between the Army Corps of Engineers and the Board of Public Works, including giving Shepherd thirty-five thousand dollars in 1872 to install a new copper roof on the White House, one of many actions that invited scrutiny in future years.[26]

The industrious Babcock aggressively steered the corps into remodeling and beautifying the "reservations"—the ugly plots of dirt, mud, and weeds in various circles, squares, and triangles—created by L'Enfant's plan. In just his first year, Babcock oversaw the laying of forty-six thousand square feet of sod, ten thousand yards of pavement, and four miles of drains. He oversaw the installation of countless fences, fountains, and trees, plus gaslights and running water, and rustic furniture and decor.[27] He even created tree nurseries and mini-zoos thick with deer and prairie dogs and imported eagles, owls, and European sparrows to perch above the parks, paying for some of the new critters from his own pocket when funds ran short.[28]

Turning his attention to the forlorn site of the stumpy, unfinished Washington Monument, Babcock improved the grounds by draining and grading them, installing ponds and a fish hatchery, planting trees, and constructing a scenic drive,[29] all of which quickly helped people forget that the site had served as an ugly cattle pen during the Civil War. Just east, he planned to add greenery, walkways, and a unified layout to the jumble of uneven turf and rutted pathways of the decrepit Mall.[30] Babcock also smartly oversaw the publication of a comprehensive survey of the park system, showing how the corps had made "green and beautiful" sites from "places of sand and mud."[31]

Height of Hubris

Despite Babcock's accomplishments, there was still but one boss in town, and that was Alexander Shepherd. In a town that had never had party bosses, Shepherd ran an electoral machine that turned out core supporters to ensure victory at the polls and applied a heavy hand to control appointed boards and assemblies.[32] Construction jobs and political patronage served as the carrot that went with the electoral stick, and Shepherd expertly glad-handed legislators in the local and national governments to do his bidding, trading their support of his costly projects with helping them gain admission to the upscale clubs and organizations they wanted to join.

He regularly favored bids from contractors smart enough to buy materials and services from companies in which he had a stake. To publicize his projects, he used government funds to buy advertising in local newspapers that promoted the sale of the board's construction bonds. He purchased $140,000 in ads from November 1871 to March 1872, more than all the state governments in New England spent on advertising combined.[33] Of course, with near-absolute power came great hubris, and Shepherd took actions by fiat that no local DC politician had attempted before or since.

On September 3, 1872, Shepherd aimed to have the shambling Northern Liberties Market north of downtown razed and replaced with new structures. Only one judge in the District could stop him with an injunction, so Shepherd cheerfully invited him to dinner while leveling the structure. But he didn't warn the vendors that their building was going to come down. A butcher was killed in the demolition along with the son of a former court justice, and thieves descended on the chaotic scene to purloin whatever the unprepared merchants hadn't managed to secure. The public reacted with outrage: The funeral train for those killed stretched half a mile, and local opinion soon turned furiously against the Boss, to the point where an armed guard had to escort him from his office.[34]

In November, his fortunes improved when his staunch ally President Grant won reelection in a landslide and his nemesis, *The Patriot*, went out of business. Having a free hand once more, Shepherd single-handedly altered the Mall without requesting permission from anyone. His men tore up the tracks of the B&O Railroad near Capitol Hill while other workers laid new tracks across the Mall at 6th Street.[35] The head of the railroad expressed his annoyance, but Shepherd placated him with a friendly meeting, after which the B&O chief allegedly offered the Boss a position as vice president of the railroad itself.[36] With its new ally in the Board of Public Works, the B&O received permission in 1873 to build a grand new station on the Mall itself, putting smoke-belching locomotives and rail yards on land once designated for trees and gardens.[37]

Indomitable Perseverance

A greedy but benevolent tyrant, Shepherd resembled the party bosses and ward heelers who ran most cities in the northern US at the time, minus the benevolence. A master builder in the style of his contemporary Baron Haussmann in Paris, Shepherd had fewer than three years to execute his plans, whereas Haussmann had seventeen. But, driven by Shepherd's domineering attitude and boundless energy, the magnitude of the territorial government's achievement was stunning:

150 miles of road graded and paved
208 miles of sidewalks created
120 miles of sewer lines installed
30 miles of water lines laid
39 miles of gas lines laid
60,000 trees planted
1,000 buildings renovated
1,073 houses constructed[38]

Other departments of the territorial government achieved their share of accomplishments too. Most notably, the Board of Health made some headway with disease control and sanitary inspections, along with condemning unsafe houses, inspecting meat and produce, controlling polluting businesses, and outlawing barnyard animals in the streets. The health department didn't have an Alexander Shepherd at its helm, however, so its efforts didn't receive as much publicity.[39]

Ultimately, according to one estimate, the District had by the mid-1870s become the "best-lit and best-paved city in the United States and its water supply was more plentiful than that of New York."[40] Shepherd and the board trumpeted their achievements in the press and through their own publications, and their allies in the Parvenu class were just as breathless. Mary Clemmer Ames saw Shepherd as a figure of "unvarying integrity and fearless independence," as well as "positive manliness" approaching the stature of a demigod, "with a large, well formed head, sharply-defined features, massive under jaw and square chin, indicative of [his] indomitable perseverance and firmness."[41]

The square-chinned hero capped his career in late 1873 by becoming governor of the Territory of the District of Columbia following Henry Cooke's retirement.[42] It should have been the crowning triumph in the career of the civil servant turned urban savior. Instead, the District was already sinking, and the former plumber was underwater.

Mudholes and Money Traps

The problems had begun soon after the Board of Public Works came into being. Since the board was undertaking so much work throughout the District simultaneously, construction activity tore up streets and sidewalks on nearly every block. *The Patriot* alleged that three-quarters of the capital's streets were damaged or inaccessible, and that "Mudholes and mantraps, dangerous alike by day and by night, swarm in all directions . . . a putrid stench comes from all sections of the city, offensive to the sense and dangerous to the public health."[43] This situation caused turmoil for residents, who found their roadways and sidewalks ripped up, their street grades dramatically altered, and their houses perched twenty feet above the sidewalk in some cases. Construction so damaged the foundations of some houses that they risked collapsing, and the city brazenly issued condemnation warnings to their owners if they didn't repair them within thirty days. Influential citizens benefited from the usual favoritism—in this case reimbursing repair costs—while most homeowners received nothing for their trouble.[44]

Many pavements that the board laid down were inadequate or, worse, dangerous. Chunks fell out of the wooden roadways, or they rotted altogether in a short time. The quality of the work had little to do with the amount the board paid for it. Shepherd steered work to his contractor friends for inflated amounts and even rejected bids when they came in too low. He set high financial floors for these "straw bids" and did all he could to ensure they would enrich his cronies.[45]

Congressional investigations of the board began in early 1872, and the charges were myriad: The board met infrequently and without oversight, overpaid on project bids, spent more funds and carried more debt than was legally allowed, arrogated power from other agencies, acted with haste and secrecy, lacked effective recordkeeping, and used construction work—and the jobs that went with it—to win elections and reward friends.[46] The Republicans who controlled the committees that oversaw the District naturally found little wrong with the Board of Public Works or the "high-minded" men who ran it.[47]

But Congress did set a limit to the borrowing authority of the District at ten million dollars. Including preexisting debt and the four million dollars that voters had approved, that left only one million dollars to complete all of Shepherd's projects.[48] The Boss didn't let minor concerns like debt or legality deter him, though, and he went ahead with his plans. Congress raised its appropriation for the District by $3.25 million in 1872 and 1873, and Shepherd pushed through an increase in local

In slapdash fashion, Shepherd often graded city streets without regard to those who lived along them.

property taxes to their legal maximum, hiked the sewer tax, and looked into tightening tax exemptions for churches and other institutions.[49]

In the end, it wasn't enough. With the territory spending money faster than it could take it in, the board resorted to increasingly creative means of financing, including issuing "certificates of indebtedness," or bonds backed by the estimated increase in taxes on improved land. They sold poorly, but that didn't stop the board from using them as collateral in lieu of cash to pay contractors, who later learned they were redeemable for eighty-five cents on the dollar rather than for their full face value.[50]

Bubble Economy Redux

Undeterred by controversy, Shepherd made a brash, conspicuous target for his critics. His three-hundred-acre "Bleak House" farm, six miles from the city, boasted its own orchard, fish pond, rustic barns, and pony rides for kids. In 1872 he constructed a great bluestone mansion at K Street and Connecticut Avenue, featuring a towering mansard roof, rooms with blue-satin curtains and red-velvet walls, crystal chandeliers, an art gallery, and a billiard room.[51] The mansion sat, not coincidentally, in the northwest quadrant of the capital, which saw the most development and improvement during the Boss's tenure and became home to a wide array of politicians, magnates, merchants, professionals, bureaucrats, generals, and admirals[52]—some of whom later worked in the State, War, and Navy Building, west of the White House, yet another symbol of the board's corruption for its inflated costs and construction graft. (Mark Twain thought it the nation's ugliest building, which we know today as the Eisenhower Executive Office Building.) Shepherd and his allies stood to make a killing on the appreciation of their holdings as the capital expanded northwestward, and the Board of Public Works raked in even more taxes from higher assessments on property in the area.[53]

The board-approved expansion of the street railway up Connecticut Avenue intentionally drove wealthier residents from the central city to develop lots on the fringes of town.[54] Land near the avenue doubled or quadrupled in value in a short time, creating a dizzying property boom not seen in the District since the eighteenth century. Only the ghost of James Greenleaf could match Alexander Shepherd in his flair for speculative building, but Shepherd proved much more successful at it, overseeing the development of twelve hundred buildings in 1872 alone.[55]

But in improving this section of the capital and the neighborhoods that became Dupont Circle, Embassy Row, and Kalorama, Shepherd largely ignored the part of town south and east of Capitol Hill, ensuring that it remained poor and underdeveloped for years to come. Indeed, while the west was booming, property in the eastern half of the capital either stagnated or depreciated.[56] The imbalance of construction was obvious: From November 1872 to November 1873, Northwest DC saw the addition of 603 houses, 134 more than all the rest of the capital combined.[57]

The Terra Firma of Hell

The building frenzy came to a sudden end with a financial collapse. This disaster, the Panic of 1873, even had a direct link to the territorial government, as Henry Cooke's brother, power broker Jay Cooke, forced him to resign as governor to attend to the desperate straits of their teetering Northern Pacific Railroad Company.[58] The firm collapsed anyway, and a six-year national depression ensued. Unemployment exploded, banks failed and suspended customers' credit, and the market for municipal bonds and the payment of local taxes fizzled.[59] An angry public and the public servants in their thrall quickly demanded solutions to the economic mess. Another congressional investigation of the territorial government began in February 1874.

Whereas Shepherd's smooth talk and glad-handing overcame the earlier, cursory congressional review of the District, he couldn't thwart this one. The year before, on his way out of Congress, reform Democrat Robert Roosevelt, uncle of future president Theodore, leveled particularly bitter scorn on the board. He claimed it operated on "the terra firma of Hell" and estimated the District would buckle under a debt of twenty million dollars to pay for the board's actions.[60] He was right. After countless hours of research and investigation and a three-thousand-page report, congressional examiners determined that the District did indeed carry that colossal amount of debt, twice the legal amount allowed.[61]

To get the District back in the black, Congress increased property taxes, cut municipal salaries by 20 percent,[62] and authorized fifty-year bonds for the rest of the debt. It abolished the Board of Public Works, the territorial government as a whole, and the roles of governor and legislature, giving a three-person commission temporary but total charge of District affairs.[63] In an embarrassing footnote, members of the House of Delegates tried to spirit away the legislature's desks, chairs, and office supplies on their way out the door. One politician even stuffed a feather duster down his pant leg, giving his legislative body, as well as the territorial government in general, the nickname "feather-duster legislature."[64]

Ballot Box and Blame

Unfortunately, one of the most honest former members of that government was a prime victim of the economic collapse. In 1874, Frederick

Douglass accepted a position as president of the Freedmen's Savings and Trust Bank, taking a job in public service as he had always done, not knowing that the bank was about to default.

Founded at the close of the Civil War as a depository for the funds of black citizens, the bank operated well for five years. In 1870, though, it began investing in riskier ventures, and when Shepherd's associates, including Henry Cooke, took seats on its finance committee, disaster was all but inevitable. The bank's managers schemed to find an unwitting scapegoat for their own bad investments in the Northern Pacific Railroad and other failed enterprises, and they found their mark in Douglass.[65] Losing ten thousand dollars,[66] he called being tied to the bank like being "married to a corpse" and castigated those who had brought the bank to ruin by "squandering in senseless loans on bad security the hard-earned moneys of my race."[67]

The meltdown of the Freedmen's Bank wasn't the only example of territorial leaders abusing the trust of their African-American constituents. Shepherd and his peers used them to win elections and in return provided temporary construction jobs and passed the occasional civil rights bill. But the Boss and his board did almost nothing in the long term to build up the poor and working-class parts of town where most blacks lived, especially east and south of the Capitol. With their real estate improvements focused in Northwest DC, they actually stifled the development of such neighborhoods as The Island, East Capitol Hill, and parts of downtown. Even worse, Congress, which had offered the opportunity for black voters to become major players in local elections in the late 1860s, rolled back their franchise in 1871 with the creation of the territory and then, when the territory folded three years later, curtailed their suffrage entirely.

The Demise of Suffrage

In 1874 Senator Justin Morrill of Vermont introduced a bill to reorganize the District and permanently strip voting rights from its citizens. Senator Allan Thurman of Ohio, like others supporting the bill, tried to blame the failings of the territory on the African Americans who had supported the Board of Public Works. He made the specious claim that the previous municipal governments of the District did "tolerably well," and "There was never any great complaint about them until Negro suffrage came."[68]

The elderly Frederick Douglass: icon of America, victim of DC bankers.

Thomas Bayard of Delaware spoke more bluntly as a representative of a former slave state: "negro suffrage has been a very sickening business to the unhappy people of this District and to those who brought it here; and I have no doubt that as a matter of fact this bill seeks to accomplish the complete abandonment of that most absurd attempt to govern this District though the instrumentality of its most ignorant and degraded classes."[69]

Old-line white supremacists of course supported removing the franchise from DC citizens, but they had company. Outside Congress, even the stalwart *National Republican* went along with the antivoting camp, saying the Republican Party should acknowledge the "failure" of suffrage. If it didn't, "The Party would be putting a sword in the hands of the enemy to slay itself."[70] Many local whites spoke grimly of a return to suffrage in the District, and the emergence of "Murder Bay politicians," that is, blacks who would rise to power if it occurred.[71]

A few brave politicians did speak out against the tide of reaction, noting the odium of permanently removing all voting rights for District residents. Senator Oliver Morton of Indiana said of the Morrill bill:

> *It takes from them the right of local self-government; it takes from them the power of considering and acting upon their own local and, so to speak, domestic affairs . . . In that respect this bill is anti-republican; it is anti-democratic; and I do not feel that I could vote for it without violating the very spirit of our institutions. . . . when we undertake to disenfranchise 100,000 people we are taking a step backward, and I know what will be said about it . . . that it is intended to get clear of colored suffrage. In this District, where it was first established, it is to be the first stricken down.*[72]

The Shepherd Legacy

Congress wrestled with a permanent form of District government for a few more years but rendered a verdict on Alexander Shepherd much more quickly: In 1874 it exonerated him from charges of fraud or any other misdeeds. He was simply too likable, too influential, and had too many friends in the Republican Party to be held liable for the failings of the territory, however grievous and however much his fault they were.[73] Ulysses Grant even had the nerve to nominate him as one of the District's temporary commissioners, but for once the Senate didn't assent to the president's dubious choice.[74]

But as the myth took hold that the failures and fraud of the territorial government derived from "degraded" African-American voters and a few corrupt public servants, Alexander Shepherd's reputation grew. In later years he was hailed a "latter-day L'Enfant, with more brains and

more power," and an engineering genius who had "cautiously and carefully" reconstructed and improved the city.[75] Although Shephred declared
personal bankruptcy in 1876, he amazingly restored his fortunes six years
later with a speculative gold mine in Mexico, and returned to the capital
in 1882 to be "feted, honored, and commemorated in a deluge of congrat-
ulatory parties, parades, and balls." By then memories of the nasty little
village of Washington City had faded, and writers sang the praises of the
national capital as a hub of political power and prestige, with its "dazzling
vistas and public edifices reminiscent of grand European capitals."[76]

Real District Power

In the end, Shepherd received more credit than he deserved. The far-
sighted vision of Montgomery Meigs and Nathaniel Michler provided
the underlying template for the improvement of the District, even as the
Board of Public Works took credit for their ideas and gloried in them.
In subsequent years the popular press added to the legend that the board
alone had driven all change in the capital, even assigning credit for the
army corps' major accomplishments—such as replacing the wood pavers
in the street with asphalt—to the board years after Congress had abolished it.[77]

One figure who bridged the divide between the Army Corps of Engineers (as a superintendent) and the Board of Public Works (as an advisor)
was Orville Babcock. Linked to nearly as many accomplishments and as
much corruption as Shepherd, Babcock was indicted in 1875 and tried for
his role in the Whiskey Ring to evade federal liquor taxes.[78] A year later
he was tried again for planting evidence on one of Shepherd's enemies. In
both cases he was acquitted, though a later historian said that he "fished
for gold in every stinking cesspool, and served more than any other man
to blacken the record of Grant's administration."[79]

Capital Emergent

Disregarding Babcock's antics, Congress elevated the role of the corps
when it passed the Organic Act of 1878. This act codified the District
of Columbia as the capital's sole governing entity, subject to the will of
Congress, and made the federal government responsible for funding half
of the city's budget, with the other half raised from local taxation.[80] It was

The Grant administration featured a high-wire act of
corruption, with two prominent DC officials—Shepherd
and Babcock—key players.

a long-overdue change from those dreadful decades when citizens had to
beg the legislature for any scrap of funding at all.

In executing its plan for the city, Congress handed control of municipal affairs to three appointed commissioners. Leaders of each major party
chose one, and the third, by law, would be an "Engineer Commissioner"
from the US Army.[81] With all former boards of the city abolished, the
new commissioners had direct responsibility for the capital, a power they
retained for nearly a century.

This was the ultimate payoff for the Army Corps of Engineers' steady role in building up the capital, which had only increased since the war until it now gained "almost total control over Washington's public buildings, infrastructure, and physical environment."[82] In due course, it executed plans to correct the flaws in Shepherd's shoddy construction work, expand the water supply, extend the sewer system, pave and grade more streets, and reclaim the dreaded Potomac Flats. It even began finishing the embarrassing stump of the Washington Monument, finally completing the massive obelisk in 1884, a great triumph for the city.[83] Indeed, as it acquired unprecedented power in the peacetime governance of the American capital, the corps seemed capable of achieving almost anything.[84]

The End of the Franchise

But there was one thing the corps couldn't and wouldn't do: provide the citizens of the District of Columbia with a shred of power to choose their own leaders or run their own government. Early versions of the Organic Act of 1878 called for a local elective council and a member in Congress, but these disappeared from the final version of the bill and ensured that DC residents had the same influence over their local leaders as their federal ones—none.[85] Surprisingly, the act passed with the support of a racially retrograde House of Representatives run by Democrats and a nominally more progressive Senate under Republican control. Both parties stripped the vote from capital residents because, at their core, there wasn't much difference in their motivations. A quick look back shows why.

Two rival forces had whipsawed Washington City throughout its troubled history. Initially Southern congressmen paralyzed the growth of the capital to keep it weak and undeveloped so the national government, by extension, remained feeble and inhibited with respect to the states. After the war, Northern congressmen emboldened the growth of the capital so the federal government would stand dominant and uninhibited over those states.

In both cases, the interests of local voters were irrelevant. Southerners didn't care to aid a city for which they had so little use. Residents' rights became even more constricted once Northerners decided to use their power to develop the capital. Any threat to that power—even voting in municipal elections—had to be stymied. Racial politics only added to the equation and ensured that white residents could, through statutory and constitutional law, keep African Americans from exercising their franchise in the District, even as they grew to a residential majority in future decades. In stripping away the franchise, Congress ensured that the District remained a ward of the nation, the sole province of national politicians. The day-to-day rulers changed, their motivations differed, but the disenfranchisement stood.

A Founder's Legacy

Ultimately the victor was Alexander Hamilton's political philosophy, which proved remarkably resilient. Nearly a century had passed since he pontificated on the dangers of relinquishing power to the mob, imagining a place where the federal government would reign supreme. Although the capital had suffered more than seven decades of misery, his dream had come to pass by the Gilded Age. The city changed for the better, as grand new buildings, parks, infrastructure, and neighborhoods took shape. The once dysfunctional village emerged as the world-class capital that—if not quite the baroque fantasy of Pierre L'Enfant—at least kept critics at bay and gave us a respectable urban center for the nation. As part of the deal, the city's residents stood no closer to having a stake in their governance than they had a century before. The light of their democracy was finally extinguished.

In the end, the language of Hamilton's philosophy may have been dressed up in legalese and constitutional purpose, but at root it involved two simple motivations: fear of the masses and need for dominion over them. Washington, DC, acted as the test case. It took decades of mud, chaos, and struggle, but by the end of the nineteenth century the city emerged as the paradigm for Hamilton's idea of urban development as well as his imperial, profoundly antidemocratic perspective.

Little has changed since then but for one striking mood swing: Regardless of political faction, US citizens have come to view the capital as an example of everything wrong with their national governance. The reasons may stem from the imperious attitudes of American politicians, inflated delusions of grandeur, or an ongoing frustration with the elephantine federal bureaucracy. Or perhaps the public understands something deeper about the nature of political power—perhaps realizing the darker motivations of their leaders and the absurdity of running a democracy from a place that has no use for it.

EPILOGUE

THE SEA OF PAVEMENT

By the 1920s the District of Columbia looked brand new. The commissioners oversaw a city rapidly becoming the heart of a regional metropolis, the growth of the federal government providing its lifeblood. The Gilded Age had brought new commerce and industry, the Army Corps of Engineers had overseen a wealth of infrastructure improvements and public works projects, and the McMillan Commission Plan of 1901 had redesigned the capital to its core. The Mall now conformed much more closely to Pierre L'Enfant's original design. Outmoded train stations gave way to the Beaux-Arts colossus of Union Station. Stately bridges and presidential memorials added classical dignity to the landscape. Charming parks encouraged urban leisure. New roads, streetlights, sewers, and construction codes provided the essential building blocks for a modern American city.[1]

But the one neighborhood that hadn't changed much or benefited from the City Beautiful campaigns that reshaped the rest of the capital was the former Murder Bay. This triangular precinct bordered by Pennsylvania Avenue NW, 15th Street, and B Street north of the Mall still lay in the heart of the city—between the White House and the Capitol—and it still sheltered the working class and the working poor. Congress may have outlawed prostitution in the District in 1914,[2] but the neighborhood was still known as The Division, and crime remained deeply rooted.

Nonetheless, even for a down-at-heel area, The Division was quite busy, lively even. A foundry, power plant, machine shops, plumbers, and lumberyards operated in abundance here—precisely the industrial operations that old Washington City lacked—and these businesses employed a wide range of ethnic laborers who lived in the wood and brick row houses that lined the streets.[3] Italian immigrants sold fruit from their stores and carts, and "gas stations, tattoo parlors, chop suey [restaurants], rooming houses, and cheap hotels" made a busy trade along Pennsylvania Avenue and alongside the now-illegal brothels operating on Ohio Avenue.[4]

Although The Division may have resembled a Northern city, Washington society had retrenched since the carpetbagger days of the Gilded Age, as the capital once more returned to the cultural orbit of the South. From 1870 to 1930 the proportion of Northerners in town increased by 28 percent, but it doubled for Southerners, who now played a much greater role in the city's commercial and civic life and put a greater stamp on its social landscape.[5]

Freedom's Descent

In the 1920s African Americans composed a quarter of the city's population.[6] The return to power of the old Southern gentry fell upon these residents the hardest, beginning with the segregation of most public facilities at the turn of the century, and, when former Southerner Woodrow Wilson came to power in 1913, the segregation of federal offices and restriction of black hiring or advancement in government employment.[7] Black schools went underfunded; discrimination widely affected theaters, department stores, and restaurants; and whites-only neighborhoods kept black home buyers out with restrictive covenants.[8] As Constance Green writes, "The national government took the line of the Deep South, and white persons as private citizens now looked upon Negroes scarcely as citizens at all."[9]

Then it got worse. The Washington episodes of the national "Red Summer" riots of 1919 included military servicemen attacking blacks in the streets. The police could do little to stop the violence and arrested the victims instead.[10] That same year, health reports showed that local African-American levels of infectious disease were three to six times those of whites, infant mortality rates were also high, and the life span of a black person, male or female, was only forty-four years.[11] The squalid housing conditions in precincts such as The Division obviously had a lot to do with it, since subpar health and sanitation were legion and poverty was endemic. This was especially the case in the increasingly nightmarish alley dwellings, which had plagued the city since the nineteenth century and stood just as filthy and dilapidated as ever—if conveniently out of sight to most of official Washington.

In the face of such unfair treatment, blacks had no recourse to the ballot box to demand change. They, like their white counterparts, couldn't vote in the capital or do anything to change the policies of those in power. This became most evident when, instead of improving The Division, the federal government decided to tear it down.

Dignified Ideas

In 1918 the Public Buildings Commission presented a report that harshly evaluated the neighborhood: "The character of the occupancy of the area between [Pennsylvania] Avenue and the Mall is low. . . . Nothing short of radical measures to bring this area into a higher grade of occupation will save the situation."[12] Congress responded with the Public Buildings Act of 1926, which provided fifty million dollars for the construction of new federal buildings. Half the amount went to redevelop the Division,[13] both to provide more office space for government workers and to engage in an early form of urban renewal. After all, as writer Mildred Adams said, there was no place for "the little shops with slovenly fronts that offend citizens with more dignified ideas."[14]

The US government duly purchased nearly all of the land in The Division in 1927 and planned for a new "Federal Triangle" of superblocks to rise in its place. Answering critics who questioned whether such colossal structures would suit the area, federal builders promised great parks and plazas between the buildings.[15] Two years later, Treasury Secretary Andrew Mellon funded a propaganda film to win over the remaining detractors. It extolled the virtues of the huge new buildings while deriding the old neighborhood as a decrepit patch unworthy of saving.[16] During the next eight years, the government destroyed the old neighborhood.

Some of the notable buildings that came down included Harvey's restaurant, renowned for its piles of steamed clams; such popular entertainment venues as Ford's Grand Opera House, Albaugh's Opera House, and the Bijou and President Theatres; the US Electric Lighting Company, the great powerhouse built like a brick castle; and, most lamented of all, the Centre Market.[17] Although a market had been included on early city plans in the 1790s and George Washington himself had picked out the

The heart of the old city was demolished to make way for the Federal Triangle.

site for it, neither public protests nor lawsuits could stop the government from demolishing it. On January 1, 1931, two thousand vendors and their employees—who sold meat, produce, and countless other goods—were forced from their stalls. Two months later the Victorian arches and turrets of Centre Market fell. The market was not rebuilt.*[18]

The Triangle Rises

In place of the diverse, polyglot old neighborhood rose the oversized buildings of the Federal Triangle, a hodgepodge of vaguely classical structures, each six stories high and faced in stone. Their designs mixed Classical Greek with Italian Renaissance and threw in Beaux-Arts and Art Deco motifs as well. The Public Buildings Commission called it the ideal way to show "the revival of classical architecture for the use

---

* Thankfully federal developers ran out of funds before they could tear down the great Romanesque revival post office at Pennsylvania Avenue and 12th Street.

of modern business demands."[19] Official Washington rejoiced, but not everyone was impressed. Some architects later derided the Triangle for embracing "façadism" and "brutal masses . . . built in an eclectic style as boring as it was massive and unoriginal."[20] Moreover, the development completely ignored L'Enfant's original street grid, wiped out thirty-one city blocks, and removed dozens of streets that had existed since the birth of the capital, replacing them with just a few north-south corridors. Eight giant buildings occupied the rest of the space, and the promised parks never came. Not only did the Triangle stand apart from the rest of the city's layout, it acted as a wall between the redesigned Mall and the active commercial district north of Pennsylvania Avenue, making for a crowded space for federal workers during the day but an unfriendly dead zone at night.[21]

Despite its gargantuan blandness, the Federal Triangle made more than an architectural statement. Its planners intended it as a dramatic gesture to erase the embarrassing legacy of the capital by removing the shambling homes and businesses of its antique core and erecting in their place an icon to an empire on the rise. In this way, the capital's leaders succeeding in rewriting their city's visual history, replacing broken cobbles with a sea of pavement, trading ramshackle hotels and markets for imperial monuments, and helping people forget that a place called Washington City ever existed.

Walking from Pennsylvania Avenue to Constitution Avenue now, you'd never guess that colorful street life once thrived in the neighborhood—or that it had ever been a neighborhood at all. But in a previous age, before the wrecking ball arrived, life hummed along these streets. A ragtime band played in a music hall on one corner, a bordello piano on the next. Shouts and laughter from gambling dens and saloons filled the air. By contrast, these days, if you come to the area at night, you'll only hear tourists running to catch the next subway train, as the wind whistles through the Triangle's gaping arches and barren plazas past statues of people who never lived there.

ACKNOWLEDGMENTS

Empire of Mud took five years from conception to completion, and there were a lot of people who helped along the way. The most prominent were my manager, Adam Chromy, at Movable Type Management, whose energy, insight, and acumen were essential to the project; editor James Jayo, who guided the book skillfully and offered critical feedback and revisions; project editor Meredith Dias, who oversaw the book with great dexterity; and everyone else at Lyons Press who contributed their skill and energy to the endeavor. I'd also like to thank Jason Ashlock, who provided essential help in getting the project started.

A few dozen librarians and archivists offered key assistance. The most important of these were Marilyn Ibach at the Library of Congress's Prints and Photographs Division; Mark Greek, photo archivist of the Washingtoniana Collection at the DC Public Library; Laura Barry, research services librarian of the Kiplinger Research Library at the Historical Society of Washington; Julia Downie, media librarian of Special Collections at the Alexandria Library; Lieutenant Nicholas Breul, historian of the Metropolitan Police; Audrey Davis, director of the Alexandria Black History Museum; Ruth Reeder, education coordinator at the Alexandria Archaeology Museum; Frances McMillen, preservation specialist for the District's Historic Preservation Office; and various staff members at the National Archives. Also helpful were DC historian Mark Herlong, who offered a bevy of colorful tales from the late nineteenth century; librarian Clara Stemwedel, who helped uncover key dissertations and research papers; and cartographer Daniel Rosen and his tireless, expert abilities.

Others who have provided valuable assistance include the authors James Howard Kunstler, George Pelecanos, Ron Franscell, Ro Cuzon, Zora O'Neill, and Andrew Rosenberg, as well as Scott Hoffman, for the initial push forward. Finally, my friends provided useful feedback on the text, among them Matt McMillen, Noel Ponthieux, Brenna Dickey, John Miller, Teresa Christie, Leopoldo Marino, Robin Richardson, and Lisa Scarpelli. Great praise too goes to my family members and especially my parents, who continue to provide valuable thoughts, insights, and love.

NOTES

Introduction: Capital Movers

1 Mary A. Y. Gallagher, "Reinterpreting the 'Very Trifling Mutiny' at Philadelphia in June 1783," *Pennsylvania Magazine of History and Biography* 119:1/2 (1995): 8–11, 12–13.

2 Kenneth R. Bowling, "New Light on the Philadelphia Mutiny of 1783: Federal-State Confrontation at the Close of the War for Independence," *Pennsylvania Magazine of History and Biography* 101:4 (Oct. 1977): 425.

3 Bowling, "New Light," 426.

4 Ibid., 428.

5 Ibid., 431.

6 Ibid., 430.   :

7 Gallagher, "Reinterpreting," 24.

8 Bowling, "New Light," 433–34.

9 Ibid., 433.

10 Gallagher, "Reinterpreting," 25.

11 Bowling, "New Light," 437–38, 448.

12 William C. di Giacomantonio, "'To Sell Their Birthright for a Mess of Potage': The Origins of D.C. Governance and the Organic Act of 1801," *Washington History* 12:1 (Spring/Summer 2000): 32.

13 Bowling, *Creation of Washington*, 34.

14 Bowling, "New Light," 445.

15 Ibid., 449.

16 Rubil Morales Vasquez, "Imagining Washington: Monuments and Nation Building in the Early Capital," *Washington History* 12:1 (Spring/Summer 2000): 17; Donald R. Kennon, review of *Congress and the Governance of the Nation's Capital, in Washington History* 7:2 (1995/1996): 80.

17 Bowling, *Creation of Washington*, 198; Bowling, "New Light," 420.

18 Bowling, "New Light," 419.

19 Trollope, *North America*, 449, 450.

Chapter 1: The Capital Archipelago

1 Green, *Washington: Village and Capital*, 18, 20.

2 Gutheim, *Worthy of the Nation*, 21.

3 Highsmith and Landphair, *Pennsylvania Avenue*, 53.

4 Hurd, *Washington Cavalcade*, 58.

5 C. M. Harris, "Washington's 'Federal City,' Jefferson's 'Federal Town,'" *Washington History* 12:1 (2000): 49–53.

6 Ibid., 50.
7 Gutheim, *Potomac*, 12.
8 Priscilla W. McNeil, "Rock Creek Hundred: Land Conveyed for the Federal City," *Washington History* 3:1 (1991): 42–51.
9 Gutheim, *Potomac*, 327.
10 Smith, *Washington at Home*, 33.
11 Gutheim, *Potomac*, 327.
12 Vlach, "Mysterious Mr. Jenkins."
13 Margaret Brent Downing, "Significant Achievements of the Daniel Carrolls of L'Enfant's Era," *Catholic Historical Review* 16:3 (1930): 227–28.
14 Bob Arnebeck, "Tracking the Speculators: Greenleaf and Nicholson in the Federal City," *Washington History* 3:1 (1991): 113.
15 Ibid.
16 Gutheim, *Potomac*, 327.
17 Junior League of Washington, *City of Washington*, 48.
18 Arnebeck, "Speculators," 116.
19 Ibid., 117–18.
20 Ibid., 121; Reps, *Washington on View*, 32.
21 Reps, *Washington on View*, 32.
22 Arnebeck, "Speculators," 119.
23 Allen C. Clark, *Thomas Law: A Biographical Sketch* (Washington, DC; W. F. Roberts, 1900): 15
24 Bryan, *History of the National Capital*, 1:280.
25 Reps, *Washington on View*, 32.
26 Arnebeck, "Speculators," 120–21.
27 Gutheim, *Potomac*, 327.
28 Goode, *Capital Losses*, 5, 171
29 Reps, *Washington on View*, 32; Janson, *Stranger in America*, 214.
30 Gibbs, *Memoirs of the Administrations*, 2:44.
31 Janson, *Stranger in America*, 212, 214.
32 Goode, *Capital Losses*, 7.
33 Highsmith and Landphair, *Pennsylvania Avenue*, 50.
34 Ethel M. B. Morganston, "Davy Burnes, His Ancestors and Their Descendants," *Records of the Columbia Historical Society, Washington, D.C.* 40 (1948/1950): 110; Priscilla W. McNeil, "Rock Creek Hundred: Land Conveyed for the Federal City," *Washington History* 3:1 (1991): 42–51.
35 Morganston, "Davy Burnes," 111, 113.
36 Susan L. Klaus, "'Some of the Smartest Folks Here': The Van Nesses and Community Building in Early Washington," *Washington History* 3:2 (1991/1992): 25; Morganston, "Davy Burnes," 112–13.
37 Allen C. Clark, "General John Peter Van Ness, a Mayor of the City of Washington, His Wife, Marcia, and Her Father, David Burnes," *Records of the Columbia Historical Society, Washington, D.C.* 22 (1919): 136.
38 Allen B. Slauson, "Curious Customs of the Past as Gleaned from Early Issues of the Newspapers in the District of Columbia," *Records of the Columbia Historical Society, Washington, D.C.* 9 (1906): 114.

39 Gutheim, *Potomac*, 13.
40 Frances Carpenter Huntington, "The Heiress of Washington City: Marcia Burnes Van Ness, 1782–1832," *Records of the Columbia Historical Society, Washington, D.C.* 47 (1969/1970): 80, 98.
41 Alison K. Hoagland, "Nineteenth-Century Building Regulations in Washington, D.C.," *Records of the Columbia Historical Society, Washington, D.C.* 52 (1989): 58–59.
42 Goode, *Capital Losses*, 5.
43 Gutheim, *Federal City*, 78; Letter to George Washington from Pierre L'Enfant, Nov. 21, 1791. National Archives, Founders Online, accessed at http://founders.archives.gov/documents/Washington/05-09-02-0124.
44 Goode, *Capital Losses*, 5.
45 Young, *Washington Community*, 22.
46 Reps, *Washington on View*, 32.
47 Pamela Scott, "'This Vast Empire': The Iconography of the Mall: 1791–1848," in Longstreth, *Mall in Washington*, 54, n12.
48 Harris, "Washington's 'Federal City,'" 49, 51.
49 John W. Reps, "Thomas Jefferson's Checkerboard Towns," *Journal of the Society of Architectural Historians* 20:3 (1961): 108.
50 Rubil Morales Vasquez, "Imagining Washington: Monuments and Nation Building in the Early Capital," *Washington History* 12:1 (2000): 21.
51 Ibid., 24.
52 Harris, "Washington's 'Federal City,'" 52.
53 Hines, *Early Recollections*, 61–62; *Washington Federalist*, April 14, 1802, and November 23, 1802.
54 Hines, *Early Recollections*, 62–63.
55 Goode, *Capital Losses*, 23.
56 Hurd, *Washington Cavalcade*, 19.
57 Gutheim, *Potomac*, 326.
58 Weld, *Travels through the States*, 72–89.
59 Gutheim, *Potomac*, 327.
60 Reps, *Washington on View*, 60.
61 Young, *Washington Community*, 21.
62 Reps, *Washington on View*, 57.
63 Scott, "'This Vast Empire,'" 40–41.
64 Smith, *Washington at Home*, 55–56.
65 Bergheim, *Washington Historical Atlas*, 128–29.
66 Smith, *Washington at Home*, 57.
67 Green, *Washington: Village and Capital*, 36.
68 Janson, *Stranger in America*, 215.
69 Young, *Washington Community*, 23.
70 Smith, *Washington at Home*, 66.
71 Kay Fanning, "The Mall: National Mall & Memorial Parks," in *Cultural Landscape Inventory* (Washington, DC: National Park Service, 2006), 25–26.
72 Green, *Washington: Village and Capital*, 106.
73 Scott, "'This Vast Empire,'" 46.

74 *National Intelligencer*, March 24, 1841. Address of Joel R. Poinsett before the National Institution.

75 Gibbs, *Memoirs of the Administrations*, 2:377.

76 Diane K. Skvarla, "Nineteenth Century Visitors," *Washington History* 1:1 (1989): 10.

77 Reps, *Washington on View*, 70–74.

78 Dickens, *American Notes*, 279.

79 Green, *Washington: Village and Capital*, 38.

80 Bryan, *History of the National Capital*, 2:14.

81 Smith, *First Forty Years*, 10.

82 Highsmith and Landphair, *Pennsylvania Avenue*, 53.

83 Ibid., 55.

84 Mackay, *Western World*, 2:110–11.

85 Goode, *Capital Losses*, 492.

86 Hurd, *Washington Cavalcade*, 57.

87 Passonneau, *Washington through Two Centuries*, 68.

88 Green, *Washington: Village and Capital*, 41.

89 Gutheim, *Federal City*, 15.

90 Green, *Washington: Village and Capital*, 41.

91 Hurd, *Washington Cavalcade*, 27; Green, *Washington: Village and Capital*, 41.

92 Hurd, *Washington Cavalcade*, 58.

93 Vasquez, "Imagining Washington," 145–46.

94 Gutheim, *Potomac*, 332–33.

95 Bryan, *History of the National Capital*, 2:16.

96 Ibid., 18.

97 Green, *Washington: Village and Capital*, 140.

98 Young, *Washington Community*, 23.

99 Green, *Washington: Village and Capital*, 40.

100 Ibid., 39, 89–90.

101 Young, *Washington Community*, 24.

102 Gutheim, *Potomac*, 17.

103 Bryan, *History of the National Capital*, 2:20.

104 Arnebeck, *Through a Fiery Trial*, 626.

105 Ibid., 627.

106 Ibid.

107 Young, *Washington Community*, 24.

108 Hurd, *Washington Cavalcade*, 26–27.

109 Young, *Washington Community*, 25.

110 Thomas Moore, "To Thomas Hume, Esq., M.D., On the City of Washington," in *The Poetical Works of Thomas Moore* (London: Oxford University Press, 1915): 117.

Chapter 2: A Plague of Waters

1 District of Columbia Dept. of the Environment, et al. *Federal Triangle Stormwater Drainage Study* (Washington, DC: Oct. 6, 2011): 7. Accessed at www.ncpc.gov/DocumentDepot/Planning/flooding/federal_triangle_drainage_study_presentation.pdf

2 Gutheim, *Federal City*, 8.

3 Hines, *Early Recollections*, 45.

4 Ibid., 47–48.

5 Ibid., 44, 67, 95.

6 Julie D. Abell and Petar D. Glumac, "Beneath the MCI Center: Insights into Washington's Historic Water Supply," *Washington History* 9:1 (1997): 26.

7 Garnett P. Williams, "Washington D.C.'s Vanishing Springs and Waterways," in Moore and Jackson, *Geology, Hydrology and History*, 77, 84–85

8 Ibid., 82.

9 Don Alexander Hawkins, "The Landscape of the Federal City: A 1792 Walking Tour," *Washington History* 3:1 (1991): 23.

10 John C. Reed Jr. and Stephen F. Obermeier, "The Geology Beneath Washington, D.C.—The Foundation of a Nation's Capital," in Moore and Jackson, *Geology, Hydrology and History*, 28; Gutheim, *Worthy of the Nation*, 41; Robbins and Welter, *Building Stones*, 6–7.

11 Gutheim, *Worthy of the Nation*, 19.

12 Robbins and Welter, *Building Stones*, 41.

13 Gutheim, *Potomac*, 8, 24.

14 Williams, "Vanishing Springs," 90.

15 Green, *Washington: Village and Capital*, 6.

16 Warden, *Chorographical and Statistical Description*, 11.

17 Hawkins, "Landscape," 16.

18 Harrison, *History of the Commercial Waterways*, 10.

19 Reed and Obermeier, "Geology Beneath Washington, D.C.," 28.

20 Cornelius W. Heine, "The Chesapeake and Ohio Canal: Testimony to an Age Yet to Come," *Records of the Columbia Historical Society, Washington, D.C.* 66, 68 (1966/1968): 58.

21 Richard J. Dent, "On the Archaeology of Early Canals: Research on the Pawtomack Canal in Great Falls, Virginia," *Historical Archaeology* 20:1 (1986): 52.

22 Heine, " Chesapeake and Ohio Canal," 58.

23 Dent, "Archaeology of Early Canals," 52.

24 Ibid., 50, 52.

25 Heine, " Chesapeake and Ohio Canal," 58.

26 Dent, "Archaeology of Early Canals," 53.

27 Gutheim, *Potomac*, 328.

28 Warden, *Chorographical and Statistical Description*, 7; Hibben, *Navy-Yard, Washington*, 26.

29 Warden, *Chorographical and Statistical Description*, 24.

30 Zach Spratt, "Ferries in the District of Columbia," *Records of the Columbia Historical Society, Washington, D.C.* 53/56 (1953/1956): 190–92.

31 Gutheim, *Federal City*, 4.

32 Williams, "Vanishing Springs," 87.

33 Ibid.

34 Cornelius W. Heine, "The Washington City Canal," *Records of the Columbia Historical Society, Washington, D.C.* 53, 56 (1953/1956): 2.

35 Bryan, *History of the National Capital*, 1:289.

36   Ibid., 288.
37   Heine, "Washington City Canal," 3.
38   Green, *Washington: Village and Capital*, 28.
39   Clark, *Greenleaf and Law*, 257.
40   Law, "Observations on the Intended Canal," 161–62.
41   Heine, "Washington City Canal," 5–7.
42   Frederick May, Letter to William H. Crawford, Secretary of the Treasury, December 2, 1818.
43   Reps, *Washington on View*, 54.
44   Bryan, *History of the National Capital*, 2:104.
45   Heine, "Washington City Canal," 9.
46   Bryan, *History of the National Capital*, 2:113.
47   Cowdrey, *City for the Nation*, 14; Williams, "Vanishing Springs," 87.
48   Gutheim, *Worthy of the Nation*, 40–41.
49   Green, *Washington: Village and Capital*, 72.
50   Heine, "Washington City Canal," 10.
51   Harrison, *History of the Commercial Waterways*, 14.
52   Harrison, *United States Waterways and Ports*, 10
53   Clark, *Greenleaf and Law*, 257.
54   Junior League of Washington, *City of Washington*, 146.
55   Green, *Washington: Village and Capital*, 116.
56   Ibid., 114–15.
57   Bryan, *History of the National Capital*, 2:111.
58   Vasquez, "Monuments, Markets, and Manners," 244.
59   Green, *Washington: Village and Capital*, 114.
60   Arthur G. Peterson, "The Old Alexandria-Georgetown Canal and Potomac Aqueduct," *Virginia Magazine of History and Biography* 40:4 (1932): 310.
61   Heine, "Washington City Canal," 13.
62   Ibid., 12.
63   Green, *Washington: Village and Capital*, 128.
64   Harzbecker, "Life and Death," 73.
65   Tindall, *Standard History of the City of Washington*, 245.
66   Ibid.; Bryan, *History of the National Capital*, 2:125.
67   Charles Augustus Murray, *Travels in North America During the Years 1834, 1835 & 1836*, Vol. 1 (London: Richard Bentley, 1839): 146.
68   Green, *Washington: Village and Capital*, 129.
69   Ibid.; Bryan, *History of the National Capital*, 2:126.
70   Heine, "Chesapeake and Ohio Canal," 59–60.
71   Gutheim, *Potomac*, 260.
72   Goode, *Capital Losses*, 454; Bryan, *History of the National Capital*, 2:115–17.
73   Gutheim, *Potomac*, 331.
74   Warden, *Chorographical and Statistical Description*, 63.
75   Ibid., 10.
76   Ibid., 24; Gutheim, *Worthy of the Nation*, 50.
77   George J. Moorhead, "Overflows from Combined Sewers in Washington, D.C.," *Journal of the Water Pollution Control Federation* 33:7 (1961): 713.

78 Abell and Glumac, "Beneath the MCI Center," 29.
79 Bryan, *History of the National Capital*, 2:303.

Chapter 3: A Mechanic's Guide to Washington City

1 Joint Force Headquarters–National Capital Region and The US Army Military District of Washington, "History of Fort Lesley J. McNair," accessed at http://mdwhome.mdw.army.mil/docs/media-documents/history-of-fort-mcnair-fact-sheet.pdf?sfvrsn=2.
2 Pitch, *Burning of Washington*, 20, 82–85, 117.
3 Smith, *Forty Years*, 115.
4 Junior League of Washington, *City of Washington*, 146
5 Pitch, *Burning of Washington*, 150–51.
6 Warden, *Chorographical and Statistical Description*, 31.
7 Smith, *Forty Years*, 115.
8 M. I. Weller, "Unwelcome Visitors to Early Washington," *Records of the Columbia Historical Society, Washington, D.C.* 1 (1897): 56.
9 Royall, *Sketches of History*, 156, 158.
10 Sarah Harvey Porter, "The Life and Times of Anne Royall, 1769–1854," *Records of the Columbia Historical Society, Washington, D.C.* 10 (1907): 10.
11 Elizabeth J. Clapp, "'A Virago-Errant in Enchanted Armor'?: Anne Royall's 1829 Trial as a Common Scold," *Journal of the Early Republic* 23:2 (summer 2003): 209–10.
12 Porter, "Life and Times," 17.
13 Royall, *Sketches of History*, 156.
14 Ibid.
15 Warden, *Chorographical and Statistical Description*, 42.
16 Margo, *Wages and Labor Markets*, 12.
17 Delano, *Washington Directory*, 2–84.
18 Ibid., 21, 59, 104, 109.
19 Margaret H. McAleer, "'The Green Streets of Washington': The Experience of Irish Mechanics in Antebellum Washington," in Cary, *Washington Odyssey*, 42–45.
20 Warden, *Chorographical and Statistical Description*, 27.
21 Charles H. Leedecker, et al., *Phase I Archaeological Investigation for the National Museum of African American History and Culture* (Washington: Smithsonian Institution, 2007), 39; Harzbecker, "Life and Death," 173.
22 Smith, *Forty Years*, 336.
23 McAleer, "'Green Streets,'" 47.
24 Ibid., 48.
25 Royall, *Sketches of History*, 182.
26 Hamilton, *Men and Manners*, 2:70–72.
27 Carson, *Ambitious Appetites*, 137.
28 Gibbs Myers, "Pioneers in the Federal Area," *Records of the Columbia Historical Society, Washington, D.C.* 44/45 (1942/1943): 136.
29 Hamilton, *Men and Manners*, 2:71, 72.

30 Mona E. Dingle, "*Gemeinschaft and Gemutlichkeit*: German American Community and Culture, 1850–1920," in Cary, *Washington Odyssey*, 115–18.

31 Harzbecker, "Life and Death," 87.

32 Smith, *Forty Years*, 336–37.

33 Porter, "Life and Times," 13; Cynthia Earman, "An Uncommon Scold: Treasure-Talk Describes Life of Anne Royall," *Library of Congress Information Bulletin* 59:1 (2000), accessed at www.loc.gov/loc/lcib/0001/royall.html.

34 Porter, "Life and Times," 14.

35 Royall, *Sketches of History*," 156.

36 Cable, *Avenue of the Presidents*, 52.

37 Green, *Washington: Village and Capital*, 70, 90.

38 Plummer, "History of Public Health," 26.

39 Green, *Washington: Village and Capital*, 91.

40 Royall, *Sketches of History*, 143, 144.

41 David R. Goldfield, "Antebellum Washington in Context: The Pursuit of Prosperity and Identity," in Gillette, *Southern City, National Ambition*, 15–16.

42 Myers, "Pioneers," 149.

43 Elliot, *Historical Sketches*, 211.

44 Byron Sunderland, "Washington as I First Knew It, 1852–1855," *Records of the Columbia Historical Society, Washington, D.C.* 5 (1902): 204.

45 Royall, *Black Book*, 93.

46 Ibid., 20, 246.

47 Clapp, "'Virago-Errant,'" 216.

48 Earman, "An Uncommon Scold."

49 James, *Anne Royall's U.S.A.*, 253.

50 Earman, "An Uncommon Scold."

51 Clapp, "'Virago-Errant,'" 216–17, 229.

52 Ibid., 219, 221.

53 Porter, "Life and Times," 25.

54 Clapp, "'Virago-Errant,'" 224.

55 Ibid., 226–27.

56 James, *Anne Royall's U.S.A.*, 257.

57 Earman, "An Uncommon Scold."

58 Porter, "Life and Times," 158.

59 Bernard L. Herman, "Southern City, National Ambition: Washington's Early Town Houses," in Gillette, *Southern City, National Ambition*, 45.

60 Carson, *Ambitious Appetites*, 4.

61 McAleer, "'Green Streets,'" 48–50.

62 Carson, *Ambitious Appetites*, 4.

63 Herman, "Southern City," 31.

64 Busey, *Pictures of the City*, 218–22; Green, *Washington: Village and Capital*, 160.

65 Royall, *Sketches of History*, 130

66 E. D. Merrill, "Changing Fashions in Transportation," *Records of the Columbia Historical Society, Washington, D.C.* 48/49 (1946/1947): 160.

67 William Tindall, "Beginnings of Street Railways in the National Capital," *Records of the Columbia Historical Society, Washington, D.C.* 21 (1918): 25.

68 Warden, *Chorographical and Statistical Description*, 53–54.
69 Oliver W. Holmes, "Stagecoach Days in the District of Columbia," *Records of the Columbia Historical Society, Washington, D.C.* 50 (1948/1950): 17.
70 Twining, *Travels in America*, 95–97.
71 Carson, *Ambitious Appetites*, 34, 36.
72 Watterston, *New Guide to Washington*, 87.
73 Carson, *Ambitious Appetites*, 6–7.
74 Faux, *Memorable Days in America*, 394.
75 Walter F. McArdle, "The Development of the Business Sector in Washington, D.C., 1800–1973," *Records of the Columbia Historical Society, Washington, D.C.* 49 (1973/1974): 564.
76 Watterston, *New Guide to Washington*, 87.
77 Junior League of Washington, *City of Washington*, 101.
78 Goode, *Capital Losses*, 302.
79 Highsmith and Landphair, *Pennsylvania Avenue*, 77.
80 Bryan, *History of the National Capital*, 2:335.
81 Goode, *Capital Losses*, 302.
82 Thomas A. Bogar, "The Origins of Theatre in the District of Columbia," *Washington History* 22 (2010): 8–9, 11.
83 Roger Meersman and Robert Boyer, "The National Theatre in Washington: Buildings and Audiences, 1835–1972," *Records of the Columbia Historical Society, Washington, D.C.* 48 (1971/1972): 191, 194–95.
84 A. I. Mudd, "Early Theatres in Washington City," *Records of the Columbia Historical Society, Washington, D.C.* 5 (1902): 64, 65.
85 Meersman and Boyer, "National Theatre," 204.
86 Ibid., 217.
87 Trollope, *Domestic Manners*, 2:29–30.
88 Aloysius I. Mudd, "The Theatres of Washington from 1835 to 1850," *Records of the Columbia Historical Society, Washington, D.C.* 6 (1903): 239.
89 Richard Moody, quoted in Meersman and Boyer, "National Theatre," 218.
90 James Waldo Fawcett, "The Circus in Washington," *Records of the Columbia Historical Society, Washington, D.C.* 50 (1948/1950): 269.
91 Meersman and Boyer, "National Theatre," 195.
92 Joseph Earl Arrington, "Henry Lewis' Moving Panorama of the Mississippi River," *Louisiana History: The Journal of the Louisiana Historical Society* 6:3 (1965): 250, 266, 267.
93 Hines, *Early Recollections*, 42–43.
94 Quoted in Bryan, *History of the National Capital*, 1:610.
95 Larkin, *Reshaping of Everyday Life*, 283.
96 Poore, *Reminiscences of Sixty Years*, 1:61.
97 Royall, *Sketches of History*," 158.
98 Porter, "Life and Times," 29, 30, 32.
99 James, *Anne Royall's U.S.A.*, 273, 307.
100 Ibid., 379.

Chapter 4: Driving Souls

1 James, *Anne Royall's U.S.A.*, 63, 242.
2 James Oliver Horton, "The Genesis of Washington's African American Community," in Cary, *Washington Odyssey*, 20, 21.
3 Green, *Secret City*, 13, 33.
4 H. Con. Res., 111th Congress, 1st session, May 21, 2009: 1–3.
5 Edward E. Baptist, "'Cuffy,' 'Fancy Maids,' and 'One-Eyed Men': Rape, Commodification and the Domestic Slave Trade in the United States," *American Historical Review* 106:5 (2001): 1636.
6 James Cox, "Corporations Challenged by Reparations Activists," *USA Today*, February 21, 2002.
7 Virginia Groark, "Slave Policies," *New York Times*, May 5, 2002.
8 Warden, *Chorographical and Statistical Description*, 44–46.
9 Green, *Secret City*, 20.
10 David R. Goldfield, "Antebellum Washington in Context: The Pursuit of Prosperity and Identity," in Gillette, *Southern City, National Ambition*, 9–10.
11 Harrold, *Subversives*, 30.
12 Alexandria Ship Records, 1732–1861, transcribed 1973–1989 by Betty Harrington Macdonald. Alexandria Library, Local History/Special Collections, Boxes 218, 219. "Inward Manifests, Alexandria Port," 1800–1809. Horne record from March 25, 1809.
13 John Michael Vlach, "From Slavery to Tenancy: African-American Housing in Washington, D.C., 1790–1890," in Longstreth, *Housing Washington*, 3, 6.
14 John Michael Vlach, "Evidence of Slave Housing in Washington," *Washington History* 5:2 (1993/1994): 66–67.
15 Wade, *Slavery in the Cities*, 59–60.
16 Vlach, "From Slavery to Tenancy," 7–9.
17 Lionel Moses, "The Octagon, Washington, D.C. Headquarters of the American Institute of Architects," *Art World* 2:3 (1917): 296.
18 Torrey, *Portraiture of Domestic Slavery*, 57; Andrews, *Slavery and the Domestic Slave Trade*, 113–14.
19 "Domestic Slave Trading Businesses," Collection of Freedom House Museum (Franklin & Armfield site), Alexandria, VA, accessed at www.nvul.org/freedomhouse.
20 Baptist, "'Cuffy,' 'Fancy Maids,'" 1619, 1629, 1634, 1638–39.
21 Collection of Freedom House Museum (Franklin & Armfield site), Alexandria, VA, accessed at www.nvul.org/freedomhouse.
22 Andrews, *Slavery and the Domestic Slave Trade*, 138–43.
23 Northup, *Twelve Years a Slave*, 42–43.
24 Walter C. Clephane, "The Local Aspect of Slavery in the District of Columbia," *Records of the Columbia Historical Society, Washington, D.C.* 3 (1900): 237.
25 Baptist, "'Cuffy,' 'Fancy Maids,'" 1634.
26 Abdy, *Journal of a Residence*, 100.
27 Clephane, "Local Aspect of Slavery," 239–40.
28 Abdy, *Journal of a Residence*, 97.
29 Goode, *Capital Losses*, 198.

30 Vlach, "From Slavery to Tenancy," 11.
31 Jeannie Tree Rives, "Old-Time Places and People in Washington," *Records of the Columbia Historical Society, Washington, D.C.* 3 (1900): 75–76.
32 Torrey, *Portraiture of Domestic Slavery*, 42–44.
33 Wilhelmus Bogart Bryan, "A Fire in an Old Time F Street Tavern and What It Revealed," *Records of the Columbia Historical Society, Washington, D.C.* 9 (1906): 208.
34 Abdy, *Journal of a Residence*, 91.
35 Green, *Secret City*, 29–30.
36 Cable, *Avenue of the Presidents*, 51.
37 Clephane, "Local Aspect of Slavery," 243.
38 Torrey, *Portraiture of Domestic Slavery*, 57.
39 Green, *Secret City*, 29.
40 Cable, *Avenue of the Presidents*, 51.
41 Bryan, "Fire in an Old Time F Street Tavern," 209; Green, *Secret City*, 23.
42 Green, *Washington: Village and Capital*, 77.
43 Harrold, *Subversives*, 18, 28.
44 Ibid., 18, 23.
45 Lundy, *Life, Travels, and Opinions of Benjamin Lundy*, 30.
46 William Lloyd Garrison, editorial, *The Liberator*, January 1, 1831.
47 Harrold, *Subversives*, 56.
48 Ibid., 45–46.
49 Gilje, *Rioting in America*, 89.
50 Jefferson Morley, "The 'Snow Riot,'" *Washington Post*, February 6, 2005.
51 Mary Beth Corrigan, "The Ties That Bind: The Pursuit of Community and Freedom Among Slaves and Free Blacks in the District of Columbia, 1800–1860," in Gillette, *Southern City, National Ambition*, 79–80.
52 Morley, "'Snow Riot.'"
53 Corrigan, "Ties That Bind," 80.
54 John Davis, "Eastman Johnson's Negro Life at the South and Urban Slavery in Washington, D.C.," *Art Bulletin* 80:1 (1998): 72, 74.
55 Bryan, *History of the National Capital*, 2:143.
56 Harrold, *Subversives*, 31–32.
57 Martin Van Buren, *First Inaugural Address*, March 4, 1837.
58 H. Siebert, *Underground Railroad*, 125–26.
59 Goldfield, *Cotton Fields and Skyscrapers*, 45.
60 Harrold, *Subversives*, 46, 55.
61 Sylvester, *District of Columbia Police*, 29.
62 Harrold, *Subversives*, 91.
63 Hilary Russell, "Underground Railroad Activists in Washington, D.C.," *Washington History* 13:2 (2001/2002): 30–31.
64 Smallwood, *Narrative of Thomas Smallwood*, 21.
65 Ibid., 32.
66 Harrold, *Subversives*, 82, 90.
67 Smallwood, *Narrative of Thomas Smallwood*, 32.
68 Russell, "Underground Railroad Activists," 31.
69 Smallwood, *Narrative of Thomas Smallwood*, 46.

70 Torrey, *Memoir of Rev. Charles T. Torrey*, 81.

71 Harrold, *Subversives*, 86, 90.

72 Horton, "Genesis,"23.

73 Allen, *History of Slave Laborers*, 8–9.

74 Bob Arnebeck, "The Use of Slaves to Build the Capitol and White House, 1791–1801: Part One, Stumbling to a Policy of Hiring Slave Laborers," accessed at http://bobarnebeck.com/slaves.html.

75 Letitia W. Brown, "Residence Patterns of Negroes in the District of Columbia," *Records of the Columbia Historical Society, Washington, D.C.* 69/70 (1969/1970): 71.

76 Phillips, *Freedom's Port*, 25.

77 Wade, *Slavery in the Cities*, 38.

78 Brown, "Residence Patterns," 73.

79 Vlach, "From Slavery to Tenancy," 11.

80 Horton, "Genesis," 25; Green, *Secret City*, 16.

81 Wade, *Slavery in the Cities*, 48.

82 Douglass, *My Bondage and My Freedom*, 318, 328.

83 Green, *Secret City*, 16.

84 Jonathan D. Martin, *Divided Mastery: Slave Hiring in the American South* (Cambridge, MA: Harvard University Press, 2004), 46.

85 Green, *Secret City*, 33.

86 Corrigan, "Ties That Bind," 73.

87 Ibid., 73–76.

88 Harrold, *Subversives*, 14.

89 Corrigan, "Ties That Bind," 73.

90 Gibbs Myers, "Pioneers in the Federal Area," *Records of the Columbia Historical Society, Washington, D.C.* 44/45 (1942/1943): 139.

91 Fields, *Slavery and Freedom on the Middle Ground*, 4.

92 Green, *Secret City*, 53–54.

93 Dorothy Provine, "The Economic Position of the Free Blacks in the District of Columbia," *The Journal of Negro History* 58:1 (1973): 63.

94 Melvin R. Williams, "A Statistical Study of Blacks in Washington, D.C., in 1860," *Records of the Columbia Historical Society, Washington, D.C.* 50 (1980): 175.

95 Brown, "Residence Patterns," 75–76.

96 Provine, "Economic Position," 64.

97 Harrold, *Subversives*, 40–42.

98 Horton, "Genesis," 33.

99 Ibid.

100 Green, *Washington: Village and Capital*, 43–44, 162.

101 Harrold, *Subversives*, 26–27.

102 Horton, "Genesis," 36.

103 Druscilla J. Null, "Myrtilla's Miner's 'School for Colored Girls': A Mirror on Antebellum Washington," *Records of the Columbia Historical Society, Washington, D.C.* 52 (1989): 258, 259, 262.

104 Harrold, *Subversives*, 192; Green, Secret City, 51.

105 Null, "Myrtilla's Miner's 'School for Colored Girls,'" 259, 264, 266–68.

106 Horton, "Genesis," 29.

107 *The Black Code of the District of Columbia* (New York: William Harned, 1848).
108 Brown, "Residence Patterns," 70.
109 Vlach, "Evidence of Slave Housing," 67.
110 Green, *Secret City*, 43.
111 J. Valerie Fifer, "Washington, D.C.: The Political Geography of a Federal Capital," *Journal of American Studies* 15:1 (1981): 9–10.
112 Green, *Secret City*, 175.
113 Corrigan, "Ties That Bind," 83.
114 Harrold, *Subversives*, 141.
115 Ibid., 166.

Chapter 5: The Company They Kept

1 George Alfred Townsend, "Thomas Law, Washington's First Rich Man," *Records of the Columbia Historical Society, Washington, D.C.* 4 (1901): 237, 239.
2 William Wirt, letter to Laura H. Wirt, May 23, 1820.
3 Townsend, "Washington's First Rich Man," 237.
4 Gibbs Myers, "Pioneers in the Federal Area," *Records of the Columbia Historical Society, Washington, D.C.* 44/45 (1942/1943): 134.
5 Ibid., 134–35.
6 Logan, "Redemption of a Heretic," 7.
7 Martineau, *Retrospect of Western Travel*, 238.
8 Ibid., 235.
9 Carson, *Ambitious Appetites*, 88, 90.
10 Royall, *Black Book*, 122.
11 Elizabeth J. Clapp, "'A Virago-Errant in Enchanted Armor'?: Anne Royall's 1829 Trial as a Common Scold," *Journal of the Early Republic* 23:2 (summer 2003): 230.
12 Susan L. Klaus, "'Some of the Smartest Folks Here': The Van Nesses and Community Building in Early Washington, *Washington History* 3:2 (1991/1992): 35.
13 Ibid., 38–40.
14 Royall, *Black Book*, 139.
15 Goode, *Capital Losses*, 23.
16 Myers, "Pioneers," 156.
17 Gutheim, *Potomac*, 328–29.
18 Carson, *Ambitious Appetites*, 108.
19 Mary Bailey Tinkcom, "Caviar Along the Potomac: Sir Augustus John Foster's 'Notes on the United States,' 1804–1812," *William and Mary Quarterly*, third series 8:1 (1951): 77.
20 David Hosford and Mary Bagot, "Exile in Yankeeland: The Journal of Mary Bagot, 1816–1819," *Records of the Columbia Historical Society, Washington, D.C.* 51 (1984): 36.
21 Crowninshield, *Letters of Mary Boardman Crowninshield*, 20.
22 Carson, *Ambitious Appetites*, 69–70.
23 Smith, *Forty Years*, 389–90.
24 Green, *Washington: Village and Capital*, 82.
25 Watterston, *New Guide to Washington*, 140.
26 Carson, *Ambitious Appetites*, 126–27.

27   Poore, *Reminiscences of Sixty Years*, 74, 75.

28   Ibid., 74

29   Aloysius I. Mudd, "The Theatres of Washington from 1835 to 1850," *Records of the Columbia Historical Society, Washington, D.C.* 6 (1903): 227.

30   Steven C. Bullock, "A Pure and Sublime System: The Appeal of Post-Revolutionary Freemasonry," *Journal of the Early Republic* 9:3 (1989): 361, 364.

31   Steven C. Bullock, "Remapping Masonry: A Comment," *Eighteenth-Century Studies* 33:2 (2000): 277.

32   Steven C. Bullock, "The Revolutionary Transformation of American Freemasonry, 1752–1792," *William and Mary Quarterly* 47:3 (1990): 367–68.

33   Ibid., 351; Bullock, "Remapping Masonry," 278.

34   Kathleen Smith Kutolowski, "Freemasonry and Community in the Early Republic: The Case for Antimasonic Anxieties," *American Quarterly* 34:5 (1982): 547.

35   H. Paul Caemmerer, "The Sesquicentennial of the Laying of the Cornerstone of the United States Capitol by George Washington," *Records of the Columbia Historical Society, Washington, D.C.* 44/45 (1942/1943): 177.

36   Ronald P. Formisano and Kathleen Smith Kutolowski, "Antimasonry and Masonry: The Genesis of Protest, 1826–1827," *American Quarterly* 29:2 (1977): 142; Bullock, "Pure and Sublime System," 359–60.

37   Formisano and Kutolowski, "Antimasonry and Masonry," 160.

38   William Wirt, letter to the Anti-Masonic Convention, September 28, 1831.

39   William Wirt, letter to Judge Dabney Carr, January 12, 1832.

40   Watterston, *New Guide to Washington*, 112–13; Green, *Washington: Village and Capital*, 101, 133–34.

41   Klaus, "'Some of the Smartest Folks Here,'" 33.

42   Green, *Washington: Village and Capital*, 135.

43   Ibid., 64–65.

44   Vasquez, "Monuments, Markets, and Manners," 173; Goode, *Capital Losses*, 329.

45   Green, *Washington: Village and Capital*, 65–67.

46   Townsend, "Washington's First Rich Man," 234.

47   Clark, *Greenleaf and Law*, 221.

48   Ibid., 228.

49   Ibid., 236.

50   Twining, *Travels in America*, 109–10.

51   Clark, *Greenleaf and Law*, 245.

52   Townsend, "Washington's First Rich Man," 230–31.

53   Clark, *Greenleaf and Law*, 245.

54   Ibid., 256; Townsend, "Washington's First Rich Man," 226–27.

55   Clark, *Thomas Law*, 20.

56   Thomas Law, letter to President James Madison, November 26, 1814.

57   Clark, *Greenleaf and Law*, 315.

58   Ibid., 260.

59   Clark, *Thomas Law*, 11.

60   Ibid., 27.

61   Clark, *Greenleaf and Law*, 305.

62   Smith, *Forty Years*, 4.

63 Townsend, "Washington's First Rich Man," 236.

64 Clark, *Greenleaf and Law*, 287; Clark, *Thomas Law*, 26.

65 Townsend, "Washington's First Rich Man," 235; Twining, *Travels in America*, 110.

66 Hosford and Bagot, "Exile in Yankeeland," 37.

67 Townsend, "Washington's First Rich Man," 241.

68 Scott, "'This Vast Empire,'" 47.

69 Junior League of Washington, *City of Washington*, 188–89.

70 Bryan, *History of the National Capital*, 2:324.

71 Martineau, *Retrospect of Western Travel*, 314–15.

72 Vasquez, "Monuments, Markets, and Manners," 251, 253.

73 *The Journal of the House of Delegates of the Commonwealth of Virginia, 1831–1832*
     (Richmond: Thomas Ritchie, 1831): 163; Willie P. Mangum to Charity A. Mangum,
     February, 18, 1832, *The Papers of Willie Person Mangum 1807–1832* (Raleigh: North
     Carolina State Deptartment of Archives and History, 1950): 486–87.

74 Bryan, *History of the National Capital*, 2:328–29.

75 Ibid., 245–46, 325.

76 Green, *Washington: Village and Capital*, 172.

77 Carson, *Ambitious Appetites*, 138.

78 Young, *Washington Community*, 71.

79 Carson, *Ambitious Appetites*, 138–41.

80 Young, *Washington Community*, 24.

81 Delano, *Washington Directory*, vii–xiv.

82 Young, *Washington Community*, 100–102.

83 Cable, *Avenue of the Presidents*, 56–57.

84 Smith, *Forty Years*, 192.

85 Young, *Washington Community*, 47.

86 Cable, *Avenue of the Presidents*, 54; Green, *Washington: Village and Capital*, 107.

87 Royall, *Black Book*, 126–27.

88 Green, *Washington: Village and Capital*, 107.

89 Young, *Washington Community*, 73–74, 224–25.

90 Hutchins and Moore, *National Capital, Past and Present*, 59–60.

91 Young, *Washington Community*, 73.

92 Plumer, *Life of William Plumer*, 354.

93 Faux, *Memorable Days in America*, 153.

94 Young, *Washington Community*, 76–77.

95 Myers, "Pioneers," 151-52

96 Young, *Washington Community*, 50.

97 Ibid.

98 David R. Goldfield, "Antebellum Washington in Context: The Pursuit of Prosperity
     and Identity," in Gillette, *Southern City, National Ambition*, 8.

99 Green, *Washington: Village and Capital*, 66.

100 Gillette, Introduction, *Southern City, National Ambition*, iv.

101 Constance McLaughlin Green, "The Jacksonian 'Revolution' in the District of
     Columbia," *The Mississippi Valley Historical Review* 45:4 (1959): 604–5.

102 Clark, *Thomas Law*, 12–13.

103 Clark, *Greenleaf and Law*, 286.

104 Ibid., 304, 307, 312, 313.
105 Wharton, *Social Life in the Early Republic*, 68.
106 Clark, *Greenleaf and Law*, 334.

Chapter 6: Coming to the Scratch

1 Twining, *Travels in America*, 91, 108.
2 Myra L. Spaulding, "Dueling in the District of Columbia," *Records of the Columbia Historical Society, Washington, D.C.* 29/30 (1928): 126.
3 Roger Lane, "Criminal Violence in America: The First Hundred Years," *Annals of the American Academy of Political and Social Science, Crime and Justice in America: 1776–1976* 423 (1976): 6.
4 Spaulding, "Dueling in the District of Columbia," 125.
5 Force, *Picture of Washington and Its Vicinity*, 102.
6 Spaulding, "Dueling in the District of Columbia," 156.
7 Ibid., 132–35.
8 Ibid., 140–41, 157.
9 Faux, *Memorable Days in America*, 125.
10 Spaulding, "Dueling in the District of Columbia," 150.
11 Ibid., 160–61.
12 Ibid., 172–76.
13 Ibid., 172–77.
14 Jeffrey L. Pasley, "Minnows, Spies, and Aristocrats: The Social Crisis of Congress in the Age of Martin Van Buren," *Journal of the Early Republic* 27:4 (2007): 629–30.
15 Hone, *Diary of Philip Hone*, 179.
16 Lane, "Criminal Violence in America," 6.
17 David Grimsted, "Rioting in Its Jacksonian Setting," *American Historical Review* 77:2 (1972): 367.
18 Smith, *Forty Years*, 295–96.
19 Grimsted, *American Mobbing*, 3–4.
20 Gilje, *Rioting in America*, 63.
21 Pasley, "Minnows, Spies, and Aristocrats," 627.
22 Carl E. Prince, "The Great 'Riot Year': Jacksonian Democracy and Patterns of Violence in 1834," *Journal of the Early Republic* 5:1 (1985): 18–19.
23 Grimsted, *American Mobbing*, 4; Prince, "Great 'Riot Year,'" 19.
24 Grimsted, *American Mobbing*, 181–82.
25 Abraham Lincoln, "The Perpetuation of Our Political Institutions," Address before the Young Men's Lyceum, Springfield, IL, January 27, 1838.
26 Hezekiah Niles, editorial, *Niles Weekly Register*, September 5, 1835, 1.
27 John G. Sharp, Preface, *The Diary of Michael Shiner Relating to the History of the Washington Navy Yard, 1813–1869*, Library of Congress MSS 20.957.
28 Shiner, *Diary of Michael Shiner*, 31–33.
29 Ibid., 35, 52, 52.1.
30 Ibid., 60, 61–73.
31 Grimsted, "Rioting in Its Jacksonian Setting," 365, 368.
32 Shiner, *Diary of Michael Shiner*, 26–27, 41–44, 66–70.

33 Donald Yacovone, "The Transformation of the Black Temperance Movement, 1827–1854: An Interpretation," *Journal of the Early Republic* 8:3 (1988): 288–91.

34 Ibid., 294; Brown, *Strain of Violence*, 206–7.

35 Shiner, *Diary of Michael Shiner*, 74.

36 Wilhelmus Bogart Bryan, "Hotels of Washington Prior to 1814," *Records of the Columbia Historical Society, Washington, D.C.* 7 (1904): 71–72.

37 Oliver W. Holmes, "The City Tavern: A Century of Georgetown History," *Records of the Columbia Historical Society, Washington, D.C.* 50 (1980): 8–9.

38 Grimsted, *American Mobbing*, 186.

39 Poore, *Reminiscences of Sixty Years*, 52.

40 Delano, *Washington Directory*, 146; Goode, *Capital Losses*, 193, 196–97.

41 Rorabaugh, *Alcoholic Republic*, 7–8.

42 Lane, "Criminal Violence in America," 12; Grimsted, *American Mobbing*, 97.

43 Greenberg, *Cause for Alarm*, 68.

44 Ibid.

45 Scott A. G. M. Crawford, "Blood Sport," from *Guide to United States Popular Culture*, ed. Ray B. Browne and Pat Browne (Madison, WI: Popular Press, 2001): 99.

46 Smyth, *Tour in the United States of America*, 67.

47 Poore, *Reminiscences of Sixty Years*, 191–92.

48 E. Lee Shepard, "'This Being Court Day': Courthouses and Community Life in Rural Virginia," *Virginia Magazine of History and Biography* 103:4 (1995): 465.

49 William L. Ellis, "Home Rule in Action: Georgetown, 1789 to 1871," *Records of the Columbia Historical Society, Washington, D.C.* 66/68 (1966/1968): 53.

50 Hines, *Early Recollections*, 70–72.

51 Timony, *American Fistiana*, 3–4.

52 Ibid., 22–25.

53 Ibid., 25–27.

54 Sharp, "Metropolitan Police Department."

55 Green, *Washington: Village and Capital*, 160; Alfers, *Law and Order*, 13.

56 Sharp, "Metropolitan Police Department."

57 Alfers, *Law and Order*, 13.

58 Sylvester, *District of Columbia Police*, 29.

59 Alfers, *Law and Order in the Capital City*, 16.

60 Sylvester, *District of Columbia Police*, 29.

61 Michael A. Bellesiles, "The Origins of Gun Culture in the United States, 1760–1865," *Journal of American History* 83:2 (1996): 441.

62 Alfers, *Law and Order in the Capital City*, 18.

63 James Croggan, "Christmas in 1849; Day Celebrated in Washington with Much Noise, Drinkables in Plenty," *Evening Star*, December 25, 1909.

64 James Croggan, "Christmas Long Ago; How Washington Celebrated Before the Civil War; Riotous Day for Youth; Noise Continued from Dawn Until Late at Night," *Evening Star*, December 25, 1908.

65 Bryan, *History of the National Capital*, 2:147.

66 Cable, *Avenue of the Presidents*, 71.

67 Shiner, *Diary of Michael Shiner*, 57.

68 Bryan, *History of the National Capital*, 2:148.

69 Grimsted, *American Mobbing*, 267.
70 Pasley, "Minnows, Spies, and Aristocrats," 628–29, 647.
71 F. Regis Noel, "Some Notable Suits in Early District Courts," *Records of the Columbia Historical Society, Washington, D.C.* 24 (1922): 69–70.
72 Spaulding, "Dueling in the District of Columbia," 186–93.
73 Pasley, "Minnows, Spies, and Aristocrats," 649.
74 Spaulding, "Dueling in the District of Columbia," 193–98.
75 Green, *Washington: Village and Capital*, 94.
76 District of Columbia Fire Department, "History of the D.C. Fire Department: The Volunteers," accessed at www.dcfire.com/custom.html?id=173.
77 Green, *Washington: Village and Capital*, 160.
78 Bryan, *History of the National Capital*, 2:276–77.
79 Busey, *Pictures of the City*, 222.
80 Sharp, "District of Columbia Volunteer Fire Companies."
81 Bryan, *History of the National Capital*, 2:278.
82 *National Intelligencer*, September 25, 1844.
83 *National Intelligencer*, November 11, 1839.
84 Bryan, *History of the National Capital*, 2:277.
85 *National Intelligencer*, March 20, 1850.
86 David R. Goldfield, "Antebellum Washington in Context: The Pursuit of Prosperity and Identity," in Gillette, *Southern City, National Ambition*, 16.
87 Bryan, *History of the National Capital*, 2:277.
88 Washington Topham, "Centre Market and Vicinity," *Records of the Columbia Historical Society, Washington, D.C.* 26 (1924): 44.
89 Capitol Fire Museum, *Firefighting in Washington, D.C.*, 14; Goldfield, "Antebellum Washington," 17.
90 Bryan, *History of the National Capital*, 2:403–4, 427.
91 Grimsted, *American Mobbing*, 238.
92 Gilje, *Rioting in America*, 69.
93 Paul Gilje, "The Baltimore Riots of 1812 and the Breakdown of the Anglo-American Mob Tradition," *Journal of Social History* 13:4 (1980): 556.
94 Greenberg, *Cause for Alarm*, 86.
95 Fields, *Slavery and Freedom on the Middle Ground*, 46.
96 Benjamin Tuska, "Know-Nothingism in Baltimore 1854–1860," *Catholic Historical Review* 11:2 (1925): 239.
97 *Star*, June 3, 1857, quoted in Barry, "The Know Nothing Party," 34.
98 Sylvester, *District of Columbia Police*, 16.
99 Shiner, *Diary of Michael Shiner*, 156.
100 *Star*, June 1, 1857, quoted in Barry, "The Know Nothing Party," 32–33.
101 Sylvester, *District of Columbia Police*, 17.
102 Shiner, *Diary of Michael Shiner*, 156.
103 Sylvester, *District of Columbia Police*, 17.
104 Bryan, *History of the National Capital*, 2:430; A.G. Brown, Report of the Senate Committee on the District of Columbia, US Senate, 35th Congress, First Session, reprinted in *Congressional Globe*, April 5, 1860, 1460.

105 Brown, Report of the Senate Committee on the District of Columbia, 1460.
106 Preston S. Brooks, letter to J. H. Brooks, May 23, 1856.
107 Allan L. Damon, "Filibuster," *American Heritage* 27:1 (1975): 4.
108 Sharp, *Diary of Michael Shiner.*

Chapter 7: Illicit Congress

1 Leech, *Reveille in Washington*, 260–61; Elizabeth Barthold O'Brien, "Illicit Congress in the Nation's Capital: The History of Mary Ann Hall's Brothel," *Historical Archaeology* 39:1 (2005): 47–58.
2 Donna J. Seifert, "Within Sight of the White House: The Archaeology of Working Women," *Historical Archaeology* 25:4 (1991): 87, 88.
3 Ellis, *Sights and Secrets of the National Capital*, 445–46.
4 "Biography—Mary Ann Hall, 19th Century Entrepreneur,"Smithsonian Associates, *Civil War E-Mail Newsletter* 4:1 (2005), accessed at http://civilwarstudies.org/articles/Vol_4/mary-ann-hall.shtm; O'Brien, "Illicit Congress," 48.
5 Elizabeth J. Himelfarb, "Capitol Sex," *Archaeology* 52 (July/August 1999): 18.
6 O'Brien, "Illicit Congress," 55.
7 Donna J. Seifert and Joseph Balicki, "Mary Ann Hall's House," *Historical Archaeology* 39:1 (2005): 65.
8 Ibid., 66–71; Smithsonian Institution, "Madam on the Mall" (Washington, DC, 2005), accessed at www.si.edu/oahp/madam.
9 O'Brien, "Illicit Congress," 49.
10 Buel, *Mysteries and Miseries*, 167, 176, 180.
11 Townsend, *Washington, Outside and Inside*, 457.
12 Leech, *Reveille in Washington*, 261.
13 Ibid., 264.
14 Green, *Washington: Village and Capital*, 251.
15 Ibid.
16 Leech, *Reveille in Washington*, 264.
17 Gutheim, *Worthy of the Nation*, 69.
18 Neil L. Shumsky, "Tacit Acceptance: Respectable Americans and Segregated Prostitution, 1870–1910," *Journal of Social History* 19:4 (Summer 1986): 666.
19 Seifert, "Within Sight of the White House," 82.
20 Leech, *Reveille in Washington*, 263–64.
21 Lowry, Thomas P., *Sexual Misbehavior in the Civil War: A Compendium* (Bloomington, IN: Xlibris, 2005), 98.
22 Leech, *Reveille in Washington*, 260–61.
23 Ibid., 265.
24 Ibid., 121.
25 Ibid.; *Policemen's Association News*, September 1861, quoted in Alfers, *Law and Order*, 26.
26 Leech, *Reveille in Washington*, 262–63.
27 O'Brien, "Illicit Congress," 50, 52.
28 Ibid., 52.

29 Charles D. Cheek and Amy Friedlander, "Pottery and Pig's Feet: Space, Ethnicity and Neighborhood in Washington, D.C.: 1880–1940," *Historical Archaeology* 24:1 (1994): 34.
30 De Gaffenreid, *Typical Alley Houses*, 10–11.
31 Green, *Washington: Village and Capital*, 363.
32 Borchert, *Alley Life in Washington*, 19, 23–24.
33 Green, *Washington: Village and Capital*, 255.
34 Garnett P. Williams, "Washington D.C.'s Vanishing Springs and Waterways," in Moore and Jackson, *Geology, Hydrology and History*, 87–88.
35 Porter, "Life and Times," 154; "The Washington Canal—Report to Major Generals Gilmore, Warren and Tower," Sen. Ex. Doc. 35, US Senate, 39th Congress, First Session, 1866, quoted in *National Republican*, April 7, 1866.
36 Seifert, "Within Sight of the White House," 83; Shumsky, "Tacit Acceptance," 666.
37 Rosen, *Lost Sisterhood*, 98–99.
38 Donna J. Seifert, "Mrs. Starr's Profession," in Scott, *Those of Little Note*, 161–62; Advertisement, *Boston Medical and Surgical Journal*, November 27, 1913, 2.
39 Rosen, *Lost Sisterhood*, 147–48.
40 Sanger, *History of Prostitution*, 640–642.
41 O'Brien, "Illicit Congress," 54.
42 Ibid., 55.

Chapter 8: Seeing the Elephant

1   Leech, *Reveille in Washington*, 56.
2   James H. Whyte, "Divided Loyalties in Washington During the Civil War," *Records of the Columbia Historical Society, Washington, D.C.* 60/62 (1960/1962): 104.
3   Green, *Washington: Village and Capital*, 231.
4   Benjamin Franklin Cooling, "Civil War Defenses During the Civil War," *Records of the Columbia Historical Society, Washington, D.C.* 71/72 (1971/1972): 316–17; Ed Hendrickson, "Defending Washington: The District of Columbia Militia," *Washington History* 23 (2011): 38.
5   Cooling, "Civil War Defenses," 317.
6   Hendrickson, "Defending Washington," 39; Whyte, "Divided Loyalties," 105.
7   Miller, *Second Only to Grant*, 75–76.
8   Cooling, "Civil War Defenses," 317.
9   Whyte, "Divided Loyalties," 106.
10 Cooling, "Civil War Defenses," 318; Leech, *Reveille in Washington*, 55–65.
11 Whyte, "Divided Loyalties," 108.
12 Leech, *Reveille in Washington*, 143, 145.
13 Whyte, "Divided Loyalties," 120.
14 Green, *Washington: Village and Capital*, 248.
15 Whyte, "Divided Loyalties," 120.
16 Green, *Washington: Village and Capital*, 287.
17 Leech, *Reveille in Washington*, 134–35.
18 Green, *Washington: Village and Capital*, 250–52.
19 Goode, *Capital Losses*, 329–30.

20 Curtis Carroll Davis, "The 'Old Capitol' and Its Keeper: How William P. Wood Ran a Civil War Prison," *Records of the Columbia Historical Society, Washington, D.C.* 52 (1989): 207, 211–12.

21 Lomax, *Old Capitol and Its Inmates*, 66–67.

22 Davis, "'Old Capitol' and Its Keeper," 219–22.

23 Leech, *Reveille in Washington*, 266, 408.

24 Ibid., 143–45.

25 Whyte, "Divided Loyalties," 119.

26 Donal E. J. MacNamara, "American Police Administration at Mid-Century," *Public Administration Review* 10:3 (Summer 1950): 181.

27 Sylvester, *District of Columbia Police*, 36–37, 42.

28 Donald E. Press, "From Murder Bay to the Federal Triangle," *Records of the Columbia Historical Society* 51 (1984): 57; Green, *Washington: Village and Capital*, 21, 264.

29 Report of the Board of Metropolitan Police, House Ex. Doc. 1, 37th Congress, 2nd Session (1861), US Serial Set 1157: 649; Alfers, *Law and Order*, 27.

30 Alfers, *Law and Order*, 27.

31 Report of the Board of Metropolitan Police, 649.

32 Sylvester, *District of Columbia Police*, 36, 49; *Report of the Board of Metropolitan Police*, 651–52.

33 "Seven of the Finest, They Have Seen Nearly Thirty Years' Service; Origin of the Police Force," *Evening Star*, March 8, 1890.

34 Robert Hill, "Eighty-Four Years of Washington Life by a Man Who Has Seen Them All," *Washington Post*, August 19, 1917.

35 Ibid.

36 Leech, *Reveille in Washington*, 243.

37 *Report of the Board of Metropolitan Police*, 655; Green, *Washington: Village and Capital*, 251.

38 *Report of the Board of Metropolitan Police*, 658.

39 Alfers, *Law and Order*, 24.

40 *Report of the Board of Metropolitan Police*, 660.

41 Hill, "Eighty-Four Years of Washington Life."

42 Sylvester, *District of Columbia Police*, 247.

43 "Old Coppers' Stories; Two Original Members of the Force Tell Some Good Tales; Lively Times in the Sixties," *Washington Post*, October 7, 1895.

44 Alfers, *Law and Order*, 25–26.

45 Sylvester, *District of Columbia Police*, 245.

46 Leech, *Reveille in Washington*, 77.

47 Bryan, *History of the National Capital*, 2: 496–97.

48 Michael A. Cooke, "The Health of the Union Military in the District of Columbia, 1861–1865," *Military Affairs* 48:4 (1984): 195.

49 James M. Goode, "Civil War Washington: Rare Images from the Albert H. Small Collection," *Washington History* 15:1 (2003): 74.

50 Cooke, "Health of the Union Military," 195; Leech, *Reveille in Washington*, 71.

51 Cooke, "Health of the Union Military," 195.

52 Leech, *Reveille in Washington*, 209.

53 Marilyn Mayer Culpepper and Pauline Gordon Adams, "Nursing in the Civil War," *American Journal of Nursing* 88:7 (1988): 983.

54 Wheelock, *Boys in White*, 37.

55 Green, *Washington: Village and Capital*, 261.

56 Leech, *Reveille in Washington*, 205–6; Culpepper and Adams, "Nursing in the Civil War," 983.

57 Culpepper and Adams, "Nursing in the Civil War," 983; Wheelock, *Boys in White*, 201.

58 Martin G. Murray, "Traveling with the Wounded: Walt Whitman and Washington's Civil War Hospitals," *Washington History* 8:2 (1996/1997): 66.

59 Culpepper and Adams, "Nursing in the Civil War," 983.

60 Wheelock, *Boys in White*, 208; Ropes, *Civil War Nurse*, 116.

61 Cooke, "Health of the Union Military," 196–98.

62 Bray, *Armies of Pestilence*, 191.

63 Newby, *Anderson Ruffin Abbott*, 52.

64 Murray, "Traveling with the Wounded," 64; Green, *Washington: Village and Capital*, 261.

65 Culpepper and Adams, "Nursing in the Civil War," 982.

66 Jane E. Schultz, "The Inhospitable Hospital: Gender and Professionalism in Civil War Medicine," *Signs* 17:2 (1992): 369–70.

67 Ibid., 370.

68 Culpepper and Adams, "Nursing in the Civil War," 982, 984.

69 Leech, *Reveille in Washington*, 209.

70 John R. Brumgardt, "Introduction: Mother, Author, Antislavery Reformer," in Ropes, *Civil War Nurse*, 32.

71 Culpepper and Adams, "Nursing in the Civil War," 982.

72 Cooke, "Health of the Union Military," 196; Ropes, *Civil War Nurse*, 102, 105; G. C. Caldwell, "The Hospitals of Washington," from *United States Sanitary Commission Bulletin* (New York: 1866): 243.

73 Donald H. Mugridge, "The United States Sanitary Commission in Washington," *Records of the Columbia Historical Society, Washington, D.C.* 60/62 (1960/1962): 144; J. Foster Jenkins, "Report of Special Relief Department: Washington, D.C.," from *United States Sanitary Commission Bulletin* (New York: 1866): 19.

74 "Notes on Nursing," United States Sanitary Commission Bulletin (New York: 1866): 217–18.

75 Goode, *Capital Losses*, 351.

76 Murray, "Traveling with the Wounded," 65–66, 67.

77 Stearns, *Lady Nurse of Ward E*, 7–8, 86, 101.

78 Ibid., 52–53, 88, 150, 161.

79 Murray, "Traveling with the Wounded," 67.

80 Stearns, *Lady Nurse of Ward E*, 56–57.

81 Ibid., 60.

82 Wheelock, *Boys in White*, 39.

83 Ropes, *Civil War Nurse*, 89–90; Brumgardt, "Introduction: Mother, Author, Antislavery Reformer," 41.

84 Brumgardt, "Introduction: Mother, Author, Antislavery Reformer," 40.

85 Alcott, *Hospital Sketches*, 34, 72.

86 Brumgardt, "Introduction: Mother, Author, Antislavery Reformer," 12.

87 Ropes, *Six Months in Kansas*, 111, 116, 117.

88 Ropes, *Civil War Nurse*, 50.

89 Brumgardt, "Introduction: Mother, Author, Antislavery Reformer," 29–33.

90 Ropes, *Civil War Nurse*, 69.

91 Brumgardt, "Introduction: Mother, Author, Antislavery Reformer," 45.

92 Culpepper and Adams, "Nursing in the Civil War," 984.

93 Schultz, "Inhospitable Hospital," 384, 385.

94 Ropes, *Civil War Nurse*, 84.

95 Ibid., 84–85, 87.

96 Schultz, "Inhospitable Hospital," 382–83, 389.

97 Culpepper and Adams, "Nursing in the Civil War," 982.

98 Elden E. Billings, "Social and Economic Conditions in Washington During the Civil War," *Records of the Columbia Historical Society, Washington, D.C.* 63/65 (1963/1965): 196–97.

99 Barbara Welter, "The True Cult of Womanhood, 1820–1860," *American Quarterly* 18:2 (1966): 174.

100 Ropes, *Civil War Nurse*, 115.

101 Ibid., 119.

102 Ibid., 121–22.

103 Ropes, *Civil War Nurse*, 114–15.

104 Joseph P. Reidy, "Coming from the Shadow of the Past: The Transition from Slavery to Freedom at Freedmen's Village, 1863–1900," *Virginia Magazine of History and Biography* 95:4 (1987): 404.

105 Eric Wills, "The Contraband of America and the Road to Freedom," *Preservation: The Magazine of the National Trust for Historic Preservation* (May/June 2011): accessed at www.preservationnation.org/magazine/2011/may-june/the-forgotten .html.

106 Green, *Washington: Village and Capital*, 273, 277.

107 Damani Davis, "Slavery and Emancipation in the Nation's Capital: Using Federal Records to Explore the Lives of African American Ancestors," *Prologue Magazine*, National Archives 42:1 (2011): accessed at www.archives.gov/publications/ prologue/2010/spring/dcslavery.html.

108 Mary Mitchell, "I Held George Washington's Horse: Compensated Emancipation in the District of Columbia," *Records of the Columbia Historical Society, Washington, D.C.* 63/65 (1963/1965): 221, 222, 225–26.

109 Green, *Washington: Village and Capital*, 274.

110 Wills, "Contraband of America."

111 Reidy, "Coming from the Shadow of the Past," 408–9.

112 Rebecca K. Sharp, "'Their Bedding Is Wet, Their Floors Are Damp': 'Pre-Bureau' Records and Civil War African American Genealogy," *Prologue Magazine*, National Archives 39:2 (2007): accessed at www.archives.gov/publications/prologue/2007/ summer/pre-bureau.html.

113 Reidy, "Coming from the Shadow of the Past," 407.

114 Holt, Smith-Parker, and Terborg-Penn, *Special Mission*, 2–3.

115 Press, "From Murder Bay to the Federal Triangle," 58.

116 US Congress, Senate, Sen. Morrill introduction of *Superintendent Report*, Office of Metropolitan Police, 39th Congress, 1st Session, March 20, 1866, *Congressional Globe*, 1508.

117 *Harper's Weekly*, May 7, 1864; Reidy, "Coming from the Shadow of the Past," 409–11.

118 Reidy, "Coming from the Shadow of the Past," 413–14.

119 US Congress, Senate, *Report of the Bureau of the Refugees, Freedmen, and Abandoned Lands*, S. Ex. Doc. 6, 39th Congress, 2nd Session, October 22, 1866, p.36; Robert M. Poole, "How Arlington Cemetery Came to Be," *Smithsonian* (November 2009): 1, accessed at www.smithsonianmag.com/history-archaeology/The-Battle-of-Arlington.html.

120 Reidy, "Coming from the Shadow of the Past," 411.

121 Newby, *Anderson Ruffin Abbott*, 62–65.

122 M. Elizabeth Carnegie, "Black Nurses at the Front," *American Journal of Nursing* 84:10 (1984): 1251.

123 Newby, *Anderson Ruffin Abbott*, 60–65, 83–84.

124 Ibid., 80–81.

125 Ibid., 81; Bryan, *History of the National Capital*, 2:531.

126 Bryan, *History of the National Capital*, 2:512–13.

127 Green, *Washington: Village and Capital*, 280–82.

128 Leech, *Reveille in Washington*, 250–52.

129 US Congress, Senate, *Report of the Bureau of the Refugees, Freedmen, and Abandoned Lands*, S. Ex. Doc. 6, 39th Congress, 2nd Session, October 22, 1866, 34–35.

130 Leech, *Reveille in Washington*, 251.

131 Newby, *Anderson Ruffin Abbott*, 53; Leech, *Reveille in Washington*, 253–54.

132 Green, *Secret City*, 88.

133 Sherrod E. East, "Montgomery C. Meigs and the Quartermaster Department," *Military Affairs* 25:4 (Winter 1961–1962): 194.

134 Wills, "Contraband of America."

135 Miller, *Second Only to Grant*, 264; East, "Montgomery C. Meigs," 195.

136 Cynthia R. Field, "A Rich Repast of Classicism: Meigs and Classical Sources," pp. 73–75, and Barbara A. Wolanin, "Meigs the Art Patron," pp. 138–143, in Dickinson, *Montgomery C. Meigs and the Building of the Nation's Capital*.

137 Dean A. Herrin, "The Eclectic Engineer: Montgomery C. Meigs and His Engineering Projects," in Dickinson, *Montgomery C. Meigs and the Building of the Nation's Capital*, 13.

138 Miller, *Second Only to Grant*, 20; Harry C. Ways, "Montgomery C. Meigs and the Washington Aqueduct," in Dickinson, *Montgomery C. Meigs and the Building of the Nation's Capital*, 22–23.

139 Miller, *Second Only to Grant*, 20.

140 Bryan, *History of the National Capital*, 2:306.

141 Miller, *Second Only to Grant*, 72–74.

142 East, "Montgomery C. Meigs and the Quartermaster Department," 187–90.

143 Cooling, "Civil War Defenses," 324–25.

144 Goode, "Civil War Washington," 64.

145 Miller, *Second Only to Grant*, 18–19, 239.
146 Poole, "How Arlington Cemetery Came to Be," 2.
147 Ibid., 3.
148 Miller, *Second Only to Grant*, 259–60.
149 Poole, "How Arlington Cemetery Came to Be," 3.

Chapter 9: Suspicious Characters

1 "Rival to Boom Towns; Washington Has Had Its Wild and Woolly Days," *Washington Post*, September 7, 1902.
2 Sylvester, *District of Columbia Police*, 53–54.
3 "Rival to Boom Towns; Washington Has Had Its Wild and Woolly Days," *Washington Post*, September 7, 1902.
4 Ibid.
5 Alfers, *Law and Order*, 35–37.
6 William G. Brock, *Report of the Major and Superintendent of Police of the District of Columbia: The Year Ending June 30, 1880* (Washington, DC: Government Printing Office, 1881): 3.
7 "Rival to Boom Towns; Washington Has Had Its Wild and Woolly Days," *Washington Post*, September 7, 1902.
8 *The Evening Union*, July 3, 1863, quoted in John G. Sharp, "The Metropolitan Police Department, District of Columbia: Law, Crime and Policing in the District, 1790–1900," Washington D.C. Genealogy Trails (April 2, 2010), accessed at www.genealogytrails.com/washdc/lawsprisons/historyofpolicedept.html.
9 Green, *Washington: Village and Capital*, 252, 363.
10 Alfers, *Law and Order*, 27.
11 Leech, *Reveille in Washington*, 262.
12 David K. Sullivan, "Behind Prison Walls: The Operation of the District Penitentiary, 1831–1862," *Records of the Columbia Historical Society, Washington, D.C.* 71/72 (1971/1972): 262.
13 Green, *Washington: Village and Capital*, 253; Sullivan, "Behind Prison Walls," 266.
14 Sylvester, *District of Columbia Police*, 62, 67–69.
15 Brock, *Report of the Major and Superintendent of Police*, 14.
16 Byrnes, *Professional Criminals of America*, 1–2, 8, 12, 22, 30, 40, 44, 47–49.
17 David R. Johnson, "The Origins and Structure of Intercity Criminal Activity, 1840–1920: An Interpretation," *Journal of Social History* 15:4 (Summer 1982): 595.
18 Alfers, *Law and Order*, 38–39.
19 Moore, *Report of the Major and Superintendent of Police*, 8.
20 Sylvester, *District of Columbia Police*, 237.
21 Ibid., 228–31
22 Collection of Lt. Nicholas Bruel, Historian of the Metropolitan Police, Washington, DC, interview on June 26, 2012.
23 Donald E. Press, "From Murder Bay to the Federal Triangle," *Records of the Columbia Historical Society* 51 (1984): 51, 55, 62.
24 *Washington Post*, July 8, 1888.
25 Green, *Washington: Village and Capital*, 363.

26 "Rival to Boom Towns; Washington Has Had Its Wild and Woolly Days," *Washington Post*, September 7, 1902.

27 *Washington Post*, February 4, 1900.

28 Arrest Books, 1869–1906 (August 14–September 16, 1874); Law Enforcement Records, Metropolitan Police; Records of the Government of the District of Columbia, RG 351, National Archives and Records Administration.

29 Ibid.

30 Identification Books, 1883–90; Law Enforcement Records, Metropolitan Police; Records of the Government of the District of Columbia, Vols. 1–2, RG 351, National Archives and Records Administration.

31 Ibid.

32 *Report of the Board of Metropolitan Police*, House Ex. Doc. 1, 37th Congress, 2nd Session (1861), US Serial Set 1157: 659; Moore, *Report of the Major and Superintendent of Police*, 8.

33 Alfers, *Law and Order*, 33.

34 Sylvester, *District of Columbia Police*, 213.

35 Ibid., 216; Alfers, *Law and Order*, 34.

36 Borchert, *Alley Life in Washington*, 7, 26.

37 Alfers, *Law and Order*, 35.

38 Cecily Hilleary, "Noah E. Sedgwick: A Black Cop in D.C.'s Gilded Age," pt. 1, from *Quondam Washington: A Compendium of Tales from Forgotten City Archives*; accessed at http://quondamdc.wordpress.com.

Chapter 10: *The Fall of Washington City*

1 James H. Whyte, "The District of Columbia Territorial Government, 1871–1874," *Records of the Columbia Historical Society, Washington, D.C.* 51/52 (1951/1952): 87–88; Washington Topham, "Centre Market and Vicinity," *Records of the Columbia Historical Society, Washington, D.C.* 26 (1924): 69–70; William van Zandt Cox, "Matthew Gault Emery, The Last Mayor of Washington, 1870–1871," *Records of the Columbia Historical Society, Washington, D.C.* 20 (1917): 41–42.

2 Cox, "Matthew Gault Emery," 41–42.

3 Ibid., 43.

4 Whyte, "District of Columbia Territorial Government," 88–89.

5 Brian D. Crane, "Filth, Garbage, and Rubbish: Refuse Disposal, Sanitary Reform, and Nineteenth-Century Yard Deposits in Washington, D.C.," *Historical Archaeology* 34:1 (2000): 22.

6 Michael A. Cook, "Physical Environment and Sanitation in the District of Columbia, 1860–1868," *Records of the Columbia Historical Society, Washington, D.C.* 52 (1989): 295–98.

7 Crane, "Filth, Garbage, and Rubbish," 31; Cook, "Physical Environment and Sanitation," 299.

8 Maury, *Alexander "Boss" Shepherd*, 2.

9 Kenneth R. Bowling, "From 'Federal Town' to 'National Capital': Ulysses S. Grant and the Reconstruction of Washington, D.C.," *Washington History* 14:1 (2002): 15.

10 Ibid., 9, 15–16.

11 Carl Abbott, "Dimensions of Regional Change in Washington, D.C.," *American Historical Review* 95:5 (1990): 1375–76.

12 Whyte, *Uncivil War*, 17.

13 John Nolen Jr., "Some Aspects of Washington's Nineteenth Century Economic Development," *Records of the Columbia Historical Society, Washington, D.C.* 49 (1973/1974): 528–29.

14 Whyte, *Uncivil War*, 181–82.

15 Dahlgren, *Etiquette of Social Life*, 18–26.

16 Whyte, *Uncivil War*, 182.

17 Twain and Warner, *Gilded Age*, 254–55.

18 William M. Maury, "Alexander Shepherd and the Board of Public Works," *Records of the Columbia Historical Society, Washington, D.C.* 71/72 (1971/1972): 394.

19 Ibid., 396, 399.

20 Ibid., 399.

21 Whyte, *Uncivil War*, 92.

22 Scott, *Capital Engineers*, 71.

23 Pamela Scott, "Montgomery C. Meigs and Victorian Art Traditions," p. 62, and Cynthia R. Field, "A Rich Repast of Classicism: Meigs and Classical Sources," p. 75, in Dickinson, *Montgomery C. Meigs and the Building of the Nation's Capital*.

24 Montgomery C. Meigs, Letter to Brig. Gen. Nathaniel Michler (July 27, 1867), in Annual Report of Nathaniel Michler, Office of Public Buildings, Grounds, and Works, Capitol of the United States, Appendix T, Report of the Secretary of War (1867): 544–48.

25 Scott, *Capital Engineers*, 112–13.

26 *In Memory of Nathaniel Michler*, Funeral Program (Washington, DC, 1881): 8–10.

27 Ellen Robinson Epstein, "The East and West Wings of the White House," *Records of the Columbia Historical Society, Washington, D.C.* 48 (1971/1972): 598.

28 William D. Wise, Letter to the Board of Aldermen and the Board of Common Council, January 23, 1864.

29 Nathaniel Michler, Report in Relation to Public Park and Site of Presidential Mansion (January 29, 1867), in Annual Report of Nathaniel Michler, 535–38.

30 Epstein, "East and West Wings of the White House," 599.

31 Gutheim, *Worthy of the Nation*, 81.

32 Nathaniel Michler, Report in Relation to Public Park and Site of Presidential Mansion (January 29, 1867), in Annual Report of Nathaniel Michler, 532.

33 Nathaniel Michler, Annual Report of Nathaniel Michler, 523–25.

34 National Park Service, Historic American Buildings Survey: Market Square (Washington, DC: Department of the Interior, 1969): 3–4.

35 Nathaniel Michler, Annual Report of Nathaniel Michler, 525–26.

36 Gordon Chappell, *Historic Resource Study: East and West Potomac Parks, A History* (Denver, CO: US Department of Interior, 1973), 11–17.

37 Warden, *Chorographical and Statistical Description*, 18.

38 Cox, "Matthew Gault Emery," 41.

39 Robert Harrison, "Welfare and Employment Policies of the Freedmen's Bureau in the District of Columbia," *Journal of Southern History* 72:1 (2006): 75–76.

40 Nolen, "Some Aspects," 528–29; Frances J. Powell, "A Statistical Profile of the Black Family in Washington, D.C., 1850–1880," *Records of the Columbia Historical Society, Washington, D.C.*, 52 (1989): 278–79.

41 Powell, "Statistical Profile of the Black Family," 277.

42 Whyte, *Uncivil War*, 251–52.

43 Edward Tang, "Rebirth of a Nation: Frederick Douglass as Postwar Founder in 'Life and Times,'" *Journal of American Studies* 39:1 (2005): 33–34.

44 Douglass, *Life and Times of Frederick Douglass*, 352.

45 Whyte, *Uncivil War*, 258–62.

46 Harrison, "Welfare and Employment Policies," 80–83, 86–87; Plummer, "History of Public Health," 154.

47 Robert C. Lieberman, "The Freedmen's Bureau and the Politics of Institutional Structure," *Social Science History* 18:3 (1994): 427.

48 Whyte, *Uncivil War*, 54–57.

49 Whyte, "District of Columbia Territorial Government," 89–90.

50 Thomas R. Johnson, "Reconstruction Politics in Washington: 'An Experimental Garden for Radical Plants,'" *Records of the Columbia Historical Society, Washington, D.C.* 50 (1980): 181.

51 Melvin R. Williams, "A Blueprint for Change: The Black Community in Washington, D.C., 1860–1870," *Records of the Columbia Historical Society, Washington, D.C.* 71/72 (1971/1972): 380–82.

52 Ibid., 381.

53 Whyte, *Uncivil War*, 62–63.

54 Johnson, "Reconstruction Politics in Washington," 180.

55 Douglass, *Life and Times of Frederick Douglass*, 333.

56 Whyte, *Uncivil War*, 67–68.

57 Ibid., 68–69.

58 Johnson, "Reconstruction Politics in Washington," 82–83; Williams, "Blueprint for Change," 383; Maury, *Alexander "Boss" Shepherd*, 3.

59 Whyte, *Uncivil War*, 74–75.

60 Ibid., 71–73; Cox, "Matthew Gault Emery," 26.

61 Williams, "Blueprint for Change," 384–87.

62 Ames, *Ten Years in Washington*, 77–78.

63 John Richardson, "Alexander Shepherd and the Race Issue in Washington," *Washington History* 22 (2010): 25.

64 *Washington Star,* January 16, 1868, quoted in Richardson, "Alexander Shepherd and the Race Issue in Washington," 25.

65 Whyte, "District of Columbia Territorial Government," 91.

66 Maury, "Alexander Shepherd and the Board of Public Works," 397–98.

67 Maury, *Alexander "Boss" Shepherd*, 4.

68 Ibid.

69 Cox, "Matthew Gault Emery," 43.

70 Tindall, *Standard History of the City of Washington*, 247.

Chapter 11: A Gilded Cage

1 Maury, *Alexander "Boss" Shepherd*, 6–7.

2 James H. Whyte, "The District of Columbia Territorial Government, 1871–1874," *Records of the Columbia Historical Society, Washington, D.C.* 51/52 (1951/1952): 94.

3 Maury, *Alexander "Boss" Shepherd* , 6.

4 *Evening Star*, August 7, 1871, quoted in Whyte, *Uncivil War*, 119.

5 Maury, *Alexander "Boss" Shepherd*, 9, 10.

6 Whyte, *Uncivil War*, 125–26.

7 Maury, *Alexander "Boss" Shepherd*, 30.

8 John Richardson, "Alexander Shepherd and the Race Issue in Washington," *Washington History* 22 (2010): 17–18.

9 Ibid., 22–23.

10 Maury, *Alexander "Boss" Shepherd*, 29.

11 Merline Pitre, "Frederick Douglass: The Politician vs. the Social Reformer," *Phylon* 40:3 (1979): 270–71.

12 Richardson, "Alexander Shepherd and the Race Issue in Washington," 30–31.

13 Whyte, *Uncivil War*, 243–46.

14 Ibid., 114–15.

15 Green, *Washington: Village and Capital*, 247, 249; Maury, *Alexander "Boss" Shepherd*, 34.

16 Maury, *Alexander "Boss" Shepherd*, 30.

17 Noreen, *Public Street Illumination*, 14–15.

18 William M. Maury, *Alexander "Boss" Shepherd and the Board of Public Works* (Washington, DC: George Washington University, 1975): 30.

19 Ibid., 30–31.

20 Ibid., 43.

21 Brian D. Crane, "Filth, Garbage, and Rubbish: Refuse Disposal, Sanitary Reform, and Nineteenth-Century Yard Deposits in Washington, D.C.," *Historical Archaeology* 34:1 (2000): 22.

22 Cluss & Kammerhueber Engineering, "Report on the Present State, and the Improvement of the Washington City Canal," (Washington City: May 12, 1865): 8–10.

23 Col. Silas Seymour, letter to Richard Wallach (April 26, 1864), in "Report on the Present State, and the Improvement of the Washington City Canal," (Washington City: May 12, 1865): 46.

24 Maury, *Alexander "Boss" Shepherd*, 30–31.

25 Gutheim, *Worthy of the Nation*, 86.

26 Scott, *Capital Engineers*, 81.

27 Cowdrey, *City for the Nation*, 26; Gutheim, *Worthy of the Nation*, 86–87.

28 Gutheim, *Worthy of the Nation*, 86–87; Scott, *Capital Engineers*, 77.

29 Cowdrey, *City for the Nation*, 26.

30 Gutheim, *Worthy of the Nation*, 86–87.

31 Scott, *Capital Engineers*, 75.

32 Maury, *Alexander "Boss" Shepherd*, 20.

33 Ibid., 21, 37.

34 Whyte, *Uncivil War*, 147–48; Whyte, "District of Columbia Territorial Government," 41.

35 Green, *Washington: Village and Capital*, 352; Maury, *Alexander "Boss" Shepherd*, 41–42.

36 Maury, *Alexander "Boss" Shepherd*, 42.

37 Green, *Washington: Village and Capital*, 354.

38 Maury, *Alexander "Boss" Shepherd*, 51.

39 Plummer, "History of Public Health," 143, 161–66.

40 Whyte, "District of Columbia Territorial Government," 99.

41 Ames, *Ten Years in Washington*, 78, 81.

42 Maury, *Alexander "Boss" Shepherd*, 46.

43 Whyte, *Uncivil War*, 128.

44 Barton, *Historical and Commercial Sketches*, 29–30.

45 Maury, *Alexander "Boss" Shepherd*, 35–36.

46 Ibid., 39–40.

47 Green, *Washington: Village and Capital*, 350.

48 Whyte, "District of Columbia Territorial Government," 97.

49 Ibid., 98–99; Whyte, *Uncivil War*, 163–64.

50 Maury, *Alexander "Boss" Shepherd*, 42.

51 Whyte, *Uncivil War*, 143–44.

52 Melissa McLoud, "Craftsmen and Entrepreneurs: Builders of the Red Brick City, 1880–1900," in Longstreth, *Housing Washington*, 26.

53 Whyte, *Uncivil War*, 146–47.

54 Green, *Washington: Village and Capital*, 355.

55 Bryan, *History of the National Capital*, 2:619; Green, *Washington: Village and Capital*, 355.

56 Gutheim, *Worthy of the Nation*, 86; Whyte, *Uncivil War*, 147.

57 Maury, *Alexander "Boss" Shepherd*, 51.

58 Whyte, *Uncivil War*, 168–69.

59 Green, *Washington: Village and Capital*, 358; Whyte, "District of Columbia Territorial Government," 99.

60 Whyte, *Uncivil War*, 159.

61 Green, *Washington: Village and Capital*, 359.

62 Whyte, "District of Columbia Territorial Government," 100.

63 Green, *Washington: Village and Capital*, 360.

64 Tindall, *Standard History of the City of Washington*, 268.

65 Richardson, "Alexander Shepherd and the Race Issue in Washington," 30.

66 Whyte, *Uncivil War*, 257; Richardson, "Alexander Shepherd and the Race Issue in Washington," 30.

67 Douglass, *Life and Times of Frederick Douglass*, 357.

68 Sen. Allan Thurman, Debate on the Morrill Bill, US Senate, 43rd Congress, Second Session, *Congressional Record*, December 17, 1874: 128.

69 Sen. Thomas Bayard, Debate on the Morrill Bill, US Senate, 43rd Congress, Second Session, *Congressional Record*, December 17, 1874: 126.

70 *National Republican*, November 17, 1874.

71 Green, *Washington: Village and Capital*, 361.

72 Sen. Oliver Morton, Debate on the Morrill Bill, US Senate, 43rd Congress, Second Session, *Congressional Record*, December 17, 1874: 120.

73 William M. Maury, "Alexander Shepherd and the Board of Public Works," *Records of the Columbia Historical Society, Washington, D.C.* 71/72 (1971/1972): 406.
74 Tindall, *Standard History of the City of Washington*, 271.
75 Moore, *Picturesque Washington*, 52; Scott, *Capital Engineers*, 114.
76 Maury, *Alexander "Boss" Shepherd*, 50, 51.
77 Scott, *Capital Engineers*, 114.
78 Poore, *Reminiscences of Sixty Years*, 313–14.
79 Scott, *Capital Engineers*, 81.
80 Tindall, *Standard History of the City of Washington*, 278.
81 Ibid., 277; Scott, *Capital Engineers*, 114–15.
82 Alan Lessoff, "Review of Montgomery C. Meigs and the Building of the Nation's Capital," by William C. Dickinson et al., in *Washington History* 15:1 (2003): 89.
83 Cowdrey, *City for the Nation*, 27–29.
84 Scott, *Capital Engineers*, 116.
85 Bryan, *History of the National Capital*, 2:641.

Epilogue: The Sea of Pavement

1 Goode, *Capital Losses*, 375.
2 Donald E. Press, "From Murder Bay to the Federal Triangle," *Records of the Columbia Historical Society, Washington, D.C.* 51 (1984): 68.
3 Ibid., 66.
4 Highsmith and Landphair, *Pennsylvania Avenue*, 107.
5 Carl Abbott, "Dimensions of Regional Change in Washington, D.C.," *American Historical Review* 95:5 (1990): 1378–79.
6 Green, *Secret City*, 200.
7 Abbott, "Dimensions of Regional Change," 1383.
8 Donald Roe, "The Dual School System in the District of Columbia," *Washington History* 16:2 (2004/2005): 31.
9 Green, *Secret City*, 214.
10 David F. Krugler, "A Mob in Uniform: Soldiers and Civilians in Washington's Red Summer, 1919," *Washington History* 21 (2009): 58–59, 62.
11 Steven Mintz, "A Historical Ethnography of Black Washington, D.C.," *Records of the Columbia Historical Society, Washington, D.C.* 52 (1989): 239–40.
12 Press, "From Murder Bay to the Federal Triangle," 69.
13 Gutheim, *Worthy of the Nation*, 172.
14 Highsmith and Landphair, *Pennsylvania Avenue*, 107.
15 Green, *Washington: Capital City*, 291.
16 Highsmith and Landphair, *Pennsylvania Avenue*, 108.
17 Goode, *Capital Losses*, 299, 303, 317, 404.
18 Helen Tangires, "The Life and Death of Center Market," *Washington History* 7:1 (1995): 47, 67.
19 Gutheim, *Worthy of the Nation*, 175.
20 Green, *Washington: Capital City*, 503.
21 Gutheim, *Federal City*, 43; National Park Service, *Historic American Buildings Survey: Market Square* (Washington, DC: Department of the Interior, 1969): 6–7.

BIBLIOGRAPHY

Governmental Accounts and Records

Annals of Congress. US Congress, 1st–18th Congresses, 1789–1824. Accessed at memory.loc.gov/ammem/hlawquery.html.

Arrest Books, 1869–1906; Law Enforcement Records, Metropolitan Police; Records of the Government of the District of Columbia, RG 351, National Archives and Records Administration.

The Black Code of the District of Columbia. New York: William Harned, 1848.

Brock, William G. *Report of the Major and Superintendent of Police of the District of Columbia: The Year Ending June 30, 1880.* Washington, DC: Government Printing Office, 1881.

Brown, A. G. *Report of the Senate Committee on the District of Columbia,* US Senate, 35th Congress, First Session, reprinted in *Congressional Globe,* April 5, 1860.

Bureau of the Census. *Historical Statistics of the United States: Colonial Times to 1970.* US Department of Commerce, House Doc. 93–78, 93rd Congress, 1st Session, 1975.

Chappell, Gordon. *Historic Resource Study: East and West Potomac Parks, A History.* Denver, CO: US Department of Interior, 1973.

Cluss & Kammerhueber Engineering. *Report on the Present State, and the Improvement of the Washington City Canal.* Washington City: May 12, 1865.

Congressional Globe. US Congress, 23rd–43rd Congresses, 1833–1873. Accessed at memory.loc.gov/ammem/hlawquery.html.

Congressional Record. US Congress, 43rd Congress, 1873–. Accessed at thomas.loc.gov.

Debate on the Morrill Bill. US Senate, 43rd Congress, Second Session, *Congressional Record,* Dec. 17, 1874.

District of Columbia Department of the Environment, et al. *Federal Triangle Stormwater Drainage Study.* Washington, DC: October 6, 2011.

District of Columbia Fire Department, "History of the D.C. Fire Department." www.dcfire.com/custom.html?id=173.

Identification Books, 1883–90; Law Enforcement Records, Metropolitan Police; Records of the Government of the District of Columbia, Vols. 1–2, RG 351, National Archives and Records Administration.

Joint Force Headquarters–National Capital Region and The US Army Military District of Washington. "History of Fort Lesley J. McNair." Accessed at http://mdwhome.mdw.army.mil/docs/media-documents/history-of-fort-mcnair-fact-sheet.pdf?sfvrsn=2.

Leedecker, Charles H., et al. *Phase I Archaeological Investigation for the National Museum of African American History and Culture.* Washington, DC: Smithsonian Institution, 2007.

Meigs, Montgomery C. *Map of the Washington Aqueduct, to Accompany Supplemental Report of the Chief Engineer.* Washington City, 1864.

Michler, Nathaniel. *Annual Report of Nathaniel Michler, Office of Public Buildings, Grounds, and Works, Capitol of the United States.* Appendix T, Report of the Secretary of War, 1867.

Moore, William G. *Report of the Major and Superintendent of Police of the District of Columbia: The Year Ending June 30, 1888.* Washington, DC: Government Printing Office, 1889.

National Capital Planning Commission. *Report on Flooding and Stormwater in Washington, D.C.* Washington, DC: National Capital Planning Commission, 2008.

National Park Service. *Constitution Gardens: National Mall & Memorial Parks—West Potomac Park: Cultural Landscapes Inventory.* Washington, DC: National Park Service, 2008.

National Park Service. *Historic American Buildings Survey: Market Square.* Washington, DC: Department of the Interior, 1969.

National Park Service. *The Mall: National Mall & Memorial Parks: Cultural Landscapes Inventory.* Washington, DC: National Park Service, 2006.

Records Concerning the Washington City Canal, 1810–1871; Records Relating to Construction, Engineering, Land, and Transportation; Records of the Government of the District of Columbia, RG 351.4, National Archives and Records Administration.

Records of the Board of Commissioners for the Emancipation of Slaves in the District of Columbia, 1862–1863; Records of the Accounting Officers of the Department of the Treasury; RG 217; National Archives and Records Administration.

Records of the Provost Marshal General's Office, Washington, DC, and of the Enrollment Division, 1861–1889; Records of the Provost Marshal General's Bureau, RG 110; National Archives and Records Administration.

Records of the Territorial Government, 1871–1974; General Records, RG 351.2.2; National Archives and Records Administration.

Records of the US District Court for the District of Columbia Relating to Slaves, 1851–1863; Records of District Courts of the United States; RG 21; National Archives and Records Administration.

Register of Debates. US Congress, 18th–25th Congresses, 1824–1837. Accessed at memory.loc.gov/ammem/hlawquery.html.

Report of the Board of Metropolitan Police. House Ex. Doc. 1, 37th Congress, 2nd Session, 1861, US Serial Set 1157.

Report of the Board of Public Works of the District of Columbia, from Its Organization Until November 1, 1872. Washington, DC: Board of Public Works, 1872.

Report of the Bureau of the Refugees, Freedmen, and Abandoned Lands. S. Ex. Doc. 6, US Congress, Senate, 39th Congress, 2nd Session, October 22, 1866.

Report on Inhabited Alleys in the District of Columbia and Housing of Unskilled Workmen. Subcommittee of Committee on the District of Columbia, US Congress, Senate, 63rd Congress, 2nd Session, 1914.

Reports of Public Hazards, 1879–1886. Law Enforcement Records, Metropolitan Police; Records of the Government of the District of Columbia, RG 351, National Archives and Records Administration.

Superintendent Report, Office of Metropolitan Police, US Congress, Senate, 39th Congress, 1st Session, March 20, 1866.

United States House of Representatives, Committee on the District of Columbia. *The Federal Payment to the District of Columbia, 1790–1980.* Washington, DC: Government Printing Office, 1979.

United States Sanitary Commission. *United States Sanitary Commission Bulletin.* New York: 1866.

Van Buren, Martin. *First Inaugural Address,* March 4, 1837.

The Washington Canal—Report to Major Generals Gilmore, Warren, and Tower. Sen. Ex. Doc. 35, US Senate, 39th Congress, First Session, 1866.

Primary Accounts

Abdy, E. S. *Journal of a Residence and Tour of the United States of North America.* London: John Murray, 1835.

Alcott, Louisa May. *Hospital Sketches.* Boston: James Redpath, 1863.

Alexandria Ship Records, 1732–1861, transcribed 1973–1989 by Betty Harrington Macdonald. Alexandria Library, Local History/Special Collections, Boxes 218 and 219.

Ames, Mary Clemmer. *Ten Years in Washington: Life and Scenes in the National Capital.* Hartford, CT: A. D. Worthington & Co., 1873.

Andrews, E. A. *Slavery and the Domestic Slave Trade in the United States.* Boston: Light & Stearns, 1836.

Anonymous. *In Memory of Nathaniel Michler,* Funeral Program. Washington, DC, 1881.

Atwater, Caleb. *Mysteries of Washington City.* Washington City: G. A. Sage, 1844.

Barton, E. E. *Historical and Commercial Sketches of Washington and Environs, Our Capital City, "The Paris of America."* Washington, DC: Judd & Detweiler, 1884.

Boschke, Albert. *Topographical Map of the District of Columbia, Surveyed in the Years 1856, '57, '58 & '59.* Washington City: D. McClelland, Blanchard & Mohun, 1861.

Briggs, Emily Edson. *The Olivia Letters.* Washington, DC: Neale Publishing, 1906.

Brockett, L. P., and Mary C. Vaughan. *Woman's Work in the Civil War, A Record of Heroism, Patriotism and Patience.* Philadelphia: Zeigler, McCurdy & Co., 1867.

Buel, J. W. *Mysteries and Miseries of America's Great Cities.* St. Louis, MO: Historical Publishing Co., 1883.

Bulkley, Barry. *Washington Old and New.* Washington, DC: Washington Printing Co., 1914.

Burnett, Frances Hodgson. *Through One Administration.* New York: Charles Scribner's Sons, 1886.

Busey, Samuel C. *Pictures of the City of Washington in the Past.* Washington, DC: Wm. Ballantyne & Sons, 1898.

Byrnes, Thomas. *Professional Criminals of America.* New York: Cassell & Co., Ltd., 1886.

Coffin, John P. *Washington. Historical Sketches of the Capital City of Our Country.* Washington, DC: John P. Coffin, 1887.

Crowninshield, Mary Boardman. *Letters of Mary Boardman Crowninshield, 1815–1816,* ed. Francis Boardman Crowninshield. Cambridge: Riverside Press, 1905.

Dahlgren, Madeleine Vinton. *Etiquette of Social Life in Washington.* Lancaster, PA: Inquirer Printing and Publishing, 1873.

De Gaffenreid, Clare. *Typical Alley Houses in Washington,* Bulletin 7. Washington, DC: Women's Anthropological Society: Gibson Bros., 1897.

Delano, Judah. *Washington Directory, Showing the Name, Occupation, and Residence of Each Head of a Family and Person in Business; the Names of the Members of Congress and Where They Board; Together with Other Useful Information.* Washington City: William Duncan, 1822.

Dickens, Charles. *American Notes for General Circulation,* 2 vols. London: Chapman and Hall, 1842.

Douglass, Frederick. *My Bondage and My Freedom.* New York: Miller, Orton & Mulligan, 1855.

———. *The Life and Times of Frederick Douglass, from 1817–1882.* London: Christian Age Office, 1882.

Drew, Benjamin. *The Refugee, or the Narratives of Fugitive Slaves in Canada.* Boston: John P. Jewett & Co., 1856.

Ellicott, Andrew. *Plan of the City of Washington in the Territory of Columbia: Ceded by the States of Virginia and Maryland to the United States of America.* Boston, 1792.

Elliot, Jonathan. *Historical Sketches of the Ten Miles Square Forming the District of Columbia.* Washington City: J. Elliot, Jr., 1830.

Elliot, William. *The Washington Guide.* Washington City: Franck Taylor, 1837.

Ellis, John B. *The Sights and Secrets of the National Capital.* Chicago, IL: Jones, Junkin & Co., 1869.

Faux, William. *Memorable Days in America: Being a Journal of a Tour to the United States.* London: W. Simpkin and R. Marshall, 1823.

Fearon, Henry B. *Sketches of America, a Narrative of a Journey of Five Thousand Miles Through the Eastern and Western States of America.* London: Strahan and Spottiswoode, 1819.

Force, William Q. *Picture of Washington and Its Vicinity.* Washington City, 1845.

Foster, Sir Augustus John. "Notes on the United States of America." Private manuscript. 1804–1812. Published in Davis, Richard Beale, ed., *Jeffersonian America.* Westport, CT: Greenwood Press, 1980.

Gibbs, George. *Memoirs of the Administrations of Washington and John Adams, Edited from the Papers of Oliver Wolcott,* 2 vols. New York: William Van Norden, 1846.

Hamilton, Thomas. *Men and Manners in America.* Philadelphia: Carey, Lea & Blanchard, 1833.

Hines, Christian. *Early Recollections of Washington City.* Washington City: Chronicle Books, 1866.

Hodasevich, R. A. *Map of Fortifications and Defenses of Washington.* Washington City: US Department of War, 1865.

Hone, Philip. *The Diary of Philip Hone,* ed. Bayard Tuckerman. New York: Dodd, Mead and Company, 1889.

Hutchins, Stilson, and Joseph West Moore. *The National Capital, Past and Present: The Story of Its Settlement, Progress, and Development.* Washington, DC: Post Publishing Co., 1885.

Jackson, Richard Plummer. *The Chronicles of Georgetown, D.C., from 1751–1878.* Washington, DC: R.O. Polkinhorn, 1878.

Janson, Charles William. *The Stranger in America.* London: James Cundee, 1807.

Jones, Thomas Jesse. *Directory of the Inhabited Alleys of Washington, D.C.* Washington, DC: Monday Evening Club, 1912.

The Journal of the House of Delegates of the Commonwealth of Virginia, 1831–1832. Richmond: Thomas Ritchie, 1832.

Keim, Randolph. *Society in Washington, Its Noted Men, Accomplished Women, Established Customs, and Notable Events.* Washington, DC: Harrisburg Publishing, 1887.

Kennedy, John P. *Memoirs of the Life of William Wirt, Attorney General of the United States,* 2 vols. Philadelphia: J. B. Lippincott & Co., 1860.

L'Enfant, Pierre Charles. *Plan of the City Intended for the Permanent Seat of the Government of the United States, 1791.* Republished in Washington, DC: US Coast and Geodetic Survey, 1887.

Law, Thomas. "Observations on the Intended Canal in Washington City," 1804.

Lincoln, Abraham. "The Perpetuation of Our Political Institutions." Address before the Young Men's Lyceum, Springfield, IL, January 27, 1838.

Logan, Mary. *Thirty Years in Washington, or, Life and Scenes in Our National Capital.* Hartford, CT: A. D. Worthington & Co., 1901.

Lomax, Virginia. *The Old Capitol and Its Inmates.* New York: E. J. Hale & Son, 1867.

Lundy, Benjamin. *The Life, Travels, and Opinions of Benjamin Lundy.* Philadelphia: William D. Parrish, 1847.

Mackay, Alex. *The Western World; or, Travels in the United States in 1846–47,* 2 vols. Philadelphia: Lea & Blanchard, 1849.

Mangum, Willie P. *The Papers of Willie Person Mangum 1807–1832.* Raleigh: North Carolina State Department of Archives and History, 1950.

Martineau, Harriet. *Retrospect of Western Travel.* London: Saunders and Otley, 1838.

Moore, Frank. *Women of the War, Their Heroism and Self-Sacrifice.* Hartford, CT: S.S. Scranton & Co., 1866.

Moore, Joseph West. *Picturesque Washington: Pen and Pencil Sketches.* Providence, RI: J. A. & R. A. Reid, 1884.

Northup, Solomon. *Twelve Years a Slave.* New York: Miller, Orton & Mulligan, 1855.

Pepper, Charles M. *Every-day Life in Washington . . . with Pen and Camera.* New York: The Christian Herald, 1900.

Philp, James. *Philp's Washington Described: A Complete View of the American Capital and the District of Columbia,* ed. William D. Haley. New York: Rudd & Carleton, 1861.

Plumer, William Jr. *The Life of William Plumer,* ed. A. P. Peabody. Boston: Phillips Sampson and Co., 1856.

Poore, Benjamin Perley. *Reminiscences of Sixty Years in the National Metropolis.* Philadelphia: Hubbard Brothers, 1886.

Porter, John Addison. *New Standard Guide of the City of Washington and Its Environs.* Washington, DC: Arlington Publishing, 1886.

Richstein, William F. *Stranger's Guide-book to Washington City, and Everybody's Pocket Handy-book.* Washington City: William F. Richstein, 1864.

Ropes, Hannah. *Six Months in Kansas.* Boston: John P. Jewett & Co., 1856.

Ropes, Hannah. *Civil War Nurse: The Diary and Letters of Hannah Ropes.* Knoxville: University of Tennessee Press, 1980.

Royall, Anne. *Sketches of History, Life, and Manners in the United States.* New Haven: 1826.

———. *The Black Book; or, a Continuation of Travels in the United States.* Washington City: 1828.

———. *Mrs. Royall's Southern Tour, or, Second Series of the Black Book.* Washington City: 1831.

Sala, George Augustus. *My Diary in America, in the Midst of War.* London: Tinsley Brothers, 1865.

Sanger, William W. *The History of Prostitution: Its Extent, Causes and Effects Throughout the World.* New York: Harper & Bros., 1876.

Shiner, Michael. *The Diary of Michael Shiner Relating to the History of the Washington Navy Yard, 1813–1869.* Library of Congress MSS 20.957, accessed at www.history .navy.mil/library/online/shinerdiary.html.

Siebert, Wilbur H. *The Underground Railroad from Slavery to Freedom.* London: Macmillan, 1898.

Smallwood, Thomas. *A Narrative of Thomas Smallwood.* Toronto: James Stephens, 1851.

Smith, Gaillard, ed. *The First Forty Years of Washington Society, Portrayed by the Family Letters of Mrs. Samuel Harrison Smith, Margaret Bayard.* New York: Charles Scribner's Sons, 1906.

Smith, Margaret Bayard. *A Winter in Washington, or, The Memoirs of the Seymour Family.* New York: E. Bliss & E. White, 1824.

———. *Forty Years of Washington Society*, ed. Galliard Hunt. London: T. Fisher Unwin, 1906.

Smyth, J. F. D. *A Tour in the United States of America.* London: G. Robinson, 1784.

Stearns, Amanda Akin. *The Lady Nurse of Ward E.* New York: Baker & Taylor, 1909.

Still, William. *Underground Rail Road Records, with a Life of the Author.* Philadelphia: William Still, 1886.

Taft, Horatio Nelson. *The Diary of Horatio Nelson Taft, 1861–1865,* 3 vols. Library of Congress MSS 84885, accessed at http://memory.loc.gov/ammem/tafthtml/ tafthome.html.

Timony, Patrick. *American Fistiana: Containing a History of Prize Fighting in the United States.* New York: H. Johnson, 1849.

Torrey, Charles T. *Memoir of Rev. Charles T. Torrey.* Boston: John P. Jewett & Co., 1847.

Torrey, Jesse. *A Portraiture of Domestic Slavery in the United States.* Philadelphia: John Bioren, 1817.

Townsend, George A. *Washington, Outside and Inside.* Chicago, IL: James Betts & Co., 1874.

Trollope, Anthony. *North America.* New York: Harper & Brothers, 1862.

Trollope, Frances Milton. *Domestic Manners of the Americans,* 2 vols. London: Whittaker, Treacher & Co., 1832.

Twain, Mark, and Charles Dudley Warner. *The Gilded Age: A Tale of To-Day.* Hartford, CT: American Publishing, 1874.

Twining, Thomas. *Travels in America 100 Years Ago: Notes and Reminiscences.* New York: Harper & Bros., 1893.

Vedder, Sarah E. *Reminiscences of the District of Columbia, or Washington City Seventy-Nine Years Ago, 1830–1909.* St. Louis: A. R. Fleming, 1909.

Warden, D. B. *A Chorographical and Statistical Description of the District of Columbia, the Seat of the General Government of the United States.* Paris: Smith Pub., 1816.

Watterston, George. *The L . . . Family in Washington, or, A Winter in the Metropolis.* Washington City: Davis and Force, 1822.

Watterston, George. *A Picture of Washington.* Washington City: William M. Morrison, 1840.

———. *A New Guide to Washington.* Washington City: Robert Farnham, 1842.

Weld, Isaac Jr. *Travels through the States of North America, and the Provinces of Lower Canada, During the Years 1795, 1796, and 1797,* 2 vols. London: J. Stockdale, 1800.

Weller, Charles Frederick. *Neglected Neighbors, Stories of Life in the Alleys, Tenements and Shanties of the National Capital.* Philadelphia: John C. Winston Co., 1909.

Wheelock, Julia S. *The Boys in White; The Experience of a Hospital Agent in and Around Washington.* New York: Lange & Hillman, 1870.

Wolff, Wendy, ed. *Capitol Builder: The Shorthand Journals of Montgomery C. Meigs, 1853–1859, 1861.* Washington, DC: US Government Printing Office, 2001.

Secondary Sources

Alfers, Kenneth G. *Law and Order in the Capital City: A History of the Washington Police, 1800–1886.* Washington, DC: George Washington University, 1976.

Allen, William C. *History of the United States Capitol: A Chronicle of Design, Construction, and Politics.* Sen. Doc., US Senate, 106th Congress, Second Session, 2001.

Allen, William C. *History of Slave Laborers in the Construction of the United States Capitol.* Washington, DC: Office of the Architect of the Capitol, 2005.

Arnebeck, Bob. *Through a Fiery Trial: Building Washington, 1790–1800.* Lanham, MD: Madison Books, 1991.

Barry, John Paul. "The Know Nothing Party of the District of Columbia." PhD Dissertation, Graduate School of Arts and Sciences, Catholic University of America, 1933.

Berg, Scott W. *Grand Avenues: The Story of the French Visionary Who Designed Washington, D.C.* New York: Pantheon, 2007.

Bergheim, Laura. *The Washington Historical Atlas: Who Did What When and Where in the Nation's Capital.* Rockville, D: Woodbine Press, 1992.

Borchert, James. *Alley Life in Washington: Family, Community, Religion, and Folklife in the City, 1850–1970.* Chicago: University of Illinois Press, 1980.

Bowling, Kenneth R. *The Creation of Washington, D.C.: The Idea and Location of the American Capital.* Fairfax, VA: George Mason University Press, 1991.

Bray, R. S. *Armies of Pestilence: The Impact of Disease on History.* Cambridge, UK: Lutterworth Press, 2004.

Brown, Richard Maxwell. *Strain of Violence: Historical Studies of American Violence and Vigilantism.* New York: Oxford University Press, 1975.

Bryan, Wilhelmus Bogart. *A History of the National Capital, From Its Foundation through the Period of the Adoption of the Organic Act,* 2 vols. New York: Macmillan, 1916.

Cable, Mary. *The Avenue of the Presidents.* Boston: Houghton Mifflin, 1969.

Capitol Fire Museum. *Firefighting in Washington, D.C.* Mount Pleasant, SC: Arcadia Publishing, 2004.

Carson, Barbara G. *Ambitious Appetites: Dining, Behavior, and Patterns of Consumption in Federal Washington.* Washington, DC: American Institute of Architects Press, 1990.

Cary, Francine Curro, ed. *Washington Odyssey, A Multicultural History of the Nation's Capital.* Washington, DC: Smithsonian Books, 1996.

Clark, Allen C. *Thomas Law: A Biographical Sketch.* Washington, DC: W. F. Roberts, 1900.

———. *Greenleaf and Law in the Federal City.* Washington, DC: W. F. Roberts, 1901.

Cowdrey, Albert E. *A City for the Nation: The Army Engineers and the Building of Washington, D.C., 1790–1967.* Washington, DC: Government Printing Office, 1978.

Croggon, James. Articles from *The Evening Star,* 1862–1915. In "Early 19th Century Neighborhoods," Bytes of History, accessed at www.bytesofhistory.com/ Collections/Croggon/Croggon_Menu.html.

Dickinson, William C., ed. *Montgomery C. Meigs and the Building of the Nation's Capital.* Athens: Ohio University Press, 2001.

Feller, Carolyn M., and Constance J. Moore, eds. *Highlights in the History of the Army Nurse Corps.* Washington, DC: US Army Center of Military History, 1995.

Fields, Barbara Jeanne. *Slavery and Freedom on the Middle Ground: Maryland During the Nineteenth Century.* New Haven: Yale University Press, 1984.

Furer, Howard B., ed. *Washington: A Chronological & Documentary History, 1790–1970.* Dobbs Ferry, NY: Oceana Publications, 1975.

Gilje, Paul. *Rioting in America.* Bloomington: Indiana University Press, 1996.

Gillette, Howard Jr., ed. *Southern City, National Ambition: The Growth of Early Washington, D.C.: 1800–1860.* Washington, DC: George Washington University Center for Washington Area Studies, 1995.

Goldfield, David R. *Cotton Fields and Skyscrapers: Southern City and Region.* Baltimore: Johns Hopkins University Press, 1982.

Goode, James M. *Capital Losses: A Cultural History of Washington's Destroyed Buildings.* Washington, DC: Smithsonian Books, 2003.

Green, Constance McLaughlin. *Washington: Village and Capital, 1800–1878.* Princeton: Princeton University Press, 1962.

———. *Washington: Capital City, 1879–1950.* Princeton: Princeton University Press, 1962.

———. *The Secret City: A History of Race Relations in the Nation's Capital.* Princeton: Princeton University Press, 1967.

Greenberg, Amy S. *Cause for Alarm: The Volunteer Fire Department in the Nineteenth-Century City.* Princeton: Princeton University Press, 1998.

Grimsted, David. *American Mobbing, 1828–1861: Toward Civil War.* New York: Oxford University Press, 1998.

Gutheim, Frederick. *The Potomac.* New York: Holt, Rinehart and Winston, 1949.

———. *The Federal City: Plans & Realities.* Washington, DC: Smithsonian Institution Press, 1976.

Gutheim, Frederick, and the National Capital Planning Commission. *Worthy of the Nation: The History of Planning for the National Capitol.* Washington, DC: Smithsonian Institution Press, 1977.

Harris, Charles Wesley. *Congress and the Governance of the Nation's Capital: The Conflict of Federal and Local Interests.* Washington, DC: Georgetown University Press, 1995.

Harrison, Robert. *Congress, Progressive Reform, and the New American State.* Cambridge: Cambridge University Press, 2004.

Harrison, Robert W. *History of the Commercial Waterways and Ports of the United States: Volume 1, from Settlement to Completion of the Erie Canal.* Ft. Belvoir, VA: Institute for Water Resources, 1979.

———. *The United States Waterways and Ports: A Chronology—Volume 1, 1541–1871.* Ft. Belvoir, VA: Institute for Water Resources, 1980.

Harrold, Stanley. *Subversives: Antislavery Community in Washington, D.C., 1828–1865.* Baton Rouge: Louisiana State University Press, 2003.

Harzbecker, Joseph John Jr. "Life and Death in Washington, D.C.: An Analysis of the Mortality Census Data of 1850." M.A. Thesis, University of Massachusetts, 1999.

Hawkins, Don A. *Topography of the Federal City, 1791.* Washington, DC: Library of Congress, 1990.

Hibben, Henry B. *Navy-Yard, Washington: History from Organization, 1799 to Present Date.* Washington, DC: Government Printing Office, 1890.

High, Mike. *The C&O Canal Companion.* Baltimore: Johns Hopkins University Press, 1997.

Highsmith, Carol M., and Ted Landphair. *Pennsylvania Avenue: America's Main Street.* Washington, DC: American Institute of Architects, 1988.

Hilleary, Cecily. "Noah E. Sedgwick: A Black Cop in D.C.'s Gilded Age," from Quondam Washington: A Compendium of Tales from Forgotten City Archives, http://quondamdc.wordpress.com.

Hofstadter, Richard, and Michael Wallace, eds. *American Violence: A Documentary History.* New York: Alfred A. Knopf, 1970.

Holt, Thomas, Cassandra Smith-Parker, and Rosalyn Terborg-Penn, *A Special Mission: The Story of Freedmen's Hospital, 1862–1962.* Washington, DC: Howard University Press, 1975.

Hurd, Charles. *Washington Cavalcade.* New York: E. P. Dutton & Co., 1948.

Imaging Research Center. *Visualizing Early Washington DC.* Baltimore: University of Maryland at Baltimore, 2009–2011. Accessed at visualizingdc.com.

James, Bessie Rowland. *Anne Royall's U.S.A.* New Brunswick, NJ: Rutgers University Press, 1972.

Junior League of Washington. *The City of Washington: An Illustrated History.* New York: Alfred A. Knopf, 1977.

Kytle, Elizabeth. *Home on the Canal: An Informal History of the Chesapeake and Ohio Canal, and Recollections of Eleven Men and Women Who Worked on It.* Cabin John, MD: Seven Locks Press, 1983.

Larkin, Jack. *The Reshaping of Everyday Life, 1790–1840.* New York: Harper & Row, 1988.

Lee, Antoinette J. "Historical Perspectives on Urban Design: Washington, D.C., 1890–1910." Conference Proceedings of Columbia Historical Society, Washington, DC, October 7, 1983.

Leech, Margaret. *Reveille in Washington: 1860–1865.* New York: Harper & Bros., 1941.

Liebertz, John Paul. *Columbia Pike: The History of an Early Turnpike*. Arlington, VA: Arlington County Historic Preservation Office, 2010.

Lockwood, John, and Charles Lockwood. *The Siege of Washington: The Untold Story of the Twelve Days That Shook the Union*. New York: Oxford University Press, 2011.

Loftin, Tee. *City of Washington: 1800*. Washington, DC: Tee Loftin Publishers, 1982.

Logan, Deborah A. "The Redemption of a Heretic: Harriet Martineau and Anglo-American Abolitionism in Pre–Civil War America." From Proceedings of the Third Annual Gilder Lehrman Center International Conference, Yale University, October 25–28, 2001.

Longstreth, Richard, ed. *The Mall in Washington: 1791–1991*. Washington, DC: National Gallery of Art, 2003.

———. *Housing Washington: Two Centuries of Residential Development and Planning in the National Capital Area*. Chicago: University of Chicago Press, 2010.

Margo, Robert A. *Wages and Labor Markets in the United States, 1820–1860*. Chicago: University of Chicago Press, 2000.

Maury, William M. *Alexander "Boss" Shepherd and the Board of Public Works*. Washington, DC: George Washington University Press, 1975.

Millay, Curtis A. "Restoring the Lost Rivers of Washington: Can a City's Hydrologic Past Inform Its Future?" M.A. Thesis, Virginia Polytechnic Institute and State University, 2005.

Miller, David W. *Second Only to Grant: Quartermaster General Montgomery C. Meigs*. Shippensburg, PA: White Mane Books, 2000.

Miller, Fredric M., and Howard Gillette Jr. *Washington Seen: A Photographic History, 1875–1965*. Baltimore: Johns Hopkins University Press, 1995.

Miller, Iris. *Washington in Maps*. New York: Rizzoli, 2002.

Moore, John E., and Julia A. Jackson, eds. *Geology, Hydrology and History of the Washington, D.C. Area*. Alexandria, VA: American Geological Institute, 1989.

Newby, M. Dalyce. *Anderson Ruffin Abbott: First Afro-Canadian Doctor*. Markham, ON: University of Toronto Press, 1998.

Newman, Graeme R. *Annals of the American Academy of Political and Social Science, Crime and Justice in America: 1776–1976*. Philadelphia: American Academy of Political and Social Science, 1976.

Noreen, Sarah Pressey. *Public Street Illumination in Washington, D.C.: An Illustrated History*. Washington, DC: George Washington University Press, 1975.

Passonneau, Joseph R. *Washington through Two Centuries: A History in Maps and Images*. New York: Monacelli Press, 2004.

Phillips, Christopher. *Freedom's Port: The African American Community of Baltimore, 1790–1860*. Champaign, IL: University of Illinois Press, 1997.

Pitch, Anthony S. *The Burning of Washington: The British Invasion of 1814*. Annapolis, MD: Naval Institute Press, 1998.

Plummer, Betty L. "A History of Public Health in Washington, D.C., 1800–1890." PhD Dissertation, University of Maryland, 1984.

Porter, Sarah Harvey. *The Life and Times of Anne Royall*. Cedar Rapids, IA: Torch Press, 1909.

Reps, John W. *Monumental Washington: The Planning and Development of the Capital Center*. Princeton, NJ: Princeton University Press, 1967.

———. *Washington on View: The Nation's Capital Since 1790.* Chapel Hill, NC: University of North Carolina Press, 1991.

Robbins, Eleanora I., and Myrna H. Welter. *Building Stones and Geomorphology of Washington, D.C.: The Jim O'Connor Memorial Field Trip.* Washington, DC: May 14, 2001, www.gswweb.org/oconnor-fieldtrip.pdf.

Rorabaugh, W. J. *The Alcoholic Republic: An American Tradition.* New York: Oxford University Press, 1981.

Rosen, Ruth. *The Lost Sisterhood: Prostitution in America 1900–1918.* Baltimore: Johns Hopkins University Press, 1982.

Scott, Elizabeth M., ed. *Those of Little Note: Gender, Race and Class in Historical Archaeology.* Tucson: University of Arizona Press, 1994.

Scott, Pamela. *Capital Engineers: The U.S. Army Corps of Engineers in the Development of Washington, D.C., 1790–2004.* Alexandria, VA: US Army Corps of Engineers, 2011.

Sharp, John. "The District of Columbia Volunteer Fire Companies: 1800–1870." Washington, DC Genealogy Trails, http://genealogytrails.com/washdc/fire&police/fireco.html.

———. "The Metropolitan Police Department, District of Columbia: Law, Crime and Policing in the District, 1790–1900," Washington, DC Genealogy Trails, April 2, 2010, www.genealogytrails.com/washdc/lawsprisons/historyofpolicedept.html.

Sherwood, Suzanne Berry. *Foggy Bottom, 1800–1975: A Study of an Urban Neighborhood.* Washington, DC: George Washington University Press, 1978.

Smith, Kathryn Schneider. *Washington at Home: An Illustrated History of Neighborhoods in the Nation's Capital.* Northridge, CA: Windsor Publications, 1988.

———. *Port Town to Urban Neighborhood: The Georgetown Waterfront of Washington, D.C., 1880–1920.* Washington, DC: The Center for Washington Area Studies at George Washington University, 1989.

Stover, John F. *History of the Baltimore and Ohio Railroad.* West Lafayette, IN: Purdue University Press, 1987.

Sylvester, Richard. *District of Columbia Police: A Retrospect of the Police Organizations in the Cities of Washington and Georgetown and the District of Columbia.* Washington, DC: Gibson Bros., 1894.

Tindall, William. *Origin and Government of the District of Columbia.* Washington, DC: Judd & Detweiler, 1902.

———. *Standard History of the City of Washington.* Knoxville, TN: H. W. Crew & Co., 1914.

Vasquez, Rubil Morales. "Monuments, Markets, and Manners: The Making of the City of Washington, 1783–1837." PhD Dissertation, Rutgers State University, 1999.

Vlach, John Michael. "The Mysterious Mr. Jenkins of Jenkins Hill: The Early History of the Capitol Site." Washington, DC: United States Capitol Historical Society, 2004, accessed at www.capitolhillhistory.org/library/04/Jenkins%20Hill.html.

Wade, Richard C. *Slavery in the Cities: The South, 1820–1860.* London: Oxford University Press, 1964.

Ways, Harry C. *The Washington Aqueduct, 1852–1992.* Baltimore: US Army Corps of Engineers, 1996.

Webb, William Benning, John Wooldridge, and Harvey W. Crew. *Centennial History of the City of Washington, D.C.* Dayton, OH: H. W. Crew, 1892.

Wharton, Anne Hollingsworth. *Social Life in the Early Republic*. Philadelphia: J. B. Lippincott, 1902.

Whyte, James H. *The Uncivil War: Washington During the Reconstruction, 1865–1878*. New York: Twayne, 1958.

Young, James Sterling. *The Washington Community: 1800–1828*. New York: Columbia University Press, 1966.

Periodicals

Daily Chronicle, 1862–1874

Daily Patriot, 1870–1872

Evening Star/Washington Star, 1852–1981

Georgetown Courier, 1865–1876

National Era, 1847–1860

National Intelligencer, 1800–1869

National Republican, 1860–1888

New National Era, 1870–1874

Niles Weekly Register (Baltimore, Md.), 1811–1848

Records of the Columbia Historical Society, Washington, D.C., 1897–1989

Sunday Herald, 1866–1887

Washington Critic/Daily Critic, 1868–1896

Washington Globe, 1831–1873

Washington History, 1989–

Washington Post, 1877–

Washington Sentinel, 1873–1910

INDEX